The
Caregiver
Chronicles

22 Family Caregivers

Get Real About the Ties That Bind

A Madness To Magic Authors' Collective

Madness to Magic 2024
Printed in the United States of America
Paperback ISBN: 978-1-7354364-5-6
eBook ISBN: 978-1-7354364-6-3

Book cover design and Interior formatting by 100 Covers

Contents

FOREWORD

"Be Bold and Mighty Forces Shall Come to Your Aid."

~ Johann Wolfgang von Goethe

H ad I known what I was getting myself into at the start with this "Collaborative Book Project" – truth be told – I may not have taken it on. But since you're reading these words, I'm not revealing any spoilers in disclosing that, clearly, I did.

This initiative began in January of 2023. I had seen some social media posts from an organization called The Picerne Family Foundation. They were calling for proposals for their annual Artist Outreach Program. The Foundation was offering a $15,000 grant to artists aged fifty-five and older who wanted to share their creative gifts by offering artistic experiences to under-served communities.

The idea intrigued me. As I reviewed the criteria further, I checked off the boxes: For sure, I hit the age requirement... check; and with five published books of my own, in addition to helping coach others on writing and publishing their books, I *did* confidently consider myself an artist...check, check; and as for wanting to serve the under-served, I could also claim that desire as part of my life's purpose. I have always been a champion of underdogs and the unsung heroes, so...check, check, check! Sign me up!

Now, the only question was...what kind of creative experience did I want to propose as my submission to the Artist Outreach Project? The answer was simple. Having been a family caregiver for my mom and younger sister, both of whom were diagnosed with paranoid schizophrenia, I had become a somewhat reluctant expert on family caregiving and all it entailed. For me, that meant living a life of obligation and putting myself on the back burner. It included exhausting myself, trying to keep my home life separate and a secret from my professional life. It translated into a constant struggle with my feelings that ping-ponged between love and hate, and everything that comes with that (especially guilt and shame). I teetered on a tightrope, tending 24/7/365 to the necessary needs of two people I loved and lived with and who were unable to care for themselves, while neglecting caring for myself.

My story may not necessarily be all that unique, and in my case, I've shared much of it in my two memoirs: THE S WORD and COMMITTED: A MEMOIR OF MADNESS IN THE FAMILY. But, sadly, too many others' stories seem to go untold for countless reasons: No time, not enough resources, lack of knowing how-to, crippling self-doubt, family disapproval, etc. I would hear these great stories almost daily: The elderly lady in the grocery store who asked me where the pickles were and ended up telling me about how as a child she shepherded her siblings as they escaped Nazi Germany; the father of a daughter diagnosed with a mental illness who following the release of my memoirs wrote to me his own story, thanking me for telling mine and for helping him not feel alone; the spouse who waited with me in the lobby of the hospital as both of our husbands underwent colonoscopies and who shared – for the first time, she said – her own life-changing moment coming to terms with her faith and authority figures abusing their power.

Because I understood the desire to share one's life and lessons learned, and to give meaning to our experiences and the trials over which we've triumphed, I felt called to give others a voice and a way by offering them a chapter to author in this book.

Family caregivers are the unsung heroes who do what few others will even consider taking on, at least, not without a paycheck attached to the job. The caregiver role, sometimes, is thrust upon us, and we seem to have little choice but to take it on. And sometimes, we step into the caregiver role wholeheartedly with the best of intentions and a "piece-of-cake" kind of attitude. No matter how we came to it, more often than not, we find ourselves akin to that frog who happily swims and soaks in a pool of cool, clean water, and who never notices – until it's too late – that they are in a pot with no escape and that the temperature keeps rising with an inevitable outcome of "stick a fork in me" done.

At times, during the spearheading of this book, I have felt a bit like that frog. I know the family caregivers authoring chapters in this book shared similar feelings of their own overwhelm, self-doubt, fear, and that, "What in the world was I thinking?" sigh of surrender.

Meeting these souls in the throes of their own caregiving madness, however, also filled me with a knowing that these unsung heroes would soon become "major creatives' in our newly formed literary bubble. While each one came to this project with their own range of writing experience, their own expertise in a variety of creative realms, their own styles, scenarios, and singularly unique voices, I felt my purpose was to serve as their captain, not only steering the boat, but building it while on the water. Through this endeavor, I was reintroduced to caregiving on a new level...to care for strangers who had become co-writers, and who were becoming something more...friends for sure, and maybe even family. And to once again, practice self-care throughout the writing and publishing process, not just for me, but as a model for them.

Caregiving may, especially of late, be quite trendy, bantered about in the media and highlighted in advertising campaigns. I liken it to how "mental health" has made its way into our societal conversations, without, from my perspective, the reality of definitions, let alone, solutions to its very real problems. Caregiving is deep, timeless, and aligned with one's life and legacy. While it stretches and strengthens us, it also has the power to unhinge us. Whatever life may throw our way, we can choose to crawl and even crumble, or we can strive to soar with the grace of something greater than ourselves.

Caregiving is messy, heartbreaking, empowering, and one of life's most challenging necessities. So, too, is this little masterpiece you hold in your hands.

Twenty-two of us came to it, together. We journeyed on with it because, let's face it, that's all any of us can do in this life, no matter our circumstances. I was given the opportunity to show and tell and teach through all the madness each of us encountered in these past several months…always moving forward to get to the magic. I'm humbled to have done it. I'm elated to say that WE did it. And what a fine "it" it turned out to be (not perfect…but perfectly imperfect on all accounts).

Looking back, had I not taken on this project, I would have missed out on meeting some incredible people and stories that made me laugh out loud, shed some tears, and nod in agreement. I also would not have been lifted up by this group of talented creatives, artists in their own right, nor would I have learned a thing or two more than what my own experiences already have taught me.

And isn't it ironic that this book venture, in many ways, parallels the road taken by the family caregiver? I wonder how many family caregivers would have taken on their roles had they known what they'd encounter along their journeys? It's never all good or all bad. It's never all black or all white. And it's never,

"This is something I'll never have to deal with," because, as Rosalynn Carter said, *"There are only four kinds of people in the world — those that have been caregivers, those that are caregivers, those who will be caregivers, and those who will need caregivers."*

We're all destined to experience caregiving in some form or fashion, hence why this book is being written...*for* family caregivers *by* family caregivers. We are in this thing we call life together. So, whether you who are reading this now *are* the care-giver, or you *have been* a caregiver, or you *are the recipient* of caregiving...or, if you're just wise enough to know that *caregiving at some level most likely will be in your future*, this book is for you. May you find the stories shared here insightful, inspirational, hopeful...and maybe even find yourself knowingly nodding...

And wouldn't it be wonderful if you even find yourself pick-ing up your own pen to start writing your own family caregiver chronicles...? I, for one, look forward to the read.

Journey On,

Paolina Milana
Paolina Milana
MadnessToMagic.com

CHAPTER ONE

Big Girls Do Cry

by Tracey Y. Jones

E very night, I rejoice at 8 p.m. It's my happy hour. It's the time I gladly prep my 88-year-old father to take his butt to bed. I recently realized that by spending most of my day anticipating my father's bedtime, I may be wishing days of my life away. Nonetheless, I get excited.

To set the bedtime wheels in motion, I first make sure the temperature in his bedroom is comfortable for him. Then, I turn off the television to create a quiet environment. Next, to help father relax, I give him a quick bed bath. I love the scent of lavender and how it relaxes father when I massage him with it. All clean, with the sweet delicate aroma of the lavender filling the room, I help him into a fresh pair of pajamas and get him to bed. Once in bed, I gently place pillows under his elbows and hips. Father has gotten a little bony in those areas, so the pillows provide a cushion. A friend who works with elders taught me that. Finally, I tuck him in and leave him with a goodnight kiss on the forehead.

Sounds too perfect? Well, it's not impossible. I have experienced days like that. Unfortunately, most days are perfectly imperfect, especially, at the start of spring 2020. That's when a series of life-altering events exacerbated father's already declining abilities.

Father went from slowly walking with a cane to being wheelchair-bound. He could no longer bathe or dress himself. He also developed urinary incontinence, and now wears waterproof briefs to prevent embarrassing accidents. He maintained his ability to think, speak, and feed himself. However, the loss of his other abilities made the need for a caregiver to assist him 24 hours a day, 7 days a week, and 365 days a year, vital.

As a result of that, I was hurled into the role of father's caregiver—a role for which there was no dress rehearsal.

Father always said he wanted to age at home. His exact words were, "I do not wanna go to a damn convalescent home!" He and my mother would say that so much, I became programmed to believe there would be a curse of shame on my ass if I put my parents in a convalescent home because they were older. So I vowed not to, unless necessary.

To their credit, father and mother planned for the future as best they could. Their number one goal was to always have a roof over our heads. So, in 1961, my father (age 26) and mother (age 20) worked hard and saved enough money to achieve the American dream by purchasing what would become my childhood home and their forever home. To date, this is where father is aging in place.

They managed their money responsibly throughout the years. Insomuch, that when mother passed, father reaped the benefits of mother's financial savvy. Be that as it may, with mother's brilliance and father doing his part, the cost for 24/7 home care in California is a staggering $20,000 a month, on average. There was no way my father could afford that on his own. I had my savings and wanted to help out as much as I could. However, there needed to be a long-term plan, which he didn't have.

At the time, I made my living as a pre-need burial counselor for Inglewood Park Cemetery. COVID-19 was ramping up business for cemeteries, and I was classified as an essential worker during one of the most dangerous times in history. My office was mobile, and I was required to search for and meet with families to counsel. I liked helping families get their affairs in order, but I hated the corporate drama. The mental stress became unbearable.

My father needed help, and I was expected to expose myself to a deadly virus for a paycheck, which I was not willing to do.

And so, I quit that job to stand in the gap as my father's caregiver and fiercely crusade for the best possible outcome for him to age at home.

I recall thinking that because father had healthcare coverage through the VA and CareMore, a Medicare Advantage plan, he'd have no problem getting assistance promptly. It never crossed my mind all the rigmarole I'd have to go through to get him what he needed.

One of many examples: I wanted a professional, thorough caregiver who was skilled to handle my father's condition. Therefore, I felt it would be best to have an agency provide our caregiver. However, I found that agencies were and still are short-handed of great workers. If they had someone that fit the description we needed, they were already on assignment. With the help of the VA, I tried agency after agency and concluded that finding someone who was the right fit would take some time.

With the pandemic in full swing, we kept being assigned home health aides who'd show up unmasked, under-skilled, unvaccinated, sniffling with no COVID-19 test results, and talking about "what they would and would not do."

I, a YouTube-taught family member, had to train so-called professionals in basic caregiver duties such as bed baths, changing diapers, managing supply inventory, and boiling an egg for breakfast. Most were not dependable, and if you ask me, all of them needed some type of professional emotional support themselves. To top it off, if I wanted to confirm the caregiver was COVID-19 negative, I was told by the agencies that I'd have to provide the test kits. Also, with the fact that COVID-19 vaccinations weren't, and still aren't, mandatory for caregivers, I felt stressed and terrified to let these people in our home.

It felt like folks passed themselves off as caregivers just to have a job, and the agencies hired them just to keep their VA contracts.

I love my father, so I pay close attention to all details. I don't expect folks to be invested the way I am. But I do expect folks to do their professional best and use common sense. However, I learned quickly that common sense ain't so common.

My decision to be my father's caregiver until I could find someone acceptable was a decision that brought him comfort and joy at a time when he needed it most. But for me, that decision has been a life-changing sacrifice.

Like most of us caregivers, quitting my job to care for someone I love was a no-brainer, or so I thought. I didn't think about the emotional, mental, physical, and financial toll caring for my loved one would have on my own life.

My time is no longer my own because I spend most of my day caring for my father and handling his business. Father shouts my name all night because he wants to know I'm in the house with him. I'm often sleep-deprived, and my retirement savings have dwindled. On top of that, I had to shift my mind to fulfill basic caregiving duties, including personal care.

I didn't think it through because I was and still am motivated by love for my father. So, when I realized that personal care included having to groom my father's private parts, I felt uncomfortable and embarrassed. Father felt the same way, I think.

The thought of seeing and touching my father's penis hurt my heart. Since age 3, my mother ingrained in my brain that there was no appropriate reason for her little girl to see a grown man's penis, and especially, father's.

Because of my mother's wise words, I never imagined that I, father's only child, would be the one giving him bed baths. I never thought I would have to care for my father's nether regions.

It was rough in the beginning. Nonetheless, I agreed to be his caregiver, and personal care, which includes bed baths, is one of the services that has to be provided.

Recently, I shared my story with a new friend who was kind enough to care for an elderly lady who was not his relative. He shared with me the importance of empathy. I agree with him. Tapping into my ability to be empathic has helped me adapt tremendously by opening my heart to another level of compassion and caring. I've asked myself on many occasions, "If I were helpless, like my father, how would I want someone to care for me?" Naturally, I'd want to be cared for with kindness, compassion, and empathy. I'd also want my caregiver to be knowledgeable in a way that benefits my care. Because of this, I'm striving to adapt to the challenge as best I can. Being empathic helps me keep it together in moments of sadness.

When I think of what we've survived, I am amazed. By the same token, when I think of what's to come, I am heartbroken.

Lately, father has been having nightmares. He fights to stay awake even if he can barely keep his eyes open. Friends say he's like a child who doesn't want to miss out. However, I've been advised by my father's hospice nurse, that "at this stage, he may have a fear of dying, and more than likely the nightmares are side effects of the anti-anxiety medication."

The hospice nurse who is contracted by The VA to care for father, who is an Army veteran, has over 30 years of experience. So, I tend to believe her more than anyone when it comes to understanding what my father is going through. Besides, to think my father is like a child is denial and taking the easy way out because my father is still very much a man.

As mentioned, father's physical decline began in spring 2020. The world was shutting down due to COVID-19. At the same time, father suddenly began to appear weaker, restless, and delirious. I didn't know what was going on with him. Normally I'd rush him to the Emergency Room with no hesitation to seek medical attention. However, with COVID-19 peaking, I was apprehensive about walking into a hospital due to my concerns about being exposed to COVID-19. Nevertheless, father's symptoms were worsening. For this reason, I prayed to God for the strength, courage, and protection to get father to the ER. I'm glad I did. He was dehydrated from prescribed water pills and needed to be hospitalized to be rehydrated. Dehydration is especially dangerous and deadly for elderly people.

Unfortunately, father has a heart disease called congestive heart failure and has shortness of breath when excess fluid builds up around his heart. The water pill helps remove that excess fluid. At the time, father was capable of managing medications on his own. Or so I thought. He had forgotten that he needed to weigh himself every morning to determine if he needed the water pill. He was only supposed to take the pill if he had gained two to three pounds suddenly overnight. So, because he wasn't monitoring himself properly, he became dehydrated. Two days in the hospital and several IVs later, he was released to go home with me.

Within days of being home, father began acting strangely again. He seemed highly irritated and was being irrational. He woke up from a nap talking shit and using an abusive tone with me. I can recall thinking, "Oh hell no, he is out of his fucking mind talking crazy to me." I was pissed and ready to battle with him. Instead, I calmed down, got out of my feelings, and reminded myself, that father has always been loving toward me and would never want to hurt my feelings.

Once I had that reality check, I threw his ass in the car, again, figuratively, not literally, and headed back to the ER. Once there, he was evaluated and immediately admitted into the Intensive Care Unit (ICU) with a urinary tract infection (UTI) from the condom catheter used during the previous hospitalization. The infection got into his bloodstream.

For 11 days, he lay in ICU fighting for his life. Ultimately, he won that battle and was moved from ICU, down to a recovery unit on another floor. While on the recovery floor, he tested positive for COVID-19. What the heck? Poor guy! He was not COVID-positive before being admitted. Given the timeline, it was clear that he was exposed and infected while in the hospital. I walked the halls of that hospital every day to visit my father until he tested positive for COVID-19. Thank God, I never tested positive. Thankfully, my father never developed symptoms because the VA immediately treated him with a Monoclonal Antibody Product.

Emotionally, my father made it through that ordeal better than I did. Because of COVID-19, I could no longer go to the hospital. I was a nervous wreck. I'd call as often as I could to let him know I was home waiting for him. Each time we spoke, he'd sound strong and say loving things like, "Don't worry baby, I'll be okay. We'll get through this."

Amazing! he was still being a father. He wanted to make sure I didn't fall apart or become ill from stress. It was like he didn't know the severity of what was going on. Or maybe he did. Now that I think about it, it was obvious to him that I was stressed out. I'm sure he could feel the anxiety I was trying to hide. I was cussing a lot and always complaining when I'd tell him about the stupid shit I was experiencing as I navigated through the process to get him the care he deserved. I'm sure he picked up on many things, since I wore my stress on my sleeve.

Fourteen days passed before my father was cleared to be discharged from the hospital. Laying in hospital beds for 14 days took a toll on my father. He was unable to walk. I was told by the doctors that seniors require one week to recover for every day they are in hospital beds. That meant my father needed approximately 14 weeks to recover. I recall feeling numb.

This was all new, and I was not prepared at home to handle such a drastic change. I had no wheelchairs or Hoyer lift that would enable me to lift and move him around. So instead of being discharged back to our home, he was discharged to a convalescent home for 30 days to receive physical therapy while I prepared our home for his arrival.

Times were difficult. COVID-19 shut the world down. Everyone was ordered to shelter in place. Convalescent homes weren't accepting new patients. Social workers were overwhelmed and kept dropping the ball or moving slow as molasses. I had to step in using every tool in my toolbox. I used my business, producing, and communication skills. I also used my ability to be reasonable along with my Black Girl magic to get stuff done. Father had to remain in the VA hospital while I handled the red tape. I eventually found a place that would accept him.

I was grateful to find a convalescent home that was acceptable to me. However, no one mentioned that he would be isolated and quarantined for 15 days once admitted because he had been treated for COVID-19. I found that out after he was transported from the hospital to the convalescent home. Consequently, he only had 15 days of physical therapy, which yielded very little progress. Not to mention, at this point, father began to fall into a deep depression from being isolated. I felt lost and alone because I didn't know anyone who had gone through what we were experiencing. Thankfully, his doctor recommended in-home hospice care, which is where my father wanted to be, and I wanted him to be.

Hence, the hospice nurse mentioned earlier visits our home once a week to check my father's vitals and make recommendations just as they would in a hospital. She makes sure he has whatever medications he needs to be comfortable, mainly, morphine. We give small amounts to help him relieve shortness of breath. Mirtazapine helps to relieve depression and anxiety and is also useful to help him sleep and increase his appetite, and oxygen. She also makes sure we are well stocked with diapers, body wipes, gloves, skin creams, disposable chucks (waterproof bed pads), or whatever is needed. In addition, she guides me with valuable insight and comforts me when I'm on the verge of a mental meltdown.

As I said, she's the nurse. So, when she advised the nightmares might be from the medication, my heart filled with anxiety. All I could think was, that really sucks! Father has been on these anti-anxiety meds for about six months now. We (he and I) need something to help him sleep. Otherwise, he will be up all night shouting for me. We live together. If he's up all night shouting, he will disturb my sleep. When my sleep is disturbed, it's difficult for me to have a good day. I'm irritated, and my blood pressure becomes elevated. We've tried several different medications. Shockingly, this was seemingly the right combination with the least side effects.

It's all so bittersweet. From the anti-anxiety medication triggering nightmares and anxiety to the fear he experiences, my poor father is under attack again. No wonder, when I finally get him to bed, he lays on his back with his eyes closed, chatting until he's asleep with his mouth wide open.

When his mouth is open and no sounds are coming out, that's my cue! He's really asleep. I finally get to sit down, take a deep breath and say "Whoosah." It may not sound like a thrilling self-care moment, but I'm so grateful to just sit. My days are long because, typically, I wake up at 5:30 a.m. With luck, I've had a good eight hours of undisturbed sleep. The moment I open my eyes, I thank God for the new day. One, because it is said joy comes in the morning, and I need some joy. Two, I may need a do-over from the day before. Because, despite everything I do every day, each day is different.

Speaking of joy in the morning, every nanosecond of the morning is important for my morning rituals. If my father hears me and wakes up, I will have to delay my morning rituals, and jump into my butler/maid/caregiving duties. I value my mornings. I enjoy the peace and quiet. My brain is refreshed, and I get to take my time. If I have to delay or forgo my morning rituals, I'll spend the day whining and complaining about feeling cheated. Therefore, I try to move through the house as quietly as possible so as not to wake father.

Tiptoeing across the floor avoiding spots that creak, I get myself to the bathroom for my ritual of quality time on the toilet, a shower, a chance to brush my teeth, and to get dressed, 'cause I still gotta be cute. If all goes well, I can work my way downstairs to the kitchen to make coffee. Father loves to start his morning with coffee. So, I put my whistling tea kettle on the stove burner to heat water. I grab his favorite mug adding two teaspoons of coffee, three packs of raw sugar, and a splash of heavy cream. It doesn't take long for the kettle whistle to blow signaling that the water is hot. As I pour the hot water over the coffee grinds, I swirl my teaspoon in the mug unlocking the aroma of fresh coffee. Somehow, that freeze-dried, roasted smell travels through the house straight into father's nose, waking him up.

Like clockwork, I will hear father let out a loud yawn, followed by a loud fart, then a loud yell, "Traaaacccceeeeeyyy!!!! Get me up, I want to get up." I'll yell back, "Alright, give me a minute."

His memory is short, very short. So, no matter what, he will continue to yell loudly until I come to his room, help him out of the bed onto his wheelchair, and finally serve him his coffee.

From that moment, my day is spent washing, drying, and folding laundry, preparing meals, cleaning the house, online banking, ordering groceries and supplies to be delivered, and light landscaping when time permits. I also spend time making various businesses calls, some who keep me on hold so long that I forget who I'm calling.

By the end of the day, my body is tired, my brain is exhausted, and my feet hurt. For this reason, sitting my tired ass down uninterrupted is all the thrill I need in this season of my life.

So, yes, at 8 p.m., I do make haste to change father into comfortable pajamas and get him to sleep. I really wish it was that simple. But it's not. Remember, he fights to go to sleep. Not to mention, he wears a full set of dentures that should be (with emphasis on should be) taken out each night to soak in a cleaning solution that removes funky, smelly bacteria and stains. I can't stand dirty dentures, so my goal is to take those dentures out of his mouth. Father, on the other hand, doesn't give a damn about taking his dentures out. He hates the removal process. He tries to negotiate his way out of removing them every night. He'd rather leave the dentures in until the adhesive that bonds them to his gums is so weak that if he sneezed, the dentures would fly out of his mouth. I think that's gross.

I do not like negotiating with my father. I feel like I'm forcing him against his will. We go through some type of negotiation almost every night. It's not like a business negotiation either. It's more like the crisis negotiation you see in movies.

Thank God, shortly after my mother died in 2015, I invested my money and hired an attorney to work with my father to prepare his Living Trust. Within the Trust (in which I am named the trustee) is a Health Care Power of Attorney, in which he stated that "he wishes to be kept clean and groomed at all times." So, when he's negotiating, I tell him, "I'm doing what you want."

At that point, I feel as if I've won, and all negotiations should cease. But nope, father is very assertive. I admire his tenacity, but it's annoying and sometimes he pisses me off. He doesn't mean to be annoying. I just feel annoyed because the father I knew wouldn't think twice about removing his dentures.

Thankfully, I can lean on the Healthcare Power of Attorney. That investment has given me priceless peace of mind. Without it, I'd feel confused and distressed.

I still get frustrated though. Many times, I've exited his room to motivate myself with a pep talk. I'll tell myself, "Get a grip on your feelings. These may be the last easy days with father. He's declining, so get a grip." Sometimes it does the trick, sometimes it doesn't.

The supplies I need: gloves, a glass of warm gargling water, a cup for father to spit the water into, and a towel to wipe his mouth are in the bathroom down the hallway from his room.

As I head to the bathroom to get the supplies, I can hear him chatting indistinctly to himself. He goes on and on even as I return to his room. Standing in front of him prepared to extract those dentures, I'll interrupt his chatting by handing him the glass of warm water and instructing him to put enough water in his mouth until his cheeks look like balloons and to hold it.

He gives me a dirty side-eye look as he stops talking to take the glass of water. He then takes the smallest swig of water possible. It's so irritating. Why on earth would he put a small ass teaspoon amount of water in his mouth? It is beyond me. Lucky for him, the bottom dentures only require a slight wiggle to remove. The top dentures are a different story. The adhesive bonds the upper dentures tightly to his gums. When I instruct him to hold the warm water in his mouth, it's to loosen the grip so we can easily remove the dentures. When he reluctantly follows directions and then wants to spit out the water before I tell him to, I give up and let him. I'll hold the big cup up to his mouth for him to spit the water into. I'll be dammed, he somehow manages to spit on my hand instead of into the big ass cup. I think he does it on purpose. Then again, maybe not.

All I can say is, "Thank God for latex gloves." They are truly a useful commodity. Without gloves, I'd be an irate hot mess with spit on my hand. Calmy, I change into a fresh pair of gloves and wipe his mouth. I ask father to open his mouth, which he does reluctantly. When he opens his mouth, I gently place my thumb on one side of the dentures and my forefinger on the opposite side and then begin to gently wiggle the dentures up and down to loosen its grip from his gums. As the dentures begin to loosen, I can hear a suction sound as they pull away from his gums. It's fun to me. It's not fun for father.

He protests by growling and makes mean facial expressions, or should I say, he makes an expression that appears to be mean. Once the dentures are out, father abruptly spits out whatever food was trapped under the dentures as a protest. I've learned to quickly put a towel over his mouth so he can't spit shit across the room. I then gently rub his gums with oral swabs (a sponge on a stick) to remove leftover denture adhesive. Recently, I checked the inside of his mouth and noticed a small rip on his upper gum above his front canine tooth. Perhaps that's why he growls. It's an expression of pain. If he skimps using the warm water, the denture adhesive still holds strong, and my father's gums could rip. No wonder he hates the process.

Because of his state of mind, not only is it hard for him to comprehend the significance of the warm water, but it's also hard for him to verbally express his discomfort. Now that I am aware of the potential injuries, I obsessively check to make sure his gums have no ulcers or rips. After consulting with his doctor, I've switched from using flavored mouthwash, because it dries the mouth, to using peroxide to clean his mouth and begin healing if needed.

Truthfully, some days I don't feel like dealing with all that comes along with this process. I wish I didn't care. In moments of irritation, I think about how my father was a sweet-eating, soda-drinking freak who never flossed his teeth. Throughout the years, our family dentist warned him to rinse after drinking sugary beverages and to floss his teeth after meals. Or at the very least, floss the teeth he'd like to keep. He never rinsed or flossed, so now he has no teeth.

At the point the denture drama is over, it's usually around 8:45 p.m. I still have to help my father from his wheelchair to his bed. He's weak, so I have to stand strong as he wraps his arms around me to stand and walk. We struggle. I try to lead father toward the bed while he pulls in the opposite direction every time, which throws us off balance if I don't maintain control. I don't have a clue as to what he is thinking or hearing. I just know he doesn't mean to make things hard. Once I get him on his bed, we sit silently next to each other huffing and puffing as if we had just climbed a big hill. As soon as father catches his breath, I hand him a glass of his favorite orange juice and that prescribed pill that's supposed to help him sleep and reduce anxiety.

Leaning on me and needing my assistance breaks his heart. I know this because of the small tear drops he often has in the corner of his eyes. Father is a proud, gentle, clever man. A retired butcher, he worked over 30 years in freezers at meat packing houses, lifting dead cows off meat hooks to butcher them into choice cuts of meat.

Butchering is a dangerous job. Father labored in cold freezers Monday through Friday for 12 to 14 hours a day. He worked with knives so sharp that you could slice your entire finger off and not notice right away. I can recall the times when my father would come home from work sad because someone accidentally cut off a finger or caught their hand in the meat grinder. Father would say, "So and so's hand got caught in the grinder today, so we won't be eating ground beef this week."

I loved ground beef! I was horrified. I'd ask, "What dummy would do something like that?"

Father would just laugh at me. He never lost a finger. I've always admired him for never losing his fingers. Father was a cautious man with common sense. He took excellent care of his body. His muscles were big and bulged through his shirt. He loved being active.

As a little girl, he taught me how to lift weights so we could work out together. He was an avid bike rider and taught me to be the same. He wasn't a partier or an alcohol drinker. Father was the guy who took nutritional supplements, made freshly squeezed juices, and went to bed early. I honestly cannot recall him having more than a few beers throughout my life, and he never smoked. Father was no saint, but he is a good man. Like anyone else, he has his shit. However, that didn't take away from the fact that he's a handsome black man with hazel eyes and a movie star smile that loved his wife (my mother), and me (his only child). He also loved being fiercely independent and was until the age of 80. That's when his whole world turned upside down.

As mentioned, life altering events exacerbated father's already declining abilities in spring 2020. However, the onset of father's mental decline began shortly after mother died in 2015.

Mother had been suffering from a throbbing pain in the left side of her neck, her teeth hurt, and she couldn't sleep for months. Father did everything he could to help her. He took her to doctor after doctor, and not one evaluation found the problem. I remember thinking, "Mother will be fine. This too shall pass."

Then, the unthinkable happened. I can recall it being an unusually hot October day when father called in a panic. He was so scared he was stuttering. "Ca, ca, come home," he yelled. "Your mother can't breathe."

As a salesperson, I was across town meeting with an older couple counseling them about cemetery property. I thought for sure these old folks were ready to buy, so I instructed my father to call an ambulance. I wanted father and mother to get to the hospital, and I'd meet them there.

However, they were both adamant about wanting me, not an ambulance, to pick them up. They did not want to go to the nearest hospital, which is where the ambulance would have taken them. I understood my parents' concerns. Unfortunately, living in South (Central) Los Angeles, the nearest hospital was not desired. At one point, it seemed everyone we knew who went to that hospital wound up dead. Besides, the older couple I was visiting were old hustlers who loved the company of salespeople. They had no intentions of purchasing, so I quickly wrapped up our meeting.

Filled with fear that something terrible could happen before I got to my parents, I dashed out of their door and rushed across town to pick up my parents. I had to get them to the ER at Little Company of Mary, which was 45 minutes away in the city of Torrance.

I arrived at my parents' home safely. As I pulled up their driveway, I saw them waiting for me on the front porch. That was an immediate indication that something was seriously wrong. I could see mother didn't look right. She was calm but appeared listless as my father held her up in a standing position. Father was a nervous wreck.

Feeling time was of the essence, I quickly helped father get mother into the car. Once in the car, I burnt rubber out the driveway and took off racing as fast as I could through Los Angeles traffic. Adrenaline had my heart pumping hard as I sped down main streets, side streets, and alleys. For once, my father wasn't bitching about me driving fast. I recall it taking us 20 minutes to get to the hospital. Normally, it would have taken at least 45 minutes.

Thankfully, we arrived safely and ironically were able to park in the one ER parking space near the door. Parked, I jumped out of the car and ran into the ER lobby yelling for help. Father waited in the car with mother until a team of nurses rushed out with a wheelchair to get her.

As the emergency team pushed my mother through the big metal doors into the ER with my father following behind them, I remained at the front desk giving the administrator information. Once inside, the triage team immediately began to attend to my mother. I walked beyond the same big metal doors a short time later to join my parents.

As soon as I entered the ER, I felt like I had walked onto a movie set. It was loud and bustling with people crying out for help as medical assistants rushed around trying to attend to everyone. Sick people were lined along the walls. Some were sitting in chairs. Others were in hospital beds.

It seemed I was walking in circles as I looked for the room number I was given. Finally, I saw the number and began quickly walking in the direction where my parents were. As I approached the doorway of the makeshift room, a young woman stopped me and introduced herself. She was the doctor caring for my mother. I confirmed I was my mother's daughter.

With a concerned yet comforting tone, the doctor asked me to take a deep breath and told me not to panic. Stunned, I did as she instructed. She wanted me to know that there was a high probability my mother was having a heart attack.

I remember feeling like all the air had left my body. Choked up, with my hand over my mouth, I fought back tears that were welling up in my eyes. I stood outside the room for a few moments while catching my breath. Soon after, I entered. My mother was there lying on the hospital bed with her eyes closed. Taped to her arms were tubes for drawing blood. Her chest was covered with small, sticky patches that connected wires to a heart monitor.

Father was sitting in a chair next to the bed holding her hand. I pulled up a chair, sat on the opposite side, and began holding her hand as well. There we were. Just we three holding hands and waiting patiently for the diagnosis.

Within moments, we had the update. It was confirmed. The throbbing in mother's neck, and the toothaches, along with shortness of breath, were all warning signs. She was suffering a heart attack. Mother took the news like a gangster and agreed to have emergency open heart surgery. Without further ado, mother was rushed into surgery.

Hours went by. We prayed and waited patiently. Five bypasses later, mother pulled through surgery, and we were told that she'd be fine. I was so pissed to hear she needed five bypasses. Mother was being monitored by her cardiologist monthly, so I really could not understand why or how she wound up needing five bypasses. To date, I still don't understand.

With the surgery behind her, mother was taken to the intensive care unit to begin the journey of recovery. She looked like she had been through a serious battle. She was swollen and had a long jagged vertical scar that extended from the center of her chest down to her abdomen. Her leg also had a jagged surgical scar where a vein was removed to implant in her chest. There were tubes and needles all over her body. The room was filled with noises of monitors beeping and machines pumping and sucking fluids in and out of her body. Mother was semiconscious on life support machines for days. Father and I took turns sleeping all day and night on pull-out chairs in the ICU next to her.

Two weeks passed before it was determined mother had improved enough to be discharged from the hospital to a skilled nursing facility for 30 days of continued care and rehabilitation.

It was important to both father and I that mother knew we supported her recovery every step of the way. For this reason, my father drove an hour each way every day to be with her. He'd arrive when visiting hours began and stayed until they'd kick him out because visiting hours were over.

Mother was not having a good experience in that facility. She had hallucinations from medications and was frightened. The workers neglected her by leaving her in soiled diapers and not cleaning her properly, so much so that she developed massive ulcers on both of her inner thighs that looked like third-degree burns. She was, and still is, the only person I've ever known who chewed her food 32 times, which made her a slow eater. Rather than assist my mother with feeding as advised, the staff would take her food tray away before she had enough to eat because they were on a schedule. It was horrible. She was often in tears and called me throughout the night begging for me to come get her.

Concerned, I arranged a meeting with all who were in charge of that facility. I could sense immediately snippety attitudes from the care team. I understood what my mother was going through. It was clear that getting her out of there was crucial. So, I demanded they discharge her. I waited patiently as I kept getting the runaround for days after my request. I eventually packed her stuff and pretty much kidnapped her. Things got messy, and I didn't care. That was my mother, and no one was going to be allowed to mistreat her.

Once home, I was able to heal the wounds on her inner thighs while my father catered to her as best an 80-year-old tired, stressed, and confused man could. Father was so hard on himself. He spoke of feeling hurt. He was there every day. However, when the aides in the rehabilitation center came to clean and change mother, he'd leave the room for privacy. So, he never saw how horrific her inner thighs looked. With a heavy heart, he felt he let my mother down. He trusted that the workers would care for her, but instead, they hurt her. He was incensed and wanted to go back to that place to kick some ass.

I was just happy to have mother home. But something wasn't right. Every time mother had the urge to pee, she'd stare at me with a strange, deranged look in her eyes as if she didn't know me. Then she'd let out a blood-curdling scream from pain when she'd pee. I also noticed she was severely constipated.

Watching her suffer was unbearable. We had to rush her back to the ER. Turns out, while in rehabilitation, mother hadn't had bowel movements. She also developed a very aggressive urinary tract infection that was not detected or treated. By the time she was back in the ER, her urine was thick like paste and her blood was infected. We tried to fight, but it was too late. The infection took over her body. Mother died from being septic.

The pain of my mother's death has been so devasting. Father often cries from his gut, without tears.

Dealing with his medical issues while filled with grief, depression, and regret, father was dealt another blow. He was diagnosed with vascular dementia. Caused by hardened heart valves, vascular dementia restricts the blood flow to my father's brain.

Dementia changed his life dramatically. It destroyed his coordination. It is robbing him of memories and his ability to think clearly. It has stripped him of his confidence and left him incapable of taking care of himself. He knows he's changing. But he doesn't know why. So, he feels anxious and depressed. His short-term memory is diminishing. He repeats himself so much, it drives me up the wall. I used to try to stop him by saying, "Daddy, we've already talked about that." However, I learned to simply respond as if we've never had the conversation, or to just walk away. I used to ask, "Remember this, remember that?" I'm learning to stop asking and to accept father doesn't remember. We are in the advanced stages of the disease, and I'll never win. Vascular dementia has seven stages. Father is in stage five, which is considered a moderately severe cognitive decline.

I know my father feels misunderstood because dementia causes him to respond to normal situations abnormally. Yet, through it all, he still lives to inspire me, reminding me each day that I am human, and I can only endure so much. He tells me he is proud of me and grateful I take care of him. I assure him, I wouldn't have it any other way. He's my best friend. We love each other.

He may be in hospice, but I will not let anyone write him off. He's still a car guy and still takes pride in having a nice car to cruise the city. On good days, after hours of getting it together, we hop in our big fat Cadillac XT5 and drive around the city or up the coast while listening to music.

When I look over to the passenger seat, what I see trips me out. The seat looks huge and father looks tiny. I almost feel like I should sit him in the backseat away from the front passenger airbags, pretty much like we do with children. But instead, I just smile and let him ride. After all, if the end is near, why worry? We like to eat out at our favorite spots or sit in the marina watching boats sail by. We eat ice cream or popcorn and laugh at life. He's father. He's daddy bear. He cares for me and watches over me as he always has. And I allow him. I cry when he asks, "Is there anything I can do to make things easier?" We both know that he can't make things easier. The disease won't let him. So, I just love him for asking.

At times he will stare at me with a loving gaze and ask me to forgive him if he does things I don't understand. I feel ashamed when I misunderstand what's going on or bemoan my lack of patience. So, I assure him that I do forgive him. If anyone needs forgiveness, it's me.

Dementia or not, father still has his wits. There are times he feels my frustration so he says, "One day you will miss me." Sarcastically yet truthfully, I respond, "I already miss you."

CHAPTER TWO

Trying to Break a Link in the Chain: Living with and Learning about Mental Illness

by Susan A. Shoemaker

Smiling, I hung up my phone, happy about the plans I had just confirmed. I would pick up my granddaughter after work from my daughter's friend as agreed. Araya was a lovable, sweet four-year-old and I loved spending time with her. However, even with the best of plans, the outcome is not always in our favor. My simple plan to pick up my granddaughter ended up going south. Instead of meeting later that day, I got a call during work that Araya was no longer with my daughter's friend. For reasons I didn't know, she decided to call someone else earlier that day to pick Araya up without letting me know first.

What the hell! Why didn't she just ask me to meet with her earlier? My heart pounding, head aching and adrenaline surging through my body, I sped over to Children and Youth Services.

Why had Araya ended up there? I didn't know! I needed answers and I wanted them now!

My hands shook on the steering wheel as I tried to line my car up inside the parking space. Wrenching the seat belt off, I jumped out of the car and raced towards the office that would lead to the answers I hoped to find. I flew up the stairs...*Ouch, slow down for Pete's sake! I'm going to break my neck if I keep trying to take the stairs at this pace, then I'll never see Araya again!*

I spent hours earlier at work making calls in between seeing my homecare patients. Frantically tried to contact someone who knew something about what happened to my granddaughter with no success. *Friggin' bullshit, that's what this is!* I made so many calls that my fingers hurt trying to figure out where she had been placed.

"Goddamn it!" I yelled out loud as I got to the protective services office door. It was closed. Cold glass and steel stared at me with no access to the lobby that was visible through the windows. No answers are to be found here today! Oh, dear lord, here we go again! I pulled out my phone and started dialing.

That entire night, I couldn't sleep. Where was she? What the hell would I do if I couldn't get answers? Nothing I could do at this moment anyway. I would have to wait until morning, and that was hours away. I lay down on my bed and somehow during the night, I must have dozed off. Early morning's light shone through the window as I squinted my eyes. Somewhere, the phone is ringing. Heart pounding, I jump out of bed, exhausted, and yell out "hello" before picking up the receiver.

"Where the hell is she?" I growl. The person from protective services introduces herself from the other end of the line. *Take a breath, Sue! The last thing I need to do right now is to come on so bitchy and angry that she won't deal with me.* "Sorry," I sigh and start again.

She proceeds to tell me what I've been hoping to learn. *Finally, someone with an answer...but! - I'm so upset and my stomach aches because I hate her answer!* I listen to her, barely grasping what she's telling me, hanging up while falling back onto my bed. I can't see Araya until a court date is assigned in a few days. So now my little sweetheart is with some foster stranger. Are they nice? Will they be good to her? I pray hard.

Three days later I am walking unsteadily into the courtroom. My neck is strained from trying to look around at all the strangers and unfamiliar surroundings. Taking a seat on one of the hard, cold wooden benches, I wait, my hands clasped together to keep them from shaking. My breath is unsteady and my pulse pounds in my ears. Suddenly, I look around and there is my brown-eyed, dark-haired, thin-legged little granddaughter. Her eyes are wide and bewildered. A well-dressed, younger woman with a friendly smile has her by the hand. It's the stranger she's been with for the last three days. These have been the longest days of my life. I raise my head, and Araya and I make eye contact.

We both have tears in our eyes. I look at the woman beside my granddaughter. She understands my question without me speaking it aloud. *Can I please, please see my granddaughter?* Araya stands up and starts walking cautiously toward me. Her small, hopeful face reflects the same unanswered question. The judge notices our interaction, slowly smiles, and nods his head. My heart swells at just being able to sit with her. We hug and the world feels right again.

Within a half hour, the verdict is in. We are all giggles and hugs. She is coming to stay with me! I hustle her along with me to the car, fleeing from the building in case they change their minds!

I introduced her to our little home. And little it was, 450 square feet and all ours. She sat on the new twin bed and ran her tiny hand over the colorful child's comforter I had placed over it before her arrival. She bounced a bit on the mattress and smiled.

Gratitude fills me for this home as I think of the timing of these events. My Higher Power must have been in on the plan when I bought my home and moved out of the apartment I lived in previously. It was a one-bedroom with no children allowed. If I had still been living there, I would not have been allowed to bring my granddaughter home with me. But in our small, comfy 2-bedroom house, she was welcome and had a room of her own. I thought with a smile, Divine Intervention! Thank you!

So many hoops to jump through to get Araya out of the system. Child protective services required her to have a room of her own. After seeing the room, they put their stamp of approval on it, so she was welcome to make it hers. Besides attending Court, and having home inspections and living space requirements, I was also required to take mandatory foster parenting classes through their agency. Ugh! Weeks of classes! I reminded myself, *be grateful Sue, at least Araya could live with me during the classes.* Usually, the child wasn't placed until classes were completed. Chalk up another point for Higher Power! Dealing with two visits a month from social workers was part of the package as well. It was worth it! Araya was here now. Whatever comes our way, we will make the best of it. Ha, ha I thought this was going to be my daily mantra for a while.

My thoughts wandered to the two weeks before the move into our home. My daughter, Araya's Mom, had a mental health illness that haunted her for much of her life. Her symptoms became exacerbated in the weeks before my dealings with child protective services. Denial was the most outstanding issue. Depression, suicidal ideation, anxiety, and stress were taking a toll on my daughter's daily life. She was given many diagnoses over the years; bipolar, depression, borderline personality disorder among them. All she ever wanted was to be "normal".

At that time my daughter lived in denial of her illness. She was not seeking treatment to deal with the symptoms and exacerbations. Hospital admissions became routine when she suffered the worst. She had two children living with her, my grandson aged two, and my granddaughter, Araya, age four. She was becoming suicidal and exhausted. I didn't have the knowledge or the means to help her fight this condition.

Everything came to a head when she got into an altercation with a neighbor in her apartment building which led to a loss of her housing. My beautiful, loving, confused daughter knew she had to get help. She decided to place herself in the hospital. She took my grandson to stay with his paternal grandmother, and I was going to care for my granddaughter for a brief period; however, things did not go according to plan. Hence the start of my relationship with the Children and Youth Services agency.

Eventually, Araya and I fell into a comfortable rhythm. Off to work and school during the week and finding things to enjoy on weekends. I'd wake up first and feed our dog and cat. Start the coffee next and take my work clothes for that day into the bathroom to wash and dress. I'd hear her stirring and the patter of her feet as I finished dressing and went to the kitchen.

"What's for breakfast?" her first morning question. What would you like? my usual answer. Cereal please, and juice too! I'd make her request and let the dog back into the house. When her breakfast finished, she would get up, put the bowl into the sink, and go start her morning routine of teeth brushing, dressing, and making sure her backpack was ready. Once in the car, we were on our way.

After dinner every night, she would sit with me and watch a show on TV. At bedtime, she would pick a book that we would read together as I tucked her into bed. Then we'd wake in the morning and begin again. Happy and content. For a while.

Things changed the most when we moved out of our little home. It was not an easy decision to make. When I moved into my house, the idea came from my oldest son. He approached me with an opportunity to buy and renovate houses. We searched for one and agreed that I would live there and pay the mortgage expenses and closing costs. He was able to secure a mortgage as his credit was better than my own. Together we purchased the home.

The reason for moving is a story for another day, but I will say that my older son had addiction issues. After several years of sobriety and being in our house for almost seven years, my son relapsed and began using opiates and other substances again. This affected his personality greatly. One day he asked me to do a favor that I felt was unreasonable, so I told him no. He got angry and told us to get the f*^% out of his house. All the love and security I felt living there was gone in a heartbeat. I had to get out. I did not want to live in fear of him acting like this again. Or letting him have the power to pull the rug out from under us whenever he felt like it. I believed I had no choice but to turn the house over to him and get a place of our own.

It was a heart-wrenching and difficult situation and one of the hardest decisions I've ever had to make. Araya and I packed all our belongings, both of us silently hurting inside, and drove on to the new place I had rented. It was a tiny home as well and the rent was affordable. But sadly, compared to our own tiny home, this place was dark and strange. It sent out waves of uneasiness. There were no comfortable feelings of security here. It was our place now but not our home.

Not long after settling in, however, everything abruptly changed. Or maybe it wasn't so abrupt, I just didn't let myself see what might be coming.

All the subtle behaviors and signs that went unnoticed, even denied, came to a head when Araya was around the age of 11. On this particular morning, I had gotten up as usual let the dog out and continued my routine to prepare myself for work. I realized, however, that it was too quiet. No feet pattering on the floor announcing she was getting up. No uttering of what's for breakfast? Just silence. In my heart, I knew something was wrong. This was the day I couldn't breathe, my heart stopped beating, and everything changed. I stood up, squared my shoulders, and exhaled deeply. I forced myself to call out her name and headed towards her bedroom.

Looking back, I see the signs I missed. Subtle behaviors chalked up to typical growing phases. Her anger at being in my home instead of her own. Anxiety due to feeling abandoned.

When she first moved in, I would hear her frantically calling out, "Grandma, Grandma, where are you?" any time I went out of her sight. I constantly tried reassuring her by letting her know where I was and what I was doing. If I stepped outside to start the car, I would leave the door open so she could watch me and know I was there. To this day, I can still see her tiny face and hands pressed against the glass waiting for me to come back inside.

Araya also had some understandable anger issues related to her fear and insecurity. In the beginning, she would cry randomly or throw her toys. While driving, out of nowhere, I would feel my hair being pulled hard as she sat in her car seat. Unable to express herself verbally, she showed her anger by acting out. I ended up moving her car seat to the passenger side, out of my reach.

One day, we were shopping at the local department store when I eyed a kid's punching bag and boxing gloves set. I bought it and set it up in her room. We talked about using it when she felt angry. The rule was that she could just go over and use it whenever she felt angry, afraid, or just overwhelmed. She was also safe to say or yell anything she wanted at the bag. No repercussions during this exercise. Araya got the hang of this right away. Swinging her thin arms with her little hands encased in bright red gloves, she gave that bag hell! Amazingly, it worked wonders in reducing her anger.

Afterward, we would try and talk about what was going on inside her. She really couldn't express a lot. To this day, she is not good at verbally expressing herself but does write beautifully. This was a tool we used later when she was a teen.

I remembered other events as well. Occasionally, she had a nightmare or would see menacing "shadows" out of the corner of her eye. One evening at bedtime, she informed me that on more than one occasion she thought about keeping a knife with her at night to lessen her fears. Needless to say, I was a little freaked out. I tried not to show it and calmly asked her why she felt that way and genuinely wanted to help her feel better.

Other things changed over the years as well. Araya loved school in the beginning and was excited to attend kindergarten and first grade, but by the end of fourth grade, at age nine to ten, she started having trouble socially with other kids. She came home upset and reported feeling bullied. Almost daily she told me, so and so was calling me names. Or someone else wouldn't talk to her or play with her. Another classmate she thought of as a friend made fun of her. The kids and teachers are mean, she'd cry. They are always staring at me. Tears rolled down her cheeks, and she'd sob, "I see them whispering and laughing at me behind my back."

It was all very real to her, and she lived in a state of constant hurt, sadness, and stress. I spoke to the teachers several times and their point of view was that she was exaggerating and over-sensitive. This left me feeling helpless, frustrated, and without a clue as to what I should do. She began to withdraw into herself.

By the time fifth grade rolled around, complaints about school became increasingly frequent. Araya's distrust of her schoolmates increased. She was no longer happy or in any way enthusiastic. Eventually, on occasion, her feelings of being unliked and unwanted by her classmates led to verbal altercations. Araya and I had been to two different therapists over the last two years, but she never really opened up to them. Nothing was worked out or improved. I tried to do what I could myself. Obviously, that didn't go well either.

On that morning, there was nothing out of the usual. No arguments or nightmares. Just waking up and preparing for the day. That day started like any other. I entered her room and saw what I had secretly feared. My loving granddaughter was a stranger to me.

This is the moment time stood still, my heart stopped beating, and I couldn't breathe. What I saw hit me like a speeding train. My funny, sweet Araya was huddled in the corner of her bottom bunk, legs drawn up, and her beautiful brown eyes panicked and unfocused. She was shaking her head over and over. The only word she could get out was "no"!

"No, no, no," she cried, over and over again. She was trembling and paralyzed with fear and panic. I froze as well. I nearly commanded her to come on and get going! We had to get to our job and school…to start our day like always.

"No, no, no!" She yelled even louder.

Suddenly time kicked back up again, and I realized I had to do something. What though? I felt so dumb and ignorant and useless. At this point, we didn't have any regular therapists, and I didn't know who the hell to call. I just had to do something. Had to help her. Had to help myself. There was no one I could call to talk to or anyone who understood how devastating anxiety, fear, or depression can be. The only thing I could think of doing was to take her to the local emergency room and go from there. That was the beginning of her journey. And mine.

We waited hours in the hospital's one-on-one room. It was designed to have the patient watched 24/7 to keep them from harm. I was the one who sat with her. It seemed like an eternity. I think it was. Eventually, she was seen by a crisis worker, and they decided she should be admitted. Finding a spot for an 11-year-old in crisis was not an easy task. Sometime after midnight, she was given a bed at a children's psychiatric hospital about an hour away. They took her by ambulance. I followed in my car. We were both so exhausted already. There was still a lot to do before I finished.

Rubbing my blurry eyes, I followed the ambulance and we arrived safely. An admission nurse came outside to us and took us to a conference room. I spent over an hour answering the same questions we were asked in the emergency room. Finally, around 2 a.m. they took her away from me, and my heart just broke. Hopefully, they knew how to help her through this; I definitely did not. I spent another hour and a half finishing paperwork, getting information on their plan for her, and obtaining visiting and calling/contact hours. Tired as hell, worried, and regretful, I left her in their care and drove in numbness the hour back home.

The days that followed were a balancing act between work, contacting immediate family, and visiting my granddaughter. It was a scary experience and hard to accept. Many kids on her floor had even greater issues and behavioral problems as well as being patients there more than once or twice. Things that used to seem like a big deal to me, were no longer of any real importance. I followed this schedule for six weeks or so. Work was not so understanding. Stress increased threefold.

I was so relieved when the call from the hospital came telling me that Araya could come home. My relief was quickly replaced by anxiety when reality came crashing down. I sighed tensed up, and said aloud, "This is only the beginning." Araya and I had to embark on a new unknown path together. *How the hell was I going to manage this?* I didn't feel equipped at all to help her. I couldn't even help my beloved daughter. Silently, I sat heavily in the living room chair beside me, laid my head in my hands, and cried.

One of the most difficult things regarding mental health illness is the stigma. Most people can understand or empathize with a diagnosis such as diabetes or cancer. With mental health, you find out who your true friends are. Many don't get it unless they live with it first-hand. I got unwanted advice from healthcare professionals, as well, such as "she's spoiled" and from friends suggesting I just make her get over it and force her to do whatever she was fearful of doing. Or saying, "She doesn't look sick to me." Loneliness crept into our lives. I was more than thankful that our family was understanding and supportive. They visited her when they could, which helped more than they will ever know.

Once Araya returned home, I learned how difficult it is to find resources and support in the community. It had improved greatly since my daughter was younger, however, mental health treatment still has room for improvement. Therapists with flexible hours and child psychiatrists are extremely hard to come by. The aftercare that was recommended on her discharge was impossible to get to without losing my job. I had done a lot of research and reached out to another program. One that was a better fit timewise for our schedules. We adjusted to our new rhythm day by day. After researching therapists as well, I found a person that fits the bill. She was a psychologist, experienced with children. Araya still sees her to this day.

Looking back, I see how far we've come. I don't feel very triumphant, however, I will take the small day-to-day successes. My first husband had a history of alcoholism and mental illness, ending with his suicide. Our daughter, Araya's mom, has worked hard to accept and live with her illness. She is doing great and has not been hospitalized for many years. Araya, now 22, is still growing and learning and working on acceptance and loving herself. She has her own daughter, Hazel. My two-year-old, bold and funny, curly-haired and happy, great grandbuddy!

I have hopes for us all in the future. Each generation learns a bit more and heals a little each day. It can be a slow, painful process. We work together on our relationships and progress separately as our own individuals. We may not break the chain that our family forged, but are able to weaken a few of the links. A day at a time, we do what we can to live our best lives, loving each other along the way.

CHAPTER THREE

Where Did All the Years Go?

by Jeanne Erikson

"W̲e're looking for a pulmonary embolism," the ER doctor said around 10:30 pm that August night in 2010. I'm stunned and jarred by her gloomy and serious pronouncement, stated with confidence and certainty. I immediately conclude this must be the beginning of the end since pulmonary embolisms are known as the *silent killer*. She is an attractive, tall blonde who is busy and focused on many things simultaneously with her team.

I'm in total shock, wondering if I'll even have time to call my three older brothers to travel to Pasadena from various locations to say their final goodbyes to our mom. Mom's pulse rate has been holding at 150 bpm since this morning and all evening while here at Huntington Hospital. I can't even attempt to close my eyes to rest briefly because the man in the ER bay next to us is autistic, yelling out uncontrollably while the police try to calm him down. My sweet ten-year-old son Danny is scared out of his mind, crying as he cuddles into me for some much-needed comfort and security. He's never been in such a chaotic and loud environment before. It is well past his bedtime, and he's tired, scared, and stuck in a strange and uncomfortable ER hospital room, as we all are here, experiencing this intense anticipation of the yet unknown outcome for our loved ones.

I contacted my husband, who came and picked Danny up so he could spend the night safely at home.

At 6:30 a.m. the next morning, Mom was finally moved to a private view room. To me, this could only mean one thing: I would be spending Mom's final earthly hours alongside her and the splendor of a breathtaking view of the San Gabriel Valley mountains. My mind is flooded with the frightening thought that she will be passing on soon. I am overwhelmed by the enormity of what this really means…that she is going to pass away in the blink of an eye, and I simply cannot process this inconceivable new reality. I don't begin to know what comes next; I've never had these not-bargained-for emotions before. This is way too much to process. Can this incredibly hard reality actually be happening to me right now?

When the doctor entered the room to tell me Mom had *Atrial Fibrillation*, this was a tremendous relief, as I was so sure she was dying. I let out a huge sigh of relief, and my shoulders must have dropped way below my chin as I slumped down at hearing this wonderful news. It turns out I still have the chance to spend more quality time with Mom, maybe even years, I thought, as the doctor explained Mom's diagnosis.

All my worry shifted to elation as I felt like Mom had just given me a whole new lease on life. I no longer saw her as living out her final hours of life, but maybe even living long enough to see her then ten-year-old only grandson grow into his pre-teen or even teen years. From what I've heard on TV and radio about Atrial Fibrillation, there are medications to control the symptoms. The doctor says mom will be discharged with a new drug to control her A-Fib. The heaviness of just an hour ago when I was sure she was dying lifted.

Fast forward, suddenly it is May 2023. So much has happened over the last 13 years since August 2010. My caregiver journey has been long, and often, it's felt never-ending. But for the last six months now, Mom has been placed on hospice care for significant weight loss. Suddenly, my caregiving journey is taking a hard right turn. I've come to a major fork in the road with a sign reading "*The End*" instead of "no end in sight."

I cannot help but wonder whether Mom and I would have both been so much better off without all the agonizingly slow pain and suffering she endured over the ensuing years. How much better would it have been for us both to have had her pass on peacefully in that private hospital room overlooking the beautiful San Gabriel Valley mountains?

The peace and tranquility I saw when I looked over at her in that hospital bed the next morning was short-lived, replaced by yet another stroke in 2021 that left her with aphasia, the sudden loss of speaking and comprehension due to oxygen deprivation to the brain. Sadly, my once talkative, cheerful Mom was now left with a greatly impaired ability to talk to me and others. Over the course of many years, her walking and independence completely vanished. She was aging in the most unpleasant of ways possible and there was simply no dignity attached to this long, cruel process. Her life could have been spared all those joyless hours spent at home in a hospital bed surrounded by cold metal bed rails, being cared for and labored over by her daughter and a caregiver.

This is not the same mom I knew and loved so well, long before all the deteriorating illnesses set in over time, the most heartbreaking of which is dementia. My once vital mom is now old and frail, even needing to be lifted out of her bed into her wheelchair every morning. This is not how I thought her life would end; the grace of a quick illness taking her would have been so much kinder and more dignified.

For me, the opportunity to pursue a stable career path in my 50s was suddenly upended by the more pressing need to step in and assume full caregiving duties for my mom. To have been spared this massive 15-year-long major life interruption is something I think about often. How profoundly different would my life be now had Mom just passed on peacefully that night in 2010? I think of it often: How both of our lives would have had happier endings.

I had spent five years in my career working full-time and learning all about late-stage dementia and its many intricacies and variables with almost two dozen late-stage dementia residents in an upscale assisted living memory care facility. Yet, when MY own mom keeps asking me, "Where's your dad? Where's Evy? Where's my mother? Where's my brother?"...it is somehow much, much harder to cope with and accept. I can't believe it's now my turn and this is really happening to me. So, it's MY dementia journey with MY mom, not a resident's personal challenges or their family's heartbreaking dementia journey I am witnessing. This time it's my dear, irreplaceable 95-year-old mom plummeting into dementia. I'm now forced to wrap my head around our new "normal" reality of mom losing more and more of her short-term memory. She thinks the famous actors in all those old movies are still alive, even though they would be at least 110 years old by now.

In my former job, running cognitive stimulation programs for late-stage dementia residents, I would have easily recommended to family members and caregivers to redirect their loved ones: "Go with the flow," and "Be patient and loving," I'd say. But all the specialized training I've done detailing these typical behaviors and their strategies for successful communication that I've shared with so many heartbroken families now seem meaningless and hollow. I've seen it all play out over and over during my five years of memory care work, but to now insert my own mom into the picture and "*run this program*," prompting, pretending and redirecting, acting like I'm not completely devastated at her lack of connection to what's going on right around her feels too much to bear.

"Where's my mother?" Mom asks. I tell her she's in the kitchen making dinner, and Mom is pleased to hear it. But Grandma passed away in 1986. "Therapeutic lying" is used frequently in dementia care to give the person a sense of control and to reduce agitation. But I never imagined employing this technique with my own mom. The cruel reality of dementia is upon me and hits me like a freight train.

Since my three brothers live in Seattle, San Francisco, and a smaller town also in Northern California, I'm entirely on my own here with mom with no other family involved in her daily care and decline. It feels as if my three brothers can't really handle this hard reality and instead just checked out from this ugly, gritty end phase of her life. Their lack of any level of support has led me to spend many years in a raw state of anger, completely unwilling to accept my mom's subtle and not-so-subtle personality and memory changes. Maybe I'm just not willing to accept all the many ways Mom has changed into a completely different person. I did not expect her life to be so long and heartbreaking. Being expected to do all this emotionally exhausting and draining care alone, without any offers of help or even a short break from my family members, has made me resentful.

"Just hire more caregivers," said one of my brothers who is in complete denial. My inside voice wanted to tell him to take a hike and to please send a generous amount of money to help cover all these endless ongoing caregiving expenses.

Mom's therapist told me years ago, "You just want your mom back." Wow, she really hit the nail on the head that time. That is what I really wanted...still want...but I know I can't ever get her back. The mom I used to shop with, cook with, and talk with on the phone every day is gone. We can't go out t]o lunch, a museum, or a concert anymore. Sadly, things are so different now; she's not really the mom I knew and loved so much. More and more Mom is out of context with her surroundings, her comments just don't fit the situation. When this happens, I just agree and play along.

"Let's go shopping for Thanksgiving," she has said to me so many times in January. "Christmas is right around the corner," she said, wanting to start getting ready for Christmas in February. This year, she suddenly lost all track of time. That's a huge adjustment, and it makes me feel like I'm losing her faster now.

For months she's been asking for her mom who passed away in March of 1986, her brother who passed away at 39 from Hodgkin's disease in 1966, and her other brother who passed in 2014. Suddenly, she's in a different place, searching for her family members like they are supposed to be right here joining her. But she forgot they've all been gone for a long time, some even decades.

Other times, I deal with her emotions of confusion, anxiety, worry, and feeling distraught. She has completely lost track of time and significant events. Every day is becoming so bittersweet as I know Mom only has a matter of months ahead. She often spends a lot of time back in the 1960's catering business she and Dad ran together. Dad mismanaged the finances for years, and she tried endlessly to catch up and pay all the overdue bills and cover for all the drivers who didn't pay on time for their catering truck supplies. It all ended in a dreadful federal bankruptcy filing and the loss of our treasured, beautiful family home in San Rafael, overlooking Mt. Tamalpais.

At six years old, I did not understand why my three siblings and I were abruptly uprooted and forced to navigate the unfortunate loss of my parent's dream home. I feel right back there now, unable to predict Mom's mercurial moods or have any sense of control over how the day ahead will unfold. This uncertainty is my new normal, but I have not accepted it very well.

"Shut up, you're mean to me, you're lying, no, no, no." Some days, that's all I hear from her. I feel so small, unappreciated, and under attack. Why I'm not used to it by now, I don't know, but this is how I usually feel when caring for her. "Shut up," I'm told when I simply try to explain myself. "You talk too much," she says. I've learned that silence is best at these times. "Turn out the light," she yells. I hear this often but wish she could just ask me instead of yelling. The criticism is often biting and unnecessarily harsh:

I tell her none of her boys will come down and help me out. No one bothers to drive or fly to Los Angeles to visit her or even give me a two-day break. I can't understand why my brothers are not here helping during this long, exhausting journey. She is their mom too, but they do not seem to care. Using basic logic is not going to work, since most of the time she denies whatever I'm trying to explain. I try so hard thinking she can still understand me, but that's like banging my head against the wall. My efforts are futile. This is a frustrating cycle that goes on day after day.

"Mom, we need to turn off the TV now because it is 1:00 a.m., time to go to bed." She does not know what time it is. Yet, at other times, she watches the news on CNN, enjoys an old movie, reads the newspaper, or asks me how work was. How bizarre that she goes from living 60 years in the past to asking me about my day at work! This makes absolutely no sense at all. It feels like I'm on some kind of weird odyssey through time and space that's going in the wrong direction. I just agree; what else can I do? Do I have a choice? But the hard reality is I cannot get Mom back to who she used to be. I can only hope she continues to remember me and why I'm here for so long helping her.

I've been her live-in caregiver for 15 years now. I can't believe I was only 46 when my son, ex-husband and I moved in with her way back in May of 2008. The plan was to put Danny through the great public schools here in Temple City and help Mom after knee and back surgery for severe arthritis. But what instead unfolded over time was me becoming her "*every-thing.*" I cooked, cleaned, scheduled (and repeatedly canceled) important medical appointments and surgeries she absolutely refused to go to over and over, did all the grocery shopping, paid all the bills, and completed necessary household repairs, which on occasion were sizable and very significant. I mor-

phed into this *everything gets it done girl* over time. Meanwhile, mom unwittingly became highly dependent on my constant help and relied on me for *everything*.

With increasing frequency, Mom was spending way too much time in her wheelchair and hospital bed and losing physical strength and her natural ability to walk and stand on her own legs. Sadly, over time she could only "shuffle" or slide her legs and feet along the floor without lifting or carrying her legs forward to take steps.

She was losing her footing and her balance.

So was I.

Without even realizing it, I was quickly losing myself and my identity. I was instead becoming this indispensable little helper bee buzzing around her house to instantly meet her every need. Ultimately, I lost myself as I did more and more everyday tasks for her. Instead of helping her, I was making everything *way too easy* for her. Why was I doing this? To somehow magically extend her life?

The outcome has become that I have woken up these many years later quite resentful, frequently angry, fully unemployed, and totally absent from the workplace without a current relevant skill set to speak of.

I also have recognized in me the signs of active caregiver burnout, including sudden anger, frequent frustration, resentment, and often feeling like this long journey would never end. I have found myself going to bed early just to get a good night's rest, yet not really getting enough quality sleep on a regular basis. I also have experienced broken sleep cycles as I awake during the night to change mom or to turn her in her bed.

I have sought emotional support through a USC family caregiver support group that has been a lifesaver. There, I have discovered many family caregivers in much more demanding and sometimes dual-parent caregiving roles. I have met a wonderfully supportive social worker who met Mom and supported me tremendously as I sojourned in the trenches of this really challenging experience. But over time, I realize that I have essentially allowed myself to become *invisible*. This has been the result of my selfless, accommodating nature. I haven't erected proper, healthy boundaries to keep myself vital as an individual. I have lost myself and only recently have realized it.

"I am grateful, I am appreciative," says my client, a 98-year-old woman for whom I also care. This woman astounds me as although she has early-stage dementia, she can still be very coherent. The tears well up in my eyes as I prepare her breakfast. The sadness hits me like a ton of bricks because my own 95-year-old mom has aphasia and cannot express her full appreciation for what I do for her daily. But way beyond that, I see in my client what I so want from my own mom: The ability to walk, talk, and be an independent senior; to share some genuinely happy memories together instead of all this sadness and anticipation of her passing. This is a bittersweet moment that has played out at times with my client because she has represented what my mom can no longer be.

While it would be great to go back in a time machine and get the mom who was transported with that 911 call to the ER in August 2010, I realize I can't. it's simply no longer possible. Instead, I have no choice but to continue loving the fragments and pieces of her that are morphing and changing daily. It's frightening when she says she doesn't remember the big family lawsuit where we lost all 196 acres in a legal land partitioning court case in Santa Clara Superior Court back in 2006. I'm scared and wary to discover what she'll forget next. I fear in time she won't feed herself, or know my now 23-year-old son, or her own three sons, or me.

While I love my mom dearly, the thought of her peacefully passing that night in the ER in such a serene and beautiful setting would have spared both of us this terribly slow and debilitating journey. She is living a life so far removed from who she used to be.

For 15 years now, not only has my life not been my own, but neither has hers. We have both changed and not necessarily for the better.

It is truly a blessing to still have her, but she's slowly slipping farther into dementia and becoming less of herself and more like the disease with which she's been diagnosed. She's losing context, remembering random fragments of her former life and memories. It's all really an elongated blur of who she was way back in 2010 and who she is now.

Where did all those years go? What have I been doing for the past 15 years? I can't get my life, career, or earning potential back. They're gone forever. I'm left to cherish this time, a few very special memories and moments together. This experience has created so many conflicting emotions internally because I've had to take on a thankless role I never asked for as Mom's live-in caregiver.

What great opportunities have I missed that could have been realized in these past 15 years? Might I have remarried and lived happily ever after? I'll never know.

But now, I only have a matter of maybe a few more months left with her. How will all this time I've spent with her end? Will she know me? Will she remember she's my mom, and I'm her daughter? Will she remember anything? How much longer will she live? How hard will all this become for me daily? Why do our loved ones have to endure dementia? Why can't they just grow old with grace and dignity? I can't stop all the questions or this insidious process. I can only put one foot in front of the other and be grateful for her long life and so much time together. It's just a matter of time now.

At the same time, I need to acknowledge that without my faith, this very long and emotionally trying journey would have been impossible to endure. God has been my enduring strength, granting me so much grace and blessing when I felt I didn't know how I was going to continue. Without my church, people praying for me, and trusted, dear friends to lean on, I probably would have given up long ago. Instead, I have become so much stronger than I ever realized I could be. Over these many years, I have also found clarity and guidance by reading the Bible and searching for wisdom. Listening to Christian worship music daily, belonging and participating in a women's Bible Study, and trusting and believing God that He keeps Mom in His care, have kept me going.

Over the years, I have been blessed by many Christian caregivers and helpers along the way. Looking back, it's obvious God has sent more than one very purposeful caregiver to help me including Mom's current caregiver, Cecilia. For a short time, even a pastor's wife spent time on Sundays with Mom so I could attend church. Some of these caregivers have also been important messengers who told me how fortunate and blessed I am to still have my mom. More than one had already said goodbye to their moms.

I have to believe God's hand is on Mom because much blessing has come out of this very long, challenging journey. God has certainly shown up while I'm struggling to keep going some days. All those emotional prayers crying out to God in my car and in my bed must have been heard. I could never endure so long on my own without being granted a divine level of strength, grace, and mercy. I would never have believed I could carry on as a family caregiver for this many years and through so many ups and downs. I attribute my ability to keep going to my faith and resilience and an abiding desire to see Mom live out her life until God calls her home.

This journey has taught me that we really don't know our true inner strength until we are tested and must resort to an unknown level of strength and resilience. Over the course of many years, God has given me the ability to trust Him for the outcome of Mom's deteriorating life and health. This test has been extraordinarily long, unforeseen, and has taken many years from my life. It's truly sad knowing the finality of my journey now lies right before me. This long and exhausting emotional journey of extreme self-sacrifice and selflessness is coming to a final ending.

Of course, I had thought that 15 years ago…

It is still hard to believe 15 long years have passed in the blink of an eye.

The time has finally come for me to shift my focus from Mom to myself. I look forward to the joy of being involved in a local community gardening effort, working a full-time schedule, and spending time with my friends, going places, and finally doing whatever I want, whenever I want. I also hope to travel to Europe and parts of the United States I have never seen. I am once again excited about my future and what my life ahead could become.

And I also rejoice in what lies ahead for Mom as she enters into God's kingdom.

CHAPTER FOUR

Loving Frank, Loving Me

by Enma Espinoza

"*E very day when the light of Mr. Sun enters through my window, I thank God for another day. Good morning to joy, good morning to love and to life.*" This song *Buenos Días, Señor Sol* by Juan Gabriel is one I sing in Spanish every day to my husband Frank as I embrace him. It has become a routine that we look forward to.

Frank was diagnosed with dementia in his early 60s. I have been caring for Frank with love and devotion now for over a decade, as he is currently in the advanced stages of this terrifying and painful disease.

For many years, Frank worked in a bustling and beloved restaurant in the City of Beverly Hills, a place frequented by major movie stars and producers including Steve Martin, Madonna, Whoopi Goldberg, and other celebrities. He fondly recalls a night where the staff offered to take Sylvester Stallone through the backdoor exit to avoid the paparazzi, and the actor chose instead to stand and sign autographs with fans out front.

Frank is my Mexican Latin Lover, the love of my life, and an amazing human being and husband for over 50 years. We met while both of us were students taking English as a Second Language classes in Los Angeles. After dating for only 3 months, we married in 1971. We both looked forward to spending many amazing life moments together and here we are, over a half of a century later, in the middle of this challenging brain disease still holding hands.

Relationships last because two people made a choice to keep it, fight for it and work through it. The secret to our long relationship has been our unconditional love, respect, and loyalty. We decided that those twisted tangles in his brain were not going to mess up his world and mine and vowed to turn our lives into an adventure. We kept physically active by regularly going on delightful scenic walks and hiking the breathtaking trails of Griffith Park, Echo Mountain, Eaton Canyon, and many other places. We explored delightful pathways up mountains and through rocky places with views overlooking the ocean. On many of these adventures we were able to catch glimpses of wildlife, including rabbits, deer, coyotes, and snakes. We loved setting out to unknown places that provided us with a sense of peace and tranquility.

"Where are you taking me today, mi amor?" Frank sometimes asked. I would laugh and not answer. I trusted that we were going to be okay for that day. We always were.

Frank and I have taken health, balance, nutrition, and memory classes to help keep our brains and bodies active. During the long, beautiful summer days we ventured out to concerts in the park, community events, musicals, movies, libraries, and to dancing to the uplifting sounds of Latin music, moving our bodies to the rhythm of cumbia, salsa, and boleros. Bolero is a Latin American romantic song characterized by lyrics dealing with love.

We also explored new places traveling by train and stayed socially active. Without reservations, we have taken public transportation: "Avoid the Fuss, Take the Bus!" We have taken the yellow, red, blue, green buses as well as the Gold, Red, Expo,

Metrolink, Amtrak and Dash everywhere. It has been quite an experience riding public transit to different destinations. During each trip, we have encountered different people, faces, attitudes, voices, languages, and have enjoyed seeing some distracted riders nearly spilling their coffee on passengers, as well as, a passenger who was trying to show off and call people's attention by trying to exercise using the top bars of the train. We hoped that they would not knock us down.

These activities have helped strengthen our brains and minds. As his disease continued advancing, however, it was getting progressively harder to continue with the things we loved to do. We still tried to do them, but we'd take shorter walks to the parks and modify other activities so that we still could do them.

Trips got a bit more complicated as he sometimes struggled with getting in and out of the buses because he sometimes felt confusion as his brain was rapidly changing, and it caused him to feel nervous and stressed. My main goal was to keep him and myself happy, calm, and if possible, stress-free. Having taken a series of stress-busting and other family caregivers' classes at the USC Family Caregiver Support Center, it gave me the opportunity to learn coping strategies and stress management techniques to find more positive ways to deal with frustration.

During this journey, we learned that it is the deep waves of life that teach us to be better swimmers. Facing this disease in your early sixties is what I consider the deep waves. What Frank and I have learned along this dementia journey is that so far, we have not drowned.

I am grateful that even though Frank has been facing this horrible confusing disease, he has made sure I was okay by gently holding my hand and hugging me. We have faced many stormy seasons, while going through the different stages of this disease, however, we have kept busy with meaningful activities that we have both enjoyed. These include us taking small trips to a farm to pick our own strawberries or riding a ferry boat along lake Arrowhead. We also cook together at home his favorite comfort food albondiga soup. I chop all the vegetables, bell peppers, squash, carrots, onion, garlic and other spices, and Frank helps by making the most beautiful meat balls for our "sopita de albondigas" soup. On our outings, we always made sure we did not miss a yummy double vanilla and pistachio ice cream cone from Thrifty.

Managing the household duties and our finances and at the same time advocating for Frank's medical needs and services has become my responsibility. I vividly recall one day that I dressed up like a lawyer. I wore a dark suit, put on my high heels, and carried a portfolio with all his medical records to go to a meeting to be part of an interview to help improve the medical needs for dementia patients and older adults. These days, I wear my comfortable tennis shoes to go anywhere.

The highlights and challenges during this dementia caregiver journey have made our love more intact and stronger than ever. Patients who are facing dementia have feelings, they are human beings just like you and me. Frank and I have worked hard to enjoy each moment because we're uncertain as to what might happen next, as this disease could be a short or a long, long journey. Of course, we have faced tough days; however, we have chosen to focus on gratitude and living one day at a time to the best of our ability with or without challenges.

Faith in our Lord and a nurtured diverse community church have helped us to continue traveling along this dementia journey with a positive attitude. We still have been able to pray at home or go to church and sit by the church choir and sing along. For as long as we have been able to, we have kept dancing, laughing at simple things such as trying to blow ice cream cone shaped bubbles, making funny faces, and taking funny pictures at carnivals.

We celebrated our 40th wedding anniversary at the Mission Inn Festival of Lights on a lovely carriage ride. Being carried by two lovely white horses on a stunning white carriage felt like a fairytale.

We have lived a different life than we had originally planned, but we lived and continued living a fulfilling life. We decided not to run away from the disease or hide, and we learned that even with a brain disease, it is possible to live with dignity and have a meaningful life.

One of the challenges as this disease progresses is seeing Frank's inability to communicate fluently or be always present. It has been hard to watch someone you love eat less and struggle, and not being able to do things that were such a part of his daily life before this disease. Even though this is difficult, many times, I have noticed his eyes light up when I enter the room. To better prepare for the grief and emotional side-effects of witnessing the incremental loss of a loved one with dementia, I found that it was essential for me to nurture my own soul during these difficult times. Rest and relaxation are a must for me to be able to stay healthy and alive. I celebrate and memorize our best days so I can better deal with the challenging ones. Frank and I don't have control over situations that were brought to us; however, we do have control over our attitude, and how we choose to view our world. We can only have faith that the right solutions and wisdom will be presented to us.

Education about this disease helps me to understand what it is like to walk in the shoes of a dementia patient. Along the way, we also have met friends at support groups. My friend Julie, whose husband also battled this disease, reminds me to "Keep shining bright so others will know it is possible to go through a journey such as yours". We both have learned so much and continue to do so.

My words of wisdom to those going through a similar caregiving experience is to be willing to ask for help. Schedule time off regularly to rest. I applied for and was granted a one-day respite grant and was able to go on a one-day trip to Santa Barbara by train. At Union Station, I grabbed a hot vanilla coffee and proceeded to board the train. I was fortunate to find a window seat and enjoyed a nice view of the city heading towards the Santa Barbara beach; I felt motivated to start writing in a gratitude journal that reminded me to be grateful for the good, beautiful things that I still was able to do such as to take this trip. Two hours later when I arrived at my destination, I was able to take off my bright mint green and orange tennis shoes and walk around the sandy beach barefoot and enjoy the ocean breeze, and the sound of the waves as they crashed against the shore. The weather was stunningly beautiful. I was able to walk around and enjoy gorgeous cliff views and a delicious brunch that included a Mimosa.

In the meantime, I knew that back at home, Frank was being well taken care of by an amazing caregiver. Putting together a list of Frank's daily routine helped me and the caregiver to make sure Frank walked, played his favorite song, "Tu Sonrisa," (whose lyrics are about something in your face that fascinates me...something in your face gives me light...is it your smile?). The caregiver served Frank a nutritious meal which consisted of wild salmon, green vegetables, and fruit, and kept him hydrated during what was a hot summer day in Los Angeles by preparing an aromatic fruit infusion with strawberries and blueberries. Later, the caregiver commented that Frank enjoyed and savored the fresh flavor of the colorful berries.

I had so much fun on my self-care day. I came back from this trip with elevated positive energy and more patience.

Caregivers reading this, I hope you know that you are not alone. Don't let Alzheimer's keep you from experiencing the other side of this disease. While I don't deny the uncomfortable emotions, I have tried to focus on the good things. I embrace every moment because I don't know what will come next. Laughing helps me through this journey. I surround myself with positive people. I take and live one day at a time. There are many of us going through a similar journey who can be of great help and support. My experience is that I have met many wonderful friends who have offered to pick us up and take us to concerts in the park, grocery shopping, run errands, and offered advice and support. I also found out that living your life outside of the caregiver role helps you to be a more loving, patient and a healthier caregiver.

If you are a caregiver who may be experiencing burnout and fatigue, please find a way to take time off for yourself. I strongly recommend getting respite care to help you recharge. Respite care provides short-term relief for primary caregivers. I know how hard it can be because I have experienced it, but it is important to take that day off, to dance, play, sing, and laugh on your own. Do not be afraid to ask for and accept help. Schedule a day off to go on a trip, do something you don't do every day outside of the caregiver role. Be kind to yourself. Treat yourself with love and compassion and above all, be patient with yourself, and know you are doing the best you can. I once heard from a very dear friend: "Inch by Inch, and it is a cinch because yard by yard, it is too hard."

Caring for a loved one as you age can be challenging but can also strengthen your bond. While dementia may change some aspects of a person, it doesn't have to change the love you share. Love is the balm that heals and invites our inner joy to emerge, but most of all, it connects us, one with another. Love is the mortar that holds the human structure together. Love comes to us, just as surely as we give it away.

I have learned the importance of loving the journey and that getting lost is okay. You never know what you might discover exploring. I have learned that sometimes taking a step backward after taking a step forward is not a disaster, it is like the dance the "cha cha cha." There is so much beauty to be found.

My story highlights the importance of love, hope, optimism, and self-care. I know that I am not alone in the love, devotion, and challenges I experience in dementia caregiving. It is possible to live to live with dignity and have a meaningful life. The best possible future is to live as well as we can today!

"While a disease may change many aspects of a person, it doesn't have to change the love you share."

CHAPTER FIVE

Holding the Ache of Reality

by Wendy Lew Toda

I t's easy to get lost in the wild ride of caregiving. Writing poetry has been my lifeline, guiding me back to myself when there's just too much emotional dust in the air. The practice also helps me savor sweet moments, because they are present, too. The spareness of poetic language helps me drill down and find what I'm feeling. Through poetry, I can lean into the expressive beauty of words to name my caregiving experiences, transforming them into art. My chapter offers a collection of poems with a small narrative woven throughout. They are captured moments of my caregiving life to both of my parents, and to my Auntie while she cared for my late Uncle.

....

As my mother's confusion grew, cognitive decline became a real thing.

....

"Marbles"

She's leaving
       I see it
this can't be
       I fight it
chasing the memories
rounding them up
as they bounce and
roll across the floor

she doesn't notice

I tuck them back
in her pockets
so she can keep them
but it seems there's a hole
I can't catch and return
fast enough
so I gather as many
as I can
       weeping
       holding them for her
       hiding my tears
       gathering her close
she smiles

       from somewhere

       far

       away

and blesses me
with her love.

My uncle's doctor added his harsh news.

"Protest"

Two weeks.
Four at most.
The words crash
through the underbrush
in my heart
running about wildly
yelling down the hall
kicking and screaming on the floor
before collapsing
exhausted
in stunned silence
That's it?
That's all?
The end of the offramp
I don't want to see
I shut my eyes
a bad dream
it must be
but no
the numbers remain:
two to four weeks.
I see it on his face
in his suffering body
the leaving is happening.
It is the way of things.
I don't like it.

....

I wrestled with the heartbreak of this season...

....

"Holding the Ache of Reality"

What I wish for
want to believe
colliding with
what is.
Darn reality.
So immovable
uncooperative;
I rail against it
pace around
throw up my hands.
Reality stares back
compassionately
and honestly.
I collapse into a chair
with a harumph
give reality
the stink eye.
Reality is unfazed.

Thus we remain
for a year.

Reality gently sits down
next to me
even as I
scoot away
refuse eye contact.
"The longer you won't acknowledge me
the longer you will suffer

constant surprises.
Is that what you want?"
"No", I grumble, "I want YOU to change."
Reality sighs.
"Alas. I cannot.
I am what I am."

long silence

"Walk with me.
If you don't acknowledge
where she is
you are trying to meet your mother
somewhere she's not."
"True", I mumble
staring at the ground.

more long silence

Clear invitation:
let go
surrender the memories
into the care of my heart
still honored
cherished
no longer the measure of
what should be
or who she should be,
practice
living in what is
engaging with what is
with who she is now
today,
not being surprised.
Stay with what is real.

Return when I lose my way
Return again
     and again
     and again
to love
clear-eyed
holding the ache of reality
here
now
for all her days.

....

as we buried my uncle at sea;
my Father admitted to the hospital just the day before.

....

"To the Sea"

We come
because water sings
the song of your heart.
It is right
that our goodbyes
rest here.

For all that has been
thank you
For all you mean to us
     thank you
And for the ways we carry you in our hearts
     thank you

From water you have come
To water we return you
 in peace
 in hope
 and with so very much love
until we meet again.

....

The way through is clear,

....

 "Hello"

Across the line
the horizon cups its hands
calls hello from
the distant edge of sight
so blurry
the unknown wanders there
all that draws me
all I dream of
all I dread
I wonder at the welcome
look back
goodbye
release what no longer
needs to be held
gather treasures of before
courage for my heart
hope in the dark
sweet joy now past
beauty held dear
bear these gifts forward
rich foundation
for worlds now unfolding

inviting me
into what can be
who I can be
today
I answer
Hello

....

to see the gifts offered to me in each moment

....

"The Red Leaf"

A moment of eternity
set in memory
that wanders
and weaves its way through time
this jewel
a simple leaf
singing its vibrant red song
clear and bright
a gift of beauty
awakening
the desire to share
with me
presented with sweet joy
and delight
her soul
with shining eyes
completely present
to now.

Completely undone
am I
to receive
the wonder of
her simple offering
given with such love.

....

and to welcome my own transformation.

....

CHAPTER SIX

Putting It All Together

by Parissa Kermani

June 20, 2023

I t's my ghost staring back at me in the mirror. The hollow look. The eyes that scream defeat. The lips pulled down by the sheer force of these last four years.

My life in pieces all around me.

How did I get here?

May 18, 2019

Mom's home. The red heart marked around the date on the calendar has been a daily reminder of the countdown before her return from the Pulmonary Rehabilitation Center. As my sister Hannah and brother Liam help her out of the car, I open the front door and am left breathless by the scent of orange blossoms. A joyful smile blooms on Mom's lips as we make eye contact. I smile back though I feel a tinge of sadness for her. Little does she remember that her husband of 68 years is gone.

It was just a few weeks ago when both were admitted to the hospital for pneumonia. As she came off the ventilator, they both stayed there for a few more weeks, having their rendezvous via FaceTime. Mom's shiny golden hair was coiffed and as her joyous face appeared on the phone screen, Dad's hands had raised towards the phone as if to grab her. His hands feeble with tremors, bruised and thinned to the point that his wedding band was now on his middle finger. Speaking through his oxygen mask, I could make out an "I love you," whispered with a longing look.

After three weeks, they both left the hospital just a few hours apart from each other. Mom left first. Being wheeled out, she looked radiant as the sun shone on her. Nine hours later, Dad too left the hospital except he did so via the ICU.

The grip of the ventilator and host of IV units clutching onto his arm could not overtake the gentle plan of a divine presence. His journey of this lifetime came to an end. In turn, we all lost our father that evening.

Oh, the sorrow.

I catch myself and steer off memory lane. Now's not the time for the past. I have much to celebrate given Mom's comeback. I embrace the beauty of this thought and start my new journey with Mom.

Every day I start off Mom's day with her favorite two-part morning greeting:

"Sobeh Toon Bekheyr."

"Agebateh Toon Bekheyr."

I know the first part means "May your day be good." I don't know about the second part, but it doesn't matter, it makes her happy.

For the next four years, my household is a perpetual cheerleading squad.

The constant "Bravo Mrs. Sarah," and "You're so beautiful," and 'You're so smart," become mine and all the caregivers' mantras because we all know it makes Mom happy. We fill the house with music. We play games. Every day, we make sure she's dolled up even though she may not be going anywhere. We take breakfast in the garden and create birthday celebrations that are fit for a jovial child. Visits to the nail salon, the mall, the gardens, and the beach become part of a routine schedule.

Outings are what I cling to when her mind can no longer process the games.

✶✶✶✶✶

As time moves on, it takes a part of Mom with it. Little by little, her mobility becomes worse. She can no longer stand up on her own nor can she stay standing. It's hard to believe that she was someone who in her sixties had climbed Chichén Itzá the Mayan Pyramid.

We undergo two shower incarnations for her to have a safe shower. The regular shower chair is replaced with one that slides in and out of the shower and swivels. With this change, she no longer struggles to step into the shower. I thought we got the Rolls Royce of shower chairs until she could barely turn or move from side to side. We give away the Rolls Royce and tear out a bathtub to create a walk-in shower. She still needs a chair that would minimize the amount of turning and side-to-side movement. She now needs this for both a shower and a bathroom visit. I find the perfect solution in a rolling shower commode that allows her to do both with dignity. I finally find something that can withstand the physical ravages of the passing of years.

Little by little, her voice takes more absences from this world. Hearing her speak one word after hours of silence would be a treat, as though I was the kid who found the last bar of ice cream in the freezer. She needs help eating and drinking. Liquids must be thickened. She can't do two things at once.

Mom has had a string of caregivers. Only two of those who could physically handle her were still standing at the end. If it weren't for them, Mom would have been bedbound. That I am sure of. When they asked for a raise, there was no option other than to lay off other caregivers. They each worked 9-hour days, and I picked up the remaining 15 almost every day. They afforded Mom as full a life as possible. They provided her freedom. I would have done anything to let her have that, and I did.

February 2022

My sister Gretchen is visiting. She is the food police. If it doesn't say organic on the bottle, expect to find it in the trash because -according to her – Mom's dementia requires her to have an organic diet to maintain a healthy brain. She's put together a food bible for the caregivers to follow. When she goes over it, it sounds like someone is speaking underwater. She is clueless as to how little room there is for so many orders in the mind of a 24/7 caregiver.

That's the mild version of all things Gretchen.

The more intense version is her chasing me down the laundry room, screaming her head off because I was not placing the Vie-Light on Mom's head daily.

"Don't you know this photo biomodulation therapy will invigorate Mom's brain?" Gretchen barks at my backside. Had I turned to face her at that moment, I swear she would have slapped me.

And then, there is the worst of it with her.

"Gretchen, the caregivers have called out sick." I stammer to her on the phone, trying to explain my dire need. "I have worked the last 48 hours taking care of our mom. My wrists hurt from turning her over in bed to change her diaper and my shoulder from repeatedly pulling her up in bed."

My sister is silent. My desperation continues.

"You know she must stay in bed when there is no caregiver. Just because there isn't one to help you take her to the lab, doesn't mean you can't come. You had cleared your schedule anyway. Your visit would give me a break. Why are you canceling?"

It falls on deaf ears.

Another request for help. Nothing.

Finally, she replies. It's useless.

"Parissa, I did not have a commitment to you to come there," Gretchen scolds trying to guilt me.

The wind is knocked out of me, and suddenly the exhaustion from these last 48 hours has magnified, and the upcoming 24 hours feel like I will be walking through a damp tunnel trying to breathe. What was the muffled sound of a concerto orchestrated by some school children suddenly becomes a live heavy metal concert when the tenderness of my scalp, the racing of my heart, and the burning of my eyes pound harder and burn more profoundly.

Exhaustion does that.

I am left with nothing but the intense desire to sit and bawl my eyes out. And that's what I do. I have no choice. It's the only way these days that I can relieve my burnout.

Later that night, Gretchen pesters me to FaceTime with Mom. I ignore her given her earlier behavior. It's pointless.

"How dare you take away the privilege for a mother to speak to her child," Gretchen scolds me. "Shame on you."

She continues until she's taken my last breath. I give in. Her saccharine-sweet voice permeating the room grates my ears. For some reason, I take a deep breath and tune it out.

Something comes over me and for the first time, I see it all. How did I miss it? I understand my exhaustion fully. Yes, endless planning, problem-solving, and watching Mom deteriorate are all exhausting. There is something else that is tiring: Gretchen. Her constant beating of me with all things Mom has been a drain. The inability to stand up for myself has made it worse.

Why would it matter now? Did I not know this person's ways?

Because this go around was not a normal family matter. Mom had never had dementia, nor ever needed 24/7 care. Yet, I danced into this new normal with the same family dynamics we had with her as before. When there is a "never before" situation, rules need to be drawn up and consequences implemented. Had I realized this, there may have been a chance I would have spared myself much stress and exhaustion.

Gretchen is the Disneyland Dad. She shows up for her weekly dose of fun with Mom and then disappears. Mom is her reward. New rules could have held her accountable while providing me with some respite.

No heavy lifting? No Disneyland visits.

When you do the lion's share of the work in this new normal, YOU are the lion, YOU set the rules.

Mom is fast asleep now.

My mind wanders past Gretchen and takes inventory of the week.

ER visit. Caregivers calling out sick. Wheelchair repair.

The review seems to be lacking something. Maybe I missed it. Let's see: ER, Call outs. Wheelchair.

I freeze.

Nothing is missing. Rather someone is.

Me.

I'm nowhere to be found on this list nor on any from the last four years.

I wish there had been a "how to be a caregiver to an aging parent" class. Had I jotted down all that I did or dealt with; I would have noticed that no one was taking care of me. I realize that in such an intense role, the only way to come out whole at the other end is to have been a caregiver to myself as well.

It's not the end, and already I know this won't be the case. I am perpetually tired, and my mind is foggy. Five years ago, people would see me as younger than my age. Fast forward five years of intense caregiving, and now the take on my age is reversed.

If all had only dawned on me sooner.

March 2022-November 2022

Lately, Gretchen's nightly FaceTime with Mom leaves me with the intense desire to cover my ears and scream. There's no great suspense as to the conversation.

"Mom, guess what? I bought a house." Gretchen announces. The next night: "Mom I have exciting news for you. I bought a house!"

The same announcement continues every night for weeks. For as long as I can remember, Gretchen's biggest desire has been to have Mom live with her. The purchase of this home would make that dream become a reality. Although her escrow closes mid-spring, Mom doesn't move to Gretchen's until much later. When she does, it's only for three days per week. For all of Gretchen's songs and dances of the last four years of wanting Mom to live with her, her final crescendo turns out to be a part-time gig of us sharing custody of Mom.

The arrangement is one whereby Mom leaves my house on Thursday nights, coming back on Sunday. One Thursday, as she is not well enough to travel to Gretchen's, she stays with me. Gretchen in turn takes up her week's caregiving duties at my home. Walking by Mom's room, I notice Gretchen's stress.

"Parissa, it's 2 pm," she says all flustered and stone-faced. "I haven't had breakfast and Mom still needs a diaper change."

Cry me a river I think to myself.

Getting ready to leave on Sunday night, Gretchen has a question for me.

"Parissa, if Mom gets sick when she is with me..." Gretchen says it softly, "...would you come over to help?"

I purse my lips, take a deep breath, and then answer her with a question.

"Gretchen, where were you these last four years?"

For someone who has an answer for everything, who beats me down until she gets the answer she wants, all words escape her. She's gone mute.

Through her silence, she answers her own question. I leave the room without uttering another word.

November 2022

It takes me an hour to compose one email. My hands keep dropping off the keyboard.

My mind is perpetually foggy.

A stranger's kindness leaves me bawling.

I am spent in every respect.

Given my state, Liam, Hannah, and my brother Noah decide it's best that Mom moves in with Gretchen who now becomes the 24/7 caregiver.

With Mom gone, I have more time to run my errands. Regretfully, errands can't be a plural activity. There's no such thing as "errands." I need a nap after each one. Burnout can wreak havoc.

January 15, 2023

Mom has spent the last two weeks with me since Gretchen was not feeling well. Today, she'll be heading back to Gretchen's house. Surprisingly, this morning Mom's feeding herself joyfully while staying fully engaged with the movie playing. I videotape this scene and take a picture of it. These would be my last two recordings of her in my home.

January 23, 2023-February 4, 2023

Mom's oxygen levels keep dropping, she has trouble breathing and her wheezing won't stop. She is taken to the hospital. There's fluid buildup in her lungs. Draining it provides only temporary relief as the build-up keeps coming back.

"The patient in 410 is declining rapidly," I overhear the nurses speaking to each other about Mom.

Mom's body is shutting down. There's nothing that can be done. She's transferred to hospice.

February 4, 2023

Hospice.

I didn't understand the concept of hospice as Mom was brought to Gretchen's for it. My experience of hospitalization with Mom was simple: She'll get better and go about life as usual. Little did I know that hospice is a way station between this world and the next. It's the zone where one's life is suspended until the body gives out. Essentially, Mom has come home to pass away. Hospice doesn't hold hope. It holds comfort for the patient as the body shuts down. Morphine is the active player, shutting down the patient's awareness and providing comfort as nature goes about its course.

The hospital bed has been moved to the living room and fitted with a turquoise sheet. Mom is completely knocked out. I struggle to find a reason for her state as we had not started administering morphine yet.

"I've never seen a hospice patient receive IV fluids," says the hospice nurse as she hooks one up for Mom. Shortly after, Mom comes out of her stupor, fully present. As she lies there with the sun peeking through the windows, I notice her looking at me intently. I smile and ask if she'd like me to sing her a song. She nods yes, though all animation has left her face. I bend over her bed and sing one of her favorites.

"There are many beautiful people in the world.
But none as beautiful as you.
They say tulips are the messengers of spring.

For me, you are that eternal messenger.
The whole world knows that You are the most beautiful of all
the beautiful ones."

I let the last word roll off my tongue, cup her face, and bend down to give her a kiss.

This would be our final goodbye.

Soon after, her discomfort intensifies. The hospice nurse starts administering morphine. When the bag of IV fluids is finished, she does not replace it.

February 5, 2023

As Mom's overtaken by the spell of morphine, I seek the embrace of the couch. There, I reminisce about Dad.

The "I love you," he had whispered when he FaceTimed with Mom back in April 2019 -while they were both in the hospital - was the last thing he said to his beloved wife. How poignant. He was the patriarch to whom the children bestowed - in respect - a kiss on his forehead as a greeting and a farewell. Though he had a wicked sense of humor, there was no goofing around with him. But he'd get a kick out of what would become our signature goodbye.

I'd start: "See you later."

He'd follow: "Alligator."

On April 18, 2019, I spent the afternoon in his hospital room playing his favorite songs. With his feeding tube in place and his eyes closed, he was resting comfortably. It was getting late.

"Dad, I'm leaving."

He protested, moving his head from side to side, caressing the white pillowcase cover with his silvery hair in the process.

"See you later."

I hadn't expected a reply. Surprisingly, he replied fully coherent and alert.

"Alligator."

I had returned the next day alas to chaos.

Sitting up, he looked bewildered. The nurses were in a frenzy. The oxygen delivery to him was set at the highest possible level. His respiratory rate was through the roof.

"Who are these people?" Dad had asked while reaching for my hand.

Two ICU nurses came in.

ICU nurses?

Overnight he had aspirated. They were there to suction out his lungs. To proceed, they laid him down and ordered him to swallow.

"Swallow Dad. Swallow"

He wasn't. I struggled to comprehend why he wasn't given that he was just talking.

"Dad, SWALLOW. SWALLOW."

Clunk.

The brakes on the bed were released. We were all running towards the ICU where he was put on a ventilator. I signed the consent and was ordered to leave.

As I walked out of the ICU - its white corridors devoid of life - I felt the emptiness of my heart as I sobbed, my tears covering any semblance of a face beneath them. There was a knowing. The end was near.

Soon after, Dad left this world. At first sight of all that remained of him, I sobbed uncontrollably. Never had I cried as hard nor as loud. My brother Noah planted a kiss on my forehead to comfort me. I was too drenched in my sorrow to feel any relief. As a final farewell, I bent down to kiss his forehead as I had done thousands of times. I could feel the coolness of his forehead and the warmth both in one kiss. Soon it would be only a cool kiss.

February 6, 2023

This morning Gretchen is barking at me.

"Parissa, what you did the other night was unacceptable, snapping at me like that. Don't you ever let it happen again."

She is upset that a few nights ago, I asked her to take her educational session about "all things morphine" with the hospice nurse into another room. The voices in my head wanted to scream at her: Really? Now? Here?

People often ask me how I set boundaries with Gretchen. I've tried. Many times. It's hopeless. When she wants something to be her way, she's like a volcano spewing out and burning through any barriers in her path.

February 7, 2023

Though Mom's here in Gretchen's house, I think about how alive she is in my home even though the house is dark and still. The pink pillow on her dining chair. Her favorite little red book held together by tape. Every corner holding the memory of an activity with her. Her dusty pink bedroom with the chandelier. All the beautiful dresses, most with their matching jewelry and a story of how they came to be hers.

Then, there are all the pictures of her on her bedroom wall. I had placed them there to make her feel like a queen: "Mom, who is this beautiful lady? Is this you? Wow!"

Each time she'd smile proudly and nod yes. Her favorite is one of herself in her 30s sitting in a grass field. She's wearing a pink floral dress holding an apple, smiling at the camera. Her beloved husband had captured that photo.

I once told her that she was the light in my home. She had looked puzzled. Tonight, I would tell her that even in its shadows, she is still the light that shines brightly in my home.

February 8, 2023

The hospice nurse pulls me aside. Mom's breathing has changed. She only has a little while left. I spend part of this time at the head of her bed, resting my arms over her chest, singing to her, and thanking her for having been my mom in my lifetime.

Her breathing slows down. Three more breaths and she is gone.

She passes away at 8:30 am on February 8.

I turn off the oxygen machine. Everything feels normal again. She looks more radiant, more herself than she did in the last few days. I feel joy. Mom's back. Her soul's taken comfort in her body again and she looks like she's about to wake up any moment.

It only seems natural to greet her.

"Sobeh Toon Bekheyr."

"Agebateh Toon Bekheyr."

The joy is fleeting. What's the point? She's no longer here. I'm suspended between normalcy and reality.

Soon the coroners arrive.

"Ma'am, do you want to keep this?"

The turquoise sheet.

"No sir," I reply.

Loosening the sheet from the mattress, they use it to transfer Mom's body into the body bag. I follow them, watching them place her body in the hearse and drive away. Returning to the house, I notice Liam and Hannah working on the details of the funeral.

All that's left for me to do is to sort out her "things".

*****

Weeks down the line, I'd learn the meaning of the second part of the morning greeting:

"Sobeh Toon Bekheyr." – "May your day be good"

"Agebateh Toon Bekheyr." – "May your end be good"

What a senseless greeting to have whispered over her body on the day of her passing. What was good about the end? She needed help with everything. Old age had stolen so much from her. Dementia had made it worse.

But *was* everything entirely bad?

Just as a sunset ends a day of fun at the beach, so does it create a beautiful play of colors in the sky. When the horizon swallows the sun, all is not lost.

In the end, she lived with her loving daughter in a cottage and not a nursing home, a daughter for whom she had been the #1 priority. In Noah, she had a 24/7 physician at her disposal. A physician for whom "now's not the right time" wasn't in his vocabulary when it came to her. Liam, Hannah, and Noah had been fully and lovingly committed to covering the expenses of her care despite extreme constraints for them. In them, myself and her caregivers, she had an army that would do anything for her well-being and happiness.

Without this army, the end of this lifetime's journey would have been heartbreaking. For all that she had done so selflessly for her family, for all the times she had put so many people ahead of herself, and for all the kindness she had bestowed onto the underprivileged, she didn't deserve that ending if it came to be.

But having been witness to the meaningful and joyous life that her army created for her relentlessly, I would say that the second part of the morning greeting most definitely stands. She lived a full and vibrant life at the end hand in hand with all the mental and physical setbacks of the passing of a lifetime.

June 20, 2023

The painters are here. I am excited to start taking care of a lot of things that I let go of these last four years. Seeing myself in the mirror again, I notice the ghost is still there but not as starkly as before. I now see the wind behind my back. The endless love and care that I gave Mom is my wind. I think of her – her angelic vibrant smile and the golden hair that had become her halo. Mom never grayed. She turned blonde. That brings me a smile.

I catch my reflection and my heart sinks. I don't look like me. I close my eyes and embed in my mind that bouncing back from these last four years will have its challenges. It may be a long journey. During this time, I've lost myself. I have many pieces to pick up, and to put back together again.

And so, it will be.

CHAPTER SEVEN

Bag Packed

by Shunese Coran

I n the well-lit bedroom, a faint scent of Clinique Aromatics and faded memories hung in the air. The worn and Murphy-oiled wooden dresser stood against the wall, its drawers neatly organized. The room belonged to Grandma, a gentle soul who had once filled it, and the entire home with warmth and joy. But tonight, something was different.

"Grandma, let's go to bed," I softly spoke from the doorway.

As the sun faded and night arose, Grandma began to experience one of her dementia-like episodes, a disorienting journey through time and place. Not as a result of dementia, but an anticipated and prolonged side effect of a brain tumor, that even after two brain surgeries and radiation treatment, has returned. This time it grew aggressively and on the part of the brain that was inoperable. With a poor prognosis, the decision to enroll Grandma in palliative and hospice care was the first of many tough decisions that would be made unbeknownst to me.

"I'm almost ready!" Grandma shouted.

I took a deep breath before sitting at the edge of her bed. This routine is something we grew accustomed to. After taking her bedtime meds, ensuring the nasal cannula was nestled comfortably, and turning on the nighttime news, Grandma would soon fall asleep. Not for long though. In a few short hours, it was as if the Director called "Action" in her head. She would spring out of bed and begin getting ready. Grandma was a poised woman who prided herself on always looking nice even if just going to the corner store. Many nights she would unroll the foam curlers from her hair, put on her favorite red lipstick, and get fully dressed. She'd prancy along between her bedroom and bathroom, not speaking much, focused– with her infectious smile plastered across her sweet face. She had somewhere to be and had to pack her bag. Most nights I'd go along with it. I'd ask her if she had all of her toiletries, socks, and favorite pajamas before beginning to redirect and reorient her to time and place. However, this was night four of these often hour-long episodes, and I was tired.

"Grandma, you have nowhere to be." I defeatedly stated.

Grandma hurriedly and anxiously moved past me. Speaking not one word. She grabbed her bag and carefully placed a few items she gathered in her bag before going over to her dresser. Her delicate hands trembled as she rummaged through the drawers, searching for something that seemed elusive even in her mind.

She began to get frustrated and blurted, "I've GOT to get home."

She continued her desperate quest, her fingers sifting through old paperwork and trinkets, seeking familiarity in the forgotten. I carefully approached Grandma and grabbed her hand, my voice gentle yet firm, "Grandma, you are home."

After a brief pause, she said, "No, Shunese." voice cracking, "It's time for me to go home" she exasperatedly claimed. Tears welled up in both of our eyes.

In that fleeting moment, time stood still, and the love between us transcended the confines of the brain tumor, reminding us both of the unbreakable bonds we shared. This bond began the day my grandmother was overjoyed with the news of becoming a grandparent, a dream she had wondered if it would ever materialize as my mother approached her forties. It flourished through the years, our lives interwoven as three generations were under one roof.

Her love was a guiding light, and in each triumph, she stood beside me, her heart filled with pride. She stood as my unwavering pillar of support, ensuring her presence at every sports game, awards ceremony, and milestone. As a child, you'd always find me in her shadows whether at the kitchen table snapping green beans, sitting on the porch as she watered the grass, or helping her shelve books at the library at the end of her shift. Her love intensified the day she tragically found her only child lifeless in bed. In her late sixties, she embraced the responsibility of raising her orphaned granddaughter. It was just the two of us and over the next five years, our bond deepened through countless memories, shared joys, and the inevitable lows. We weathered life together, finding strength in prayer and each other's embrace during our shared moments of intense grief. Her dedication to God and unwavering support instilled in me a sense of resilience. She was more than a grandmother; she became my mother, a confidante, and my closest companion.

With an exchanged squeeze of our hands, we made our way to her bed. The home oxygen tank hummed softly in the corner as we sat in silence. She laid across my lap, my sanctuary was hers. My hand caressed her head as I relished the privilege of being there, by her side.

She was exhausted, we all were exhausted.

A true reflection of the love and joy Grandma gave to others, one of her many surrogate daughters and two dear friends of mine, did not hesitate when asked to move in to help me care for her. Upon enrolling Grandma in hospice we were made aware that she is eligible to receive up to five days of respite care. This short-term inpatient care is provided to relieve family or other caregivers of their caregiving duties. Not much thought had been given to exploring this option prior, however, this might be the most appropriate time.

Amidst the deafening silence, a flood of thoughts surged through my mind, each one tugging at my heart forcefully. The weight of the decision to place her in a facility bore down heavily upon me. "I'm not ready to let go," I whispered to myself, fearing the separation, unsure if I could bear to see her leave our home. Moreover, the feeling in the pit of my stomach was that once she left, she would not return. "She can't give up on me, or life now," I pleaded with God, seeking a glimmer of hope that her spirit would endure, and that we could defy the odds together.

The conflicting emotions tore at my soul. "I don't want her to suffer," I murmured, my heart aching at the thought of her enduring any type of pain. Grandma already withstood two complex brain surgeries, a heart attack, a series of radiation treatments, and nearly a dozen Grand Mal seizures over the past four years. I could not imagine her petite body being able to handle much more. Then there's the unpleasant psychological pain she's experienced as she's verbally expressed her frustration with the decline in energy and independence over the past few months. This graceful and faithful servant of God was undeserving of any pain or suffering.

"But another cycle of grief awaits," a voice warned, reminding me of the inevitable heartache that would follow this difficult choice. My mother's untimely death when I was thirteen was life-altering, faith-shaking, and debilitating. For nearly a year each day, when the clock struck 9:28 am, I would sob uncontrollably, replaying the moment the paramedics pronounced her deceased. It was the fervent prayers and discernment of my grandmother that kept me on the straight and narrow. She knew by looking at me, when it was just one of those moments or just one of those days, and knew exactly what to say or do. It could be a thoughtful card with a handwritten note full of encouraging words I would unexpectedly discover on my nightstand or a suggested trip to get ice cream. Although I lost my mother physically, Grandma's love tremendously filled the gap and I continued to receive the nurture and love of a mother. How will I withstand the loss of a mother twice?

"Respite would mean she would go into a nursing facility," I realized with a pang of guilt, that the promise I once made to keep her at home might not be fulfilled. Doubts crept in like shadows, whispering, "What if they don't treat her right?" or she believes "I've given up on her." An unbearable fear. Yet, a flicker of self-preservation stirred within me. A break would give me time to restore order to the house: get the carpet cleaned, deep clean, catch up on laundry, change bedding– what was once the every Saturday morning routine. A good night of uninterrupted sleep. I reasoned, seeking a semblance of normalcy amidst the chaos. "She cannot die in this house," the haunting memory of my mother's passing surged back, fueling a determination to protect her from the same fate. I am pulled in opposite directions, grappling with love, responsibility, and the need to find a balance that would safeguard her well-being while preserving my own.

Amid the tumultuous silence, I yearned for a guiding light to lead me through this profound and challenging journey.

Eventually, Grandma falls asleep, and I tearfully watch over her.

In the following days, the inevitable truth loomed closer, and I knew a decision had to be made urgently, as she spent nearly all her days, and nights sleeping. With compassion and understanding, the hospice social worker case explained the process ahead and the supports that would be in place at home until a facility with a vacancy could be found, should I choose to place her in respite.

During that time, our home became a hub of caregiving activity. The hospital bed arrived, marking the gravity of her condition. The catheterization and daily nursing visits to either monitor vitals or give a bath became routine, and amidst it all, she lay there, sleeping peacefully, seemingly unaffected by the flurry of activity around her.

As the days ticked by, each passing moment felt like an eternity, allowing me to reflect deeply. These few days of waiting felt both endless and fleeting as I grappled with the weight of the decision that would shape the days to come.

"Found one that will be able to take her as soon as tomorrow afternoon." says the social worker on the other end of the phone line. With a deep sigh, I said "Okay" and scrambled to look for the notebook. The notebook generally sat by the telephone to keep a log of anyone who called while Grandma slept. I enjoyed sharing with her the names of those who called as a reminder that she was well-loved and to encourage her to keep up the good fight. I yelled out asking if anyone had seen the notebook, as I overlooked it in plain sight right at the edge of the coffee table. My nerves began to get the best of me. I took down the information provided including the name of the facility and address. Anaheim, that's nearly thirty-five to forty-five minutes away, I immediately thought. I planned to visit at least twice a day to oversee the care provided but the distance would make that a challenge. I was told that a nonemergency ambulance would arrive to transport her in the morning, and I was free to ride along.

The journey as Grandma's primary caregiver truly picked up after routine testing discovered a second brain tumor had aggressively formed and surgery was the agreed treatment. In between classes and at each break, I would call the hospital to get an update on her status. After school would let out for the day, I would drive nearly fifty miles one way, in Los Angeles traffic, to check on her and to sit by her side. She would always tell me it was okay to not come every day, but that was never an option in my mind. The recovery this go-round was rough. She developed epilepsy and really shouldn't be left alone. My house quickly became the kick-it spot after school and on weekends as my friends knew, I could not be out late to make sure Grandma had eaten and taken her medication. They loved, respected, and affectionately called her Grandma as well, so it never presented an issue. This is where my effective time management skills were developed as I balanced being a teenager and caregiver; staying ahead of my coursework, Grandma's doctor's appointments and schedule, and my extracurricular activities.

Decisions I made daily centered around Grandma's care needs although she was adamant to not worry about her. If I didn't who would? Yes, she had four living siblings, yet she was the youngest and their level of support was limited. A plethora of nieces and nephews, but they have their households to tend to. She's my responsibility. What I ate generally was based upon what she had a taste for. The college I chose needed to be close enough for me to be able to get home if needed. For a while her health was pretty stable, I had the opportunity to live on campus for a year and even get my apartment. Friday evenings I would commute home to spend the weekend with Grandma, refill her medication reminder box, pick up any refills from the pharmacy, complete her grocery shopping, and conclude with taking her to church on Sundays if she had the energy. As Grandma's energy began to deplete, so did mine.

During these times, it was as if the weight of Grandma's illness forged a unique connection, and every moment became an opportunity for learning and connection. The lessons she shared extended far beyond the practical skills I acquired, such as balancing a checkbook and ensuring timely bill payments. She offered life lessons, family history, and the virtues a woman should uphold. In her wisdom, she seemed determined to impart as much knowledge as possible as if we shared an unspoken understanding of the limited time we had left.

The sun began to peak through the blinds as I nervously peeked from the couch around the railing of the hospital bed. I held my breath, hoping and praying Grandma hadn't taken her last. The couch became my bed the past few nights and its cushioned arms soaked the tears that fell throughout the night. I wanted to remain close and if the bed was a little larger we'd share it. An insurmountable and indescribable amount of strength overcame me. Grandma was in the lucid state she had been for the last few days. I wanted to ensure she looked great for what I knew would be our final ride. The ambulance to transport us to the nursing facility would arrive in just a few hours, and the bath nurse and nurse should arrive any minute. After quickly getting dressed for the day and attempting to straighten up a bit, an all too familiar voice is heard.

"Shunese" shouts Grandma.

It had been about three days since I heard her voice. I quickly ran down the hall over to her bedside with joy in my heart yet worry at the forefront of my mind. Is she okay? Did she try to get out of bed just that fast? Is she in pain?

"Yes, Grandma", I said softly stroking her cheek with the back of my hand and looking deeply into her eyes.

"Where'd your mom just go?" she asked. Taken aback by her question I briefly paused and carefully considered how to respond.

I placed my forehead directly on hers. "She's in heaven, remember?" I quietly whispered.

Gazing out of the window with a smile, Grandma nodded yes.

"You know that I love you right? Do you love me?" I asked while brushing her soft grey hair.

"Very much," she immediately responded.

The bath nurse arrived and tended to Grandma's personal care needs as I was adamant her dignity remained intact. Transport arrived as scheduled and prepared her on the gurney. A sense of peace could be felt throughout the house which was very reaffirming. However, I knew, once she left she was not coming back through the house doors again, so I made sure to grab the bag she packed.

Grandma lived less than thirty-six hours after being placed in the facility. The tough decision to do so, in hindsight, was ultimately my final act of love to her as she wanted me to live a life of happiness, equipped me with tools to be resilient, and always encouraged self-preservation. Our bond, forged through uncon-ditional love, remains an unyielding force that has shaped the woman I am today.

This chapter is dedicated to Shaleta Royster, Isaiah McKinney, Jimmesha Youngblood, and Grady Robinson, all of whom I am forever indebted to for caring, loving, and supporting both Grandma and I, in the home, during such a pivotal time.

CHAPTER EIGHT

Bubble of Regret

by Tonya Mills

W alking through the parking lot, the refraction of the heat off the cars tells me it is well over a hundred degrees. Sweat is collecting in unmentionable places as I walk the few feet from my car to the apartment building door. As I swing open the door, there is the familiar, although unwelcome, smell of the old historic building my mom has lived in for over three years. The same old, worn carpet seems to be wearing even thinner as I walk through and press the button on the elevator. Entering the elevator, I smell the aroma of those who have been here before me. It is the smell of sweat, perfume, and dirty clothes. I press the button to go to the 3rd floor. On the ride up, I am thinking about the task before me. Cleaning out Mom's apartment will be no easy chore.

As I exit the elevator and continue down the long corridor, I arrive at the door to her apartment. I am filled with anxiety about what I will find. Pulling the key out of my purse, I have an overwhelming desire to run! *So, what if I decided not to clean it out?? I could walk away and let someone else deal with this mess.*

Of course, being a good, responsible daughter, I unlock the door and walk through.

It hits me why I am here. In the last few months, Mom's health declined. She could no longer live independently; it was decided she would live with me. I was home during the day, and my sister had a full-time job. Mom living with me did not give me the warm fuzzies. I struggled with the responsibility, the stress on my marriage, and my already growing frustration and resentment towards her.

The guest room had been prepared to accommodate her needs. The floor was covered in plastic to protect it. A baby monitor, which sits on the nightstand, was purchased and set up. Furniture was moved to accommodate her lift chair. Space was created for toiletries, medications, bed pads, a walker, and clothing. It had taken weeks, time, and energy to select and arrange the guest bedroom carefully, and now it was being redistributed throughout the rest of the house.

As I walk around the apartment, deciding where to begin, I reminisce about the times I would spend here with Mom. We would watch movies, eat popcorn, and laugh uncontrollably, reliving our lives and some of the crazy things we did. We had a unique relationship. Mom was 20 when I was born, and we had more of a friend relationship than a mother-daughter one.

Bringing myself back to reality, I go through the items in her bedroom. I noticed many items purchased but never used. There are several unopened packages in her closet and clothes with tags still on them. Unopened mail is stacked by her bedside. Her dresser is cluttered with makeup, face creams, perfumes, and several boxes overflowing with jewelry. She loved to shop and was never very responsible with money. She depended on my sister and I to pick up the slack. In the beginning, we were happy to help. As years passed, it became too commonplace. I began to resent her more and was quickly frustrated by her inability to be responsible. I wonder how it got this bad.

I sat on the bed's edge and began feeling overwhelming sadness. I never really thought about Mom's life coming to an end. I knew she would no longer be with us one day, but why does it seem so sudden? I want to be furious with her but can't. I am angry with myself. *I should not have waited so long to move her in. Why didn't she call and say she needed help? Why didn't she take better care of herself?* Mom wanted to be independent all her life, but she just wasn't.

I should give her grace. Her years growing up were rough. She lost her mom when she was twelve and endured different abuses throughout her life. She was depressed often. When my sister and I were kids, she would sit in a dark room, smoking a cigarette, staring out the window into the night for hours, looking at nothing. I always felt like I needed to care for her and find ways to make her happy, so she wasn't so sad.

Hours later, having completed my mission, I had a 40-minute ride home. I used this time to contemplate my future. I saw my life as wholly centered around my mom and her needs. I wanted to weep because I had so many plans. My husband and I want to travel and see the world. I am writing a book. I have my work, friends, dreams, and goals.

Pulling into the driveway, I shut off the engine and sat there. I had to go inside but didn't want to. I wanted to go back in time and change things. *Could I have done something to make Mom listen? Could I have made different choices and changed the outcome?* So many ifs, ands, and buts.

My life became a constant barrage of additional responsibilities over the next two months. I was constantly cleaning and cooking. Mom could barely get around and had trouble walking and feeding herself. She would call for me, and I would roll my eyes and think *I was just in there a few minutes ago; what could she possibly need now?* My patience was wearing thin. Years of caring for her in one way or another had taken their toll. Sometimes, I felt she was intentionally making it complicated. I spent so much time trying to make her happy, which only increased my resentment and frustration. I wanted to be a dutiful daughter but also to have my own life without the restriction of constantly caring for someone else.

My future is dwindling, and I have no say in the matter. I do not want to do this anymore. I refused to place her in a facility. Children are supposed to take care of their parents. Mom made me promise I would never put her in a place like *that*. I was about to break that promise. I couldn't handle it anymore.

Many times a day, I would go into her room to check on her. Today, I stood outside the door to her room, staring, not wanting to enter. Walking in reminds me of the weight I carry on my shoulders. Mom may not be around much longer. So much time was wasted due to my anger, resentment, and choices I should have made differently.

I did not enter the room and instead joined my husband to discuss possible facility options for Mom. I hear my name being called through the baby monitor. I huffily rise and go to her room. She was staring at the wall. I call out to her, she does not respond. I reach over and gently touch her arm to get her attention. She looks at me, and something isn't right.

"Mom, what's wrong? Are you okay?"

She shakes her head no.

In a frightened tone with a shaky voice, I ask, "Do I need to call an ambulance?"

"No. Call my doctor." She says in a whisper.

Rushing to my room, I grab my cell phone and fumble until I get the number. The line rings, and I get an answering service. I am in full-blown panic. I am shaking and trying to keep it together. I yell into the phone, "Something is wrong with my mom! I need to speak to the doctor!"

When they told me someone would call me back, I wanted to scream at them and tell them I needed her now. I decided not to and waited.

After five long minutes, I received a call from the doctor whose only advice was to call an ambulance. I immediately called

911. It took only a few minutes for the paramedics to arrive. They took her out on the gurney, and the fear on her face was apparent. *I am thinking, this is it. This is the last time I will see my mom alive; so much is left unsaid. Why didn't I say all the things before?* I quickly followed behind to the hospital.

In her room at the ER, she is awake when I arrive but is drifting in and out. Without looking at me, the nurse attending her says, "The doctor will be here in a moment." She turns and walks out of the room.

After three hours, a doctor rushes into the room and curtly says, "She is dehydrated. We are concerned with her kidneys and liver levels, and she will need to be admitted for observation." He gruffly exits the room.

I look at my mom and feel guilty for my frustration and anger. I want to crawl in the bed beside her, hold her, and tell her how much I love her. I do not. I sit and wait patiently.

Six hours later, we are in her room. I sit beside her on the edge of the bed and, with tears in my eyes, say, "Mom, I love you! I am so sorry you are going through all of this, and everything will be okay."

I did not believe it. She looked frail and frightened. I felt things were dire. I decided not to tell her that.

"I love you too," she said with a raspy voice, smiling at me.

I don't want to leave her. What if she passes away tonight? I won't be able to say I am sorry for being so mean, for not spending more time with her, not giving her more love. "Mom, I am heading home now. I love you and will see you soon." I rise and begin walking toward the door. As I turn to look at her, I no longer see an irresponsible, codependent woman. I see my mom, who loves her children unconditionally and did the best she could.

Arriving home after 1:00 a.m., I realize it is Thanksgiving Day. With all that happened, it slipped my mind. Dinner will need to be postponed. I want to cancel but won't. Mom loves Thanksgiving and would like us to be together as a family. I message my family to let them know the situation with Mom and that dinner will be late.

My sister left dinner early to see Mom at the hospital. She is there for about an hour, and I receive a call: "They are moving mom to a skilled nursing facility!" I could tell she was angry and upset. She argued with them and told them she was not well enough to be released! It doesn't matter. Mom is sent by ambulance to the facility.

The facility contacted me four hours later, "We are sending your mom back to the hospital. She is having trouble breathing, and we are not equipped to deal with this here." I was confused and angry! I grabbed my keys and purse and drove to the hospital. Mom was awake but a bit pale when I arrived, and she looked tired. She is going through so much. I want to walk into the hall and start screaming at the staff.

Several hours later, a doctor enters the room, declaring they are sending her home.

That was it! I would no longer sit by and allow this to continue. I stand up from my chair, and with my voice raised, I yell at him, "You will not be sending her home! If you send her home and something happens, I will own this hospital! Do you understand what I am saying? She will be admitted to this hospital AGAIN, and you will find out what is happening. Two days ago, she was critical with serious issues, and now she is fine?!"

With astonishment and what I believe to be a little fear, the doctor retreated from the room, "I will get someone to speak with you right away!"

Hours later, Mom was taken to her room and soon after was sleeping. I tiptoe out of her room so as not to wake her. I am so tired and emotionally drained. I feel like my world is falling apart. I had been hard on mom. When I think about how I felt when she moved in…I know I should have been more patient and loving.

After a long day at the hospital, I finally got some sleep. I wake up the next morning and want all this to be a dream. It is not. It's reality, and I am dealing with it.

I decided to take some me time. I find my favorite blanket, make a cup of tea, and cuddle up on the couch with my dog. I turn on the TV and begin to watch the Harry Potter movies. This is my refuge. My happy place. I am halfway through the first movie, and my phone rings. It is my sister.

"The doctor was just here," she said through the holding back of tears. "Mom's liver and kidneys are shutting down, and they can do nothing." She was putting up a strong front for Mom, but I could hear fear and disbelief in her voice.

A feeling of dread washes over me, and I feel as if I am floating, "Oh my god!" is all I say.

My sister continued choking out the words, "The doctor wants to make her comfortable, and what they are doing is not working. She is not coming out of this. They can only lessen the pain."

I am speechless. Sitting on the sofa, which is no longer my refuge, I cannot believe this is happening.

My sister finally breaks the silence. "They are bringing in hospice. She would be around her family and live her final days without all the tubes and prodding." My sister sounds brave and in control, but I know she is falling apart. She continues with a shaky voice, "Mom is aware and knows what is going on. She is okay with what is happening and says she is tired of being sick all the time."

After a minute of processing, I respond through uncontrollable tears, "Did they say how long?"

My sister pauses, and I know she is unable to talk about it, and says, "Let's discuss that when you get here."

"I will be there as soon as I can." Sitting there in my living room, all I can do is cry.

I picked up the phone to call my daughter. She is very close to her Nana. The first three years of her life were spent in Nana's

101

home. She is emotional, and I must be calm when speaking with her. I dialed her number.

The first thing she says is: "Is Nana okay?" I could tell she was worried by the high pitch of her voice. I explained the situation to her. "I will be there first thing in the morning!" "Are you okay, mom?"

"Yes, sweetie, I am fine." But I am not okay. *My mom is dying, and I can do nothing about it. I am not okay. There are so many things I should have said and done. Now it is too late. I am not okay!*

I wouldn't say I like the way hospitals smell of disinfectant and sickness. It reminds me of my mortality. I have been here way more times than I would have liked. I walk into her hospital room and notice she is pale and has a yellow tint to her skin. She is awake and aware of me approaching her bed. She looks at me and smiles.

The doctor, who is there when I arrive, says softly, "We think moving her to the hospice floor is best. This process could take up to two weeks to complete."

My heart feels like it will explode from my chest, and I want to yell at him! *Complete? You mean dead. She is dying!* I keep quiet as tears well in my eyes, and I can barely keep my composure.

The doctor continues, "The medication she takes for her kidneys and liver will be stopped, and we will start a series of medications to keep her comfortable until the end."

Pulling a chair close to her bedside, I hold her hand. My sister does the same opposite me. I cannot believe this is happening. I know she has been unwell. I am so angry right now at everyone. At the hospital for releasing her to skilled nursing. At the doctor for not being able to do anything. I want to scream, throw things, and blame someone.

Mom begins to reminisce about her life. She shares how much she loves us and expresses how bad she feels about being such a burden. I choke back tears. Recently, I did feel like she was a burden. *Mom, I am so sorry. You are not a burden. I am so sorry for all the things I said and did. Please forgive me.* I keep this to myself because I don't want her to see me cry.

The next four days and nights are spent at the hospital. We sleep in chairs made into small beds and have food delivered to spend as much time with Mom as possible. We talk with Mom about her wishes, our lives, and our memories.

With a whimsical tone, my sister asks my mom, "So, when you come back as a ghost to visit us, how will we know it is you?"

With a mischievous grin, Mom responds, "I am going to come into your house, get a sheet out of your linen closet, put it on, and scare the shit out of you!" The room bursts into laughter. It is a break in seriousness and, for all of us, a much-needed moment.

Nights are the worst—so much time to think. My sister is restless, and I can hear her tossing and turning. It is late, and my thoughts go to last Christmas when Mom and I went shopping for decorations.

"This is gorgeous!" she exclaimed, pointing at a beautiful wreath decorated with gold ornaments and braided with a beautiful green and red ribbon hanging on the display. I looked at the price tag, dismissing her childlike excitement: "Too expensive," I barked. "You need to pick out something more affordable." Mom never paid attention to how much she spent. She seemed to think there would always be enough money. "You need to be more responsible," I yelled at her in frustration. "I shouldn't have to be the adult here."

I shake my head to clear the memory of sadness in her eyes that was caused by my harsh words. I am consumed with regret. I regret for not buying her the wreath myself. Shame and guilt for the way I spoke to her. I had no idea it would be her last Christmas, and I didn't make it better for her. I convinced myself I made it worse.

Mom's breathing is becoming labored, and I know it is only a matter of time now. As I am holding her hand, its warmth lets me know she is still with us. Although she is not responding to my touch, she knows I am with her. The machines keeping track of her vitals fill the room with electric energy and the beeping signals that I still have time with her.

On the opposite side of the bed, my sister looks down at Mom's hand, and silent tears flow down her face and drop onto the bed. She raises her head, and grief is staring at me.

At 38 years old, my daughter is staring into some unknown space. I can see she is trying to organize all the thoughts swirling around in her head. It reminds me of when she was only 4 or 5 years old and trying to figure out why the Weeble wobbled but didn't fall down.

So many thoughts! I want them to stop. I am besieged with regret. For all the things I did not say. For all the time I failed to spend with her. For all the times, I could have been more kind. For all the times I should have gone that extra mile to make her feel more at home—so much regret.

I am staring at the skilled nursing facility mom was in from the front seat of my car. My daughter, very distraught, is in the passenger seat, crying. Less than an hour ago, mom passed away. What just happened? This cannot be true. I am here to pick up my mom's belongings, and I cannot find the courage to go in. *What did I do? What should I have done? She had a hard time taking care of herself. I waited too long. I didn't want her living with me. My husband and I like how things are, and the added responsibilities would be too much. She should have moved in sooner. If she did, would she still be with us? Would I have been able to make sure she was taking her medicines properly? Eating properly?*

My regret became so powerful it gave me nightmares. I'm there lying in bed, and arms wrap around me. It is my mom. She is visiting me and letting me know I would be okay. When I turn to look, something dark and melting is there. I wake up terrified. I am shaking, crying, and sick to my stomach. Later, I spent time interpreting my dream. I think dreams allow you to see things you are hiding deep inside. I have analyzed my dreams for many years, and this one taught me a valuable lesson. The dark melting being was my regret and guilt. The one hugging me was Mom. It was my subconscious telling me I was preventing the love of my mom from shining.

As frightening as it was, the dream created the desire for a lighter and healthier approach to dealing with my regret.

One day, I came across a note when going through some papers. Several months ago, Mom shared something she did when feeling overwhelmed.

She said, "Remember, when you have troubles, put them in a bubble and let them float away."

My mom was telling me to let it go. My perception changed, and I began to release the regret, no longer allowing it to rule my life.

We all have regrets about one thing or another. I started visualizing my regrets in a bubble, allowing them to float away. This began a process of healing and acknowledgment. I see our love for each other and what we shared. Love and gratitude instead of the woulda, coulda, shoulda's.

Sometimes, I felt I could have done more, been more, better, stronger. I recognize every person's journey is different, and comparing myself to some imagined superwoman is ridiculous. Maybe I will always have regrets; perhaps I won't. I have these feelings, and I acknowledge them. The constant regret created in me, the idea I wasn't good enough or strong enough…? None of that is true. I found that I am better and stronger than I ever imagined possible. I now examine what I am feeling and bring it forward. I acknowledge and learn from my mistakes. I appreciate more about Mom, her life, and all she did for me. I no longer allow regret to rule me.

Thank you, Mom, for all the gifts you gave me. Thank you for raising me to be self-aware. Thank you for loving me even though you were struggling. Thank you for teaching me to be vulnerable and transparent. Thank you for instilling in me independence and knowing I can accomplish anything I set my mind to. Mom, thank you for the bubble!

CHAPTER NINE

Living Life Waiting for Someone to Die

by Makeba Pease

I t was a beautiful day in February. I got off work early and did a routine stop at my mom's house to check on her and my sister. Two steps in the door and the hairs on the back of my neck stood up. I walked into my mother's bedroom to find her lying in bed drenched in urine. I could tell from the stench; that she had been in this condition for quite some time. I knocked on my sister's bedroom door across the hall and it was obvious that she had relapsed. The room was occupied by six people, and she was barely coherent. I was livid and at the top of my voice, in a roar, I ordered: "Everyone GET OUT!" I cleared the house, including the two people who were hiding in the back bedroom.

In the days that followed, I took my mother to visit the doctor because she had bedsores and bloodwork indicating her malnutrition.

I didn't see it coming but that was the day I became a caregiver.

It has been one of the most challenging roles that I have had to play so far in my life. My Mom was a first-class superSHEro in my eyes. She was always strong and independent. She raised all six of her children solo and although there were things that we could list that we wanted and did not get; we can never say that our basic needs were not met. We were never hungry, and always had a home, a full belly with a well-stocked pantry, and an abundance of clothing and love.

Watching dementia overtake my superSHEro has been heartbreaking. I have witnessed this disease take her from her normal state to a bedbound baby that requires 24-hour care. The disease has been a slow, consistent decline that started with the wandering and turning on the stove.

Mom loves ice cream. So, I made a deal with the local ice cream truck owner to just give her what she wanted, and I would check periodically and clear the balance as needed. He refused to allow me to pay him and gave her whatever she wanted, whenever she came to his truck. She paid with buttons one day. He kept them to show them to me. We both laughed as he reminded me that he knew everyone on his route, including my mother. He said it was his gift to her.

I can recall how the disease robbed her ability to talk. She went from voluntary conversation where she would tell you what she did and did not want. Those were the hard times when I had to remove the knobs from the stove and hide the keys to HER car. It was a race to the mantel to hide the car key. My clue was when she would begin to lay out a perfectly coordinated outfit and start her bubble bath. Oh, how she HATES showers! I would start my convincing as she straightened her long black hair. "Hey, where ya going? I wanna go! Want me to drive?" or whatever convincing and insisting I had to do as long as she didn't get in the car alone. Horrified and grateful at the same time, she would allow me to take her. Always in her car because she could smoke and do as she wished "in her car." She would often remind me that she had her car and, "Who the hell was I to tell her when and where she could go?" I was glad to get past that time, but it was a sad time, too, because a part of her was lost, and I knew it would never return.

I miss her voice, her laughter, and her reminder-replies that "You ain't the boss of me!" to everything said to her. Funny how she stopped talking but would occasionally let it be known that she was still the mother! Funny how a look still stops a whole grown adult in their tracks, just because it's Mom.

As the years passed along, I recall all those early childhood and late adult conversations I had with my mom. We would sit on the phone for hours talking about life, love, politics, and the status of EVERY family member. She would often answer the phone, "Hey, pest," because I would call her daily to talk.

I am so glad I was a pest!

I never imagined that I would miss her voice as much as I do. She was my confidant, my strength, and my teacher. The one person I learned so much from is no longer able to guide me through the toughest commitment I have made to someone so far...HER. I promised her for a long time I would never put her in a home.

It took a couple of years after she stopped talking for the disease to progress to the point that she would stop walking. She would be walking and abruptly would stop and sit. It was as if the brain signal got lost in the coordination process. Mid-stride she would just attempt to sit, and being steady on her feet was like watching someone attempt to walk with a blindfold over their eyes. The abrupt sitting mid-stride was a danger to herself and others, so using the wheelchair became the new normal.

This too was a bittersweet moment because I knew that walking would not return, but relieved that the level of mainte-nance had changed. Before her full-time use of the wheelchair, the daily routine for years would be mom would pee or poop in her diaper, and on the way to the bathroom, there's always some sort of spillage coming out. The worst was the metformin diar-rhea that would leak down her leg leaving a trail of poop from the living room to the bathroom. I had a carpet cleaning service come in every three months to clean the poop stains out of the carpet and it would seem like no matter how hard I would try to keep up with that ritual there was always some level of stain that just wouldn't come out of the carpet. What was perhaps most frustrating is that it was less than a year that I had recarpeted the entire house. It was an endless cycle of pooping on the carpet, spot-cleaning the carpet, can't get the stain out, call the carpet cleaners to remove the odor and stain. It just wore me out! I can remember being so frustrated one day trying to get poop stains out of the carpet that I took a utility knife and cut the poop stain out of the carpet. Finally, I went to hardwood floors. I suppose there was a good reveal from that frustrating moment. The refinished hardwood floors turned out beautiful.

I can recall with perfect clarity the day I decided that I would be with my mother to the end, PERIOD. It was the day that solidified the promise I made: "I WON'T PUT YOU IN A HOME." It was the fourth of her hospital stays for the year. She was admitted because she passed out while sitting on the toilet during bowel movement. It's common in older people. The stress of pushing puts pressure on the vagus nerve restricts blood flow and causes the person to pass out. They call it the "vasovagal syndrome"; a heart condition that can cause a sudden, rapid drop in heart rate and blood pressure, which leads to fainting.

As I returned on the second or third day to be with her and to try and catch the neurologist, general practitioner, and other specialty doctors on the list for her stay, my mother was being changed by the Certified Nursing Assistant (CNA). Mom saw me and began to cry like a child... that kind of cry when you leave your kid with a sitter for the first time...the one that makes you want to go back, get your baby, quit your job, and just figure out how to feed, house and clothe them later. She clutched my arm begging me to take her home.

"I promise, I will be good, I promise, just please take me home and don't leave me here," Mom begged.

It took several minutes for her to calm down and allow the CNA to get her cleaned up for the day. I had to assist the CNA with her duties because mom would not let go of my arm. I had to keep one hand on her to keep her from crying and begging me to not leave her. She cried so hard the CNA cried too. At one point I had to calm them both down.

"You really love her, I can tell," the CNA said.

I assured her I did, indeed, love my mom with every fiber of my being. I had to put on a brave face to keep my mother calm and to keep the CNA from running out of the room in tears. On the inside, however, I, myself, could barely breathe. I was so hurt because my superSHEro never cried, had no fear, and could beat up all the bad guys in the neighborhood and at that moment I realized that none of that was true. My superSHEro was scared, weak, and needed to be rescued. I could feel the weight of my chest and my head felt so heavy, but I knew if I started crying and let go of my emotions it would only make a bad situation worse, so I held it all in for the moment.

When the visit was over with my mom, I rushed to the elevator, the emotion was so heavy I could feel the tension in my jaws, and I was holding back the tears so hard that my throat was on fire! I got to my car so fast it felt like I was jogging. I was frantically searching my purse for the keys to my car. I made it! I was in my car! In an instant, I felt all the pain and hurt of seeing my mom cry like that. In real life, I saw my superSHEro crumble.

Dementia was the kryptonite that had her surrounded, and I had no way to save her. I sat in the hospital parking lot and cried my eyes out. I think if I had been anywhere other than a hospital, someone would have called to get me help. But sitting in the parking lot to the portal of life and death and seeing someone cry is not abnormal behavior, so I believe people understood my moment of emotion. It seems like I sat there for hours and recounted all the tough times in my head, trying to remember if in my frustration I told her, I would put her in a home or worse had somebody done something to her overnight. Seeing my

111

mother beg me to take her home literally broke my heart. Again, at that moment my soul committed that I would never place my mother in a home.

Once again, she was released from the hospital, and I returned to work. An inbox full of "Urgent" and "Red Flagged" emails regarding things that were late and overdue deadlines awaited me. I cleaned up the mess by completing tasks, responding to emails, rescheduling meetings, and setting new deadlines. I called the CEO to explain what was going on in my world, why a couple of deadlines had slipped, and how I had gotten things back on track.

"My mother has dementia," I explained to my boss. "She can't speak for herself, and I need to be present because she's not capable of doing anything for herself."

"That's not my problem," was the response I heard. Those words cut me to the core and at that moment, I realized that I would have to choose between my job and my mother. It was simple for me. Jobs are plenty, but I only have one mother, and my loyalty is to her. Money and career would have to come second.

I would come to realize that corporate America is not set up to understand the complexity required to care for a loved one. What I found most disheartening is that there was zero understanding from the company. Although I had adequate sick and vacation leave, the response and understanding from the CEO was anything but supportive.

I believe there are approximately 75 million Baby Boomers in the United States or 29% of the current US population. There is a gap between the Family Medical Leave Act and the length of employment that allows you to u]se its benefits. I was just shy (29 days) of one year at the company, and they made sure I was out the door before I could utilize ANY benefit from the Family Medical Leave Act. With 75 million people that will soon age into some type of managed care, corporate America and conditions set in the Family Medical Leave Act will need to consider workers caught in the gap who have less than one year at a job and need time to care for a loved one. "That's not my problem" is not the solution to 75 million people.

About three more years would pass, and on the many times that I would feel like giving up, I would recall the day she begged me to take her home from the hospital, and my promise that I would take her home and I would not leave her.

Something clicked in year seven of taking care of my mom that I didn't realize. The constant care that my mother required had completely taken over my life without me truly realizing that I had set aside an entire portion of my life. The role of a caregiver is all-consuming. We are required to take on another full life. My mother had a home, income, and medical care that included one primary care physician and six specialty doctors, friends, and family, and all of it required scheduling and maintenance. The transition of my life becoming her life had been so gradual as I looked back that I didn't see it happen. I had stopped living my own life, and my life had become all about her and her care needs.

I am a single Mom and always prioritized the care of my son and his needs and well-being along with caring for my mother. What I lost was myself. I realized I stopped working professionally, and I stopped going out with friends. The frustration of dating and my desire to be a soccer/baseball/football Mom had ended because the cost of getting someone to care for my mother to do the things I do, even for a few hours a week, was more than the menial budget could handle on a caregiver salary. So, I convinced myself "Why bother!"

I wasn't living at all. I was on the sidelines of my own life waiting for my mother to die. I thought...how the hell did I let this happen? It took a bit of counseling to help me realize that I was suffering from complete and total burnout. Further, I had to ask myself "Is this what my mother would want for me?" I had to recall all those past conversations where she taught me to "be strong" and "it's okay for you to occasionally give out, but never give up" and "Get up! And get your ass back out there and get what you want!" and, "I didn't raise you to be a quitter!"

Mom supported me my entire life to have a life with options and the ability to be self-sufficient. She encouraged me to go to college because as she would always remind me, education is the one thing that can't be denied. If you get it and have it no one can take that from you or say you are not qualified because you don't have an education.

So how is it that I have an MBA, and I'm used to leading teams, large-scale projects, and discussing environmental issues, and, yet, I sit home bored most days because I care for my mother?

I needed to figure out a way to get back in the game. There is more to life than a job, but I also realized I wasn't living AT ALL. I WAS STUCK!

After countless conversations and prayerful meditation with myself, I decided to wake up and live a life WITH my mother. I realized when I committed to being her caregiver that I was not granted her expiration date and didn't know mine! I had soaked an entire savings account repairing a house that did not belong to me, and I was paying for caregivers to give me time to complete my master's degree because trying to provide care for my mother, while being a single parent to my son, and working a professional job was too much!

My son was graduating from middle school and the inner city of south Los Angeles was not what I had envisioned for him. The battle between the Black gangs, Mexican gangs and a police force that was scared to death because the gangs had better guns than they did was more than I wanted to expose him to. I wanted a different social experience for my son. One that included diversity, the ability to walk home without the visual education of guns, drugs, gangs, and a frightened police force. And since my son had spent the majority of his life in the shadow of his grandmother, I felt he minimally deserved to have the experience of a suburban life. I wanted him to feel free to stroll to the park and to just be a kid. So off to the suburbs, we went.

That decision to regain control of my life and simply live with the task at hand proved to be a huge game changer, and not in a good way. My older siblings, the three still living, were livid that I had sold my mother's home and moved to a better place. Fully aware that the old house was over 100 years old, and even with the thousands I spent to make it livable, it still required significant upgrades. In what I could only think of as an act of greed to garner their share of an inheritance that did not belong to any one of us yet because our mother was very much alive, my siblings took me to court.

During this time, I endured a hail of brutal and malicious waves of false allegations that included Adult Protective Services abuse allegations of not bathing, changing, or feeding our mother. It also alleged I was exposing her to sexual abuse. And, it included Social Security fraud allegations and probate court filings in two separate counties. All of it was lies, motivated by what I could only conclude was spite, greed and anger. These accusations all were made by two siblings who have never even spent a day in seven years caring for our mother. The third sibling was along for the ride, completely caught up in their addiction.

Although the cost of the attorney was significant to settle the issue, and all courts deemed my care exceptional and granted me conservatorship of our mother and her estate, I have nothing but pity and forgiveness for my siblings.

My mother is at the point where she only occasionally wakes up on her own. I get her up daily, and she spends most of her day in her recliner in the family room. I transfer her from the recliner to the wheelchair for all meals and from the recliner to the bed for diaper changes. I am a well-trained, uncertified nursing assistant. I know how to treat and prevent bed sores, treat bowel impaction, use a suction, oxygen machine, and adjust an air mattress.

The recliner keeps her in the main flow of the house and allows her to be part of the interaction between me and my son. We both get a kick out of her rousing up if our chatter or banter gets too loud. She is quick to yell out a corrective "Hey" or "Stop it"! It reminds me of the times early on when she would only talk to and have meaningful conversations with my son and other kids in the neighborhood.

She would always greet him, "Hey baby, give mama a hug, I love you," AND randomly with a, "I'mma whoop yo ass!" We still laugh about that phrase today. When my son and other kids would play on the floor, she would sit and give corrective instructions like, "You're gonna get hurt," and "Stop playing in this house!" I found those moments so fascinating because she couldn't tell you her date of birth, the year, or her address of over 30 years, but she would watch over small kids. I suppose her 20 years with the Los Angeles Unified School District had a bigger impact on her life than I ever knew.

Like many with dementia, my mother has sundowning. Sundowning is the confusion of the brain to determine the difference between night and day so during the day she is asleep and at night she is awake and active. It's like those first few days with a newborn where you get zero sleep because the baby just won't rest. We often would have a whole conversation at 3:00 AM. She often talks to her father during her sundowning episodes, as if he were right next to her assuring her that all is well. She gently leans over and kisses someone every morning when I wake her. That warms my heart.

Covid decided to visit us post-pandemic, and I got a glimpse of what that final hour might look like. Mom was cold and clammy because of her fever. Her skin was pale as if life were leaving her body. Her eyes were rolling up and to the back of her head. Even with an oxygen tube to assist with breathing, her breaths were faint and shallow. There was so much drool that I had to use a suction machine to keep her airway clear. The nurse ordered something for the excessive drooling, and I overheard the pharmacist ask, "Is she passing?" The hesitation in the nurse's reply "no" as she looked at me suffering from COVID-19, too, gave me little hope that she would survive.

"I know, you are feeling terrible, but prepare yourself, she might not make it," the nurse whispered to me. I could barely hear; it was so loud in her room. The sound of all those machines going at one time was unlike anything I had ever heard. *I am not ready and not even close to being prepared, I thought.*

I do not know how I managed to care for her when I had COVID-19, too, but God had something for me to see. I have spent countless hours wondering and worrying what her final hour would look like. I kind of had an idea but again, I knew I was not prepared. Perhaps that was the gift. Let me take a peek so that when the time comes, at least have seen something familiar.

Many people commend me for the sacrifice I have given to my mother. On the surface, it would appear that I have, indeed, given a lot, but I have learned so much along this journey that I am grateful for the life lessons. I have learned how to manage her life and the system I am required to work with to take care of her. I pass that along to anyone who will listen. I really can keep a promise. I haven't and won't put her in a home. I can live and be happy with a minimal income. I have learned that money does not equal happiness. I am humbled to understand that my life is a gift from God, and I have to live it keeping him first by allowing him to lead me through my journey knowing that my need is met and my natural desire to want more will have to continue to be placed on the back burner because he supplies ALL.

It's a brutal and tiring schedule that exhausts the mind and body very quickly but my faith in God continues to give me strength. Three major surgeries, a pandemic, and chronic illness, yet, God continues to keep us together. "Thank you!"

When I get to the end of this journey, and my mother's life here on earth is over, and she is resting in the mansion that has been prepared for her – and assuming that God doesn't want me first – I pray that the decision to press pause on my life from

117

time-to-time and allow my mother to remain out of a nursing home is pleasing in the eyes of God. No other opinion matters. My prayer is that my spirit will settle, and I will feel God whisper, "Well done Makeba."

CHAPTER TEN

Doing This Business of Caregiving MY Way

by Mercedes Negrete

"He's going to die on me, he's going to die!" My 19-year-old daughter's voice shouted at me through the phone. I knew my daughters would never call me at work unless it was an emergency.

"Where are you?" From the sound of her voice, she clearly was at home.

"Dad, he is dying!" she sobbed.

Luckily, my office was less than five minutes away. I told my daughter to calm down, I was on my way. And during the drive, I told myself... *You Must Calm Down!! Calm down, calm down.* I knew that it was a crisis at home, and it would need to be solved. Now was not the time for me to cry and scream, so I continued to drive and prayed, "God Help me."

I got home and ran into the house. I saw my husband. He was sitting at the table with his back to me. My daughter was standing by the sink crying. I went to her, and she pointed at him. So, I turned around just at the moment he was grabbing some salad with his hand and trying to get it to his mouth. His face was full of dressing and the fork was at the middle of the table. My heart was racing when I asked, "Are you OK?"

He turned around trying to answer, but the words just didn't come out.

My other kid had just gotten home at that time and immediately said she was calling 911.

My husband rose from his chair, screaming, "No, no, no!" His face was turning red, and he almost fell down.

"Okay, let's clean up your face, and we are going to the emergency room," I said.

I was scared, but at the same time I was in charge of the situation, so I had to think and direct the girls on what to do. They helped me to get him to my car, and they went to the other car to follow me. My husband wasn't talking, and his skin looked gray. I kept asking him what he was feeling, trying to keep him there with me in the moment. I just knew that if he were to fall asleep, he might not wake up. I knew that because of the "Red Cross First Aid Trainings" I had been taking every year at work.

We got to the ER, and one of the kids ran to get a wheelchair while the other helped me to get him out of the car. We went inside, and the person at the counter asked me, "What is wrong with him?" I told them I thought he was having a heart attack or stroke.

The staff pushed a big red button and asked me for my ID while giving me a red band to put on his wrist. I was getting to him, when more staff came out and started to wheel him inside for emergency treatment. I followed, with the red band still in my hand, and directed the girls to stay in the waiting room.

We got into a room full of machines and immediately they hooked him to several of them. A doctor came in with papers in his hands and started to check my husband's vitals. A few moments later, the doctor started to question me about my husband about his medicine intake.

Are you taking "this" he said, pointing to one of the medications. Yes, but I shake my head because my husband was supposed to take several medicines that he never did.

The doctor asked again, and then shocked me by saying, "Do you have any idea what you have you done to yourself?"

Walking to the door, the doctor signaled to me to follow him.

"Your husband just had a stroke," he said. "We will find the extent of the damage and find out what will be the best course of action. He will stay in the hospital, after we finish here. You can go home and be here in the morning. If there is anything else during the night for you to know, we will call you. The front desk will give you all the information you need."

At that moment, I just couldn't ask anything. I was falling down into what felt like a dark hole, but I had to keep calm to get the information and understand the next steps.

I returned to his bedside, gathered his belongings, and told him that he would be staying the night. He already was falling to sleep when I whispered, "I'll see you in the morning."

The kids were waiting outside. I told them we would go home, and that dad would be staying. I said we'd come back early in the morning.

"What's dad got?" That was the question they asked.

"Let's go home and talk about it there," I said.

In the car, driving home by myself, I screamed and screamed. I think I cried too. I wanted to get it out, so that when I got home, I was calm enough to explain to the girls what had happened, and what and how we were going to work this out.

When we talked and were making up a plan while I answered their questions, I saw my college kids, one 19 and the other 20, breaking down, crying and asking 'why'?

The first thing I said to them was, "Whatever happens, your schooling comes first. Yes, I will need you to help me figure out how we are going to deal with this, and we will solve the problems as they appear. But tomorrow will be another day, and there are too many things that will need to be done, so it's best now that we rest. It has been a long hard day, and we need to sleep."

As we all retired to our bedrooms for the night, it broke my heart to hear them sobbing.

The next day, I had to call in to work early. "I can't come to work today. My husband had a stroke, and I need to go to the hospital."

"Do you need some days off?" I was grateful for the response. I told them I didn't know yet. It depended on what the doctors said today.

As the kids and I ate breakfast, I told them, "It's going to be okay. Go to school. And when your classes end today just come home. I will go to the hospital, and in the afternoon, we'll see what needs to be done. Maybe they will send him home with me." I tried to sound positive.

When I got to the hospital, they told me he had a good night, and gave me his room number. As soon as I entered his room, my husband asked me where I had been. I told him I had gone home, not understanding why he was asking. He explained that he needed to go to sleep and eat with the kids. It got more confusing when his breakfast arrived. He couldn't pick up the spoon. His right side seemed impacted.

"Do you want me to help you?" I asked.

"No, I can do it myself," he said.

We sat together, and a few moments later, the doctor came in.

"Are you the wife?" he asked.

I nodded. "Yes."

The doctor handed me his card and told me he'd see me in his office in the morning.

I didn't know what to think. But I showed up next day at his office as instructed.

"Was your husband taking his medicines?" the doctor asked me.

"No, I never saw him taking any medications," I responded.

"Well, we cannot undo the damage," he told me as he put up an image of my husband's brain with a big black spot almost in the middle and proceeded to explain. "All of this black part is what was affected. It is dead. With therapy, we will try to regrow connections; he is only 54 years old."

He went on to tell me that my husband would stay in the hospital for a day or two and then be transferred to another facility.

"Do you have any questions?"

I shook my head. I needed time to process all the information. "If I have any questions, can I ask you?"

The doctor nodded, "Of course."

I returned to my husband's bedside.

"Can I go home now?" he asked.

"No, they're going to keep you here for another day or two to make sure you can walk." I sat down, lost in a sea of thoughts, questions, possibilities, and hope.

My thoughts were interrupted when my husband said he needed to use the restroom. Before I could get a nurse, he started walking to it. The nurse got there, and did help him enter, but as we both were waiting outside the door, we heard him fall down.

We raced to open the door, and there he was on the floor. Two male nurses immediately showed up and were able to put him back in bed. AND they ordered me out of the room.

After a long wait, they called my name to meet with the doctor.

"He just had a mini-stroke," he said. "So he will be staying here so we can prepare him to be transferred to the Huntington Memorial. It's the best hospital in California to treat his condition as quickly as possible. Do you have any questions?"

"Yes," I stammered out. "Is he going to survive this?"

The doctor responded saying that my husband was strong and had a good chance of survival, but that it was going to be different from here on out.

"How much different?" I asked.

I remember the doctor's response telling me that it would be "…as different as he will be willing to make it; everything is on him now. He is going to work as hard as he wants, and he has to choose to recuperate."

"Does he know that?" I asked.

"No, not right now, but he will learn that during the next few weeks," he responded. "In the meantime, you must take care of yourself. Do you have children?"

We continued to talk, and the doctor let me know they'd handle the transfer.

When it came time to transfer my husband to Huntington, another doctor showed up asking for me. He began kindly asking me about medications and telling me I could ride in the ambulance with him, and then his voice changed.

"What were you feeding this man?"

"The same food we all eat at home," I responded.

The doctor shook his head, turned and walked away from us.

"What does he mean?" The kids asked.

I straightened my back. "He is putting the blame on whoever is closest. Don't worry. Now, I am going to go in the ambulance, so you have to follow us or you can get directions to get there, because I will need a ride back home."

I kissed them and entered into the ambulance. I couldn't think. I didn't fully understand what was going to happen and I had to be "present" at the time. Later, I told myself, I would figure out what would need to be done next.

When we got him into a room at Huntington and my husband woke up, he was disoriented. He had been sedated, so everything around him was now different. I had to explain to him what had happened and where he was at and that he was going to stay at this hospital for some time.

"Are you going to be here too?"

I reminded him that I had to go to work and make sure everything was okay at home. I promised to see him after work.

A whole month went by with my husband in the hospital. Every day, he would cry and tell me he didn't want to stay there any longer. He wanted to come home. It felt as if I was a mother leaving my child.

But I am not his mother, and I found myself frustrated, mad, scared, and really tired.

On the 29th day of that month, the hospital staff told me as I was leaving that they'd be sending my husband home with me the very next day. They said to come in early to meet with the doctor and review paperwork.

The following day was the beginning of what I call, "The New Adventure" as we tried to learn what to do and what not to do with him and for him. At home, as soon as he got back, I had to develop some rules because we needed to go to work and school, so during the day there were going to be times that he was going to be alone. We did not need an accident happening.

At that time, I had been a Head Start Teacher for about 16 years, so I developed graphic warnings like "**Do not turn on the stove**" and "**Do not go upstairs**"!

My husband learned those two rules very early on in his illness. Now, after 15 years, he still obeys those rules, although we don't have the signs up any longer.

I did the same with his medicines. I got one of those plastic boxes that can hold medicines according to the time and the day of the week, explaining to him how and when to take them. If there are any changes on medicines' shapes or colors, I have to tell him about the change and show him where in the box it is going to go. This has helped me on the doses and to prevent him from looking and trying to get "his medicines" from the pharmacy bottles.

This also helps him to know what day it is, since he's always asking out of nowhere. He tells me, "Today is [day of the week]" based on how I have each day by name on the pill holder. He does not know the date, but he knows the day usually after he finishes his breakfast.

At the start of his returning home, he used to escape because when we were at home, we usually did not lock the gate. We often needed to go out in different directions looking for him. We'd usually find him several streets away from the house sitting down by the sidewalk or sitting by a wall because he had fallen down and could not get up again.

"I don't know how long this is going to be, but he can't be depending on us for his every need," I would say to myself often. "He needs to keep trying to do things that he can do safely.

Little by little, things started to change as we figured out ways for him to do things by himself in a safe manner.

All this time, I was working and still had to keep up with appointments galore at different places at different times. The kids and I had to make plans on how we were going to do this. We agreed that they would help me to take him to his physical therapies, and I would take him to his doctor's appointments. While all of these things were happening with him, I also had to deal with his employer, his medical insurance and unemployment.

Six months later, his psychiatric specialist declared that he would not ever be able to return to work. This "sentence" we had been given pulled the floor out from under my feet. She continued outlining the process about Social Security and paperwork needed. She handed me her card.

Driving home, I wanted to scream and cry, but I couldn't. My husband was in the car with me. So, I braved the ride and focused on driving carefully and quietly, very quietly, home.

As I settled my husband into his bed that had been made up in the middle of our living room, I went outside to the backyard to have a good cry. I had to accept this new challenge.

Starting the process with Social Security, officially declaring him as a "disabled person" was a whole new adventure by itself with more tests, appointments, long waiting lines, and everything else. More frustration, anger and resignation built up as we tried to do the best we could.

Exploring my feelings, I would say that I was and still am tremendously frustrated. I am angry at him for not taking care of himself and getting sick. And at the same time, I am angry at myself because I had fallen into an unescapable trap. From the beginning, no one talked to me about options, about help, about things that were available at the time. Into the fifth year of my experience, I began to get sick, frustrated and stressed out. I caught myself not giving the children in my classroom the 100 percent they needed from me. That realization really broke me down. I could NOT continue working. I loved those kids. They were the "oxygen" in my life. But they deserved the best teacher they could have, and I needed to survive.

My own children could not understand why I was leaving my job, but then accepted my choice because they could see me going downhill, and they were afraid that I might get sick too.

Quietly, I started to do my early retirement paperwork, making it effective at the end of that calendar school year. Crying in silence, knowing that I had to do this to survive, put so much pressure and stress on me. I would be the voice that my husband had lost, and the only one now in charge of my entire family's affairs both here and in Mexico.

My husband had bought a house in Mexico long ago for his mother, so that she would not need to pay rent. He had put it in both of our names. With him getting sick, and then his mother passing away at the end of the month I retired, the house we bought and paid for was now being claimed by three of his siblings as their inheritance.

The day after his mother's funeral, as maybe you can imagine, my blood was boiling, but we needed to return home that day because of my husband's health.

I questioned myself, wondering what was the right thing to do? And I answered that THAT was not! So, I decided to start getting information and making a plan about what I could do. I realize that's the way I respond to emergencies, how I react to them. As I am writing I am questioning my handling, feelings and responses to all these problems.

All these responses, questions and feelings made me wonder why I respond the way I do to emergencies, and how I react to them. They've had me reflecting back on my childhood.

I grew up in Mexico City, in a small lot with three houses that were owned by three siblings. Our household included several generations. Grandmother was the "ruler," and I was everybody's child…something I have learned through working with my therapist a few years back. My mother had a mental health problem, and I was the middle child who physically resembled my father's family the most. So, I was the target of her frustration. Very early on, I learned to understand the signs of danger and how to react to that in order to be safe. Of course, it wasn't all the time that I was able to escape, and so, I suffered the physical consequences.

My experience with my job, however, has taught me to "stop the panic and think of how to save myself"; life has given me more opportunities to react than I think I have needed.

When I was 18 years old, my grandfather got seriously ill. I was the one who was holding his hand when the paramedics inserted a catheter into him because his kidneys were failing. Following his stay in the hospital for a few weeks, my grandfather didn't want anybody else to be with him. At that time, I was working already so I stayed the night with him, and in the mornings, I would go home, take a shower, go to work, then go home to sleep for four or five hours, only to return to the hospital to be with him. There were a few days that I couldn't make it, and Grandfather would get very angry and fight with whoever was there with him. The nurses had to give him something to calm him down.

When he was sent back home, my aunts prepared a room for him, moving my grandma into another room. We fixed the bed for him using pillows to surround him so that he wouldn't fall from the bed. And, they allowed me to sleep on the bed with him, holding my hand up on top of the pillow. In the mornings, I'd leave to do what I needed to do, and my grandma would stay with him.

The last night he was alive, Grandpa played with my hand the whole night. In the morning, my two aunts, my grandma, and me were with him. The doctor came by very early and told us that he was going to go any minute. I was holding his head and one of my aunts was moistening his lips. At one point, my aunts took Grandma outside of the room.

I was with my grandpa alone, holding his head, when he passed. I could feel his life leave him. A few moments later, I rose and gently positioned his head on the pillow. I walked out of the room. I guess my screams were more like a wolf howl than anything else. My father got there at that moment, and he just held me.

I remember this moment. I experienced the passing of life. I know I was there for everything else, but I can't seem to recall anything that happened afterward, not even the burial.

Two years later, Grandmother got sick. My aunt was mad at me, I don't remember why, and I wasn't allowed to be with my grandma as I was with my grandpa. I could see her thru the window and would send her kisses and hugs.

The day Grandma passed, I saw the doctor leaving as I was getting home. I had been out making a cake for my first niece who was going to be celebrating her first birthday the next day. My aunt was crying at the door, so I asked her what was wrong. She told me that Grandma was dying.

I walked into the house and my other aunt blocked my passage with her arm. With my hand, I moved her arm away from me. "I am coming to be with my grandma, not to see if you will let me in, " I said.

My cousin was with me, and together, we walked through to where Grandma was, standing near her bed. When she saw me, she extended her hand to me and tears fell down her face. I told her not to worry, that I was here now. I helped her get back into bed with my cousin's help. I moistened my grandma's lips. My aunts did not come back into the room until about two hours later. During this time, I started to notice some things, and told my cousin, "She is leaving us." My cousin got up and ran out of the room.

I stayed with Grandma by myself talking to her and holding her hand until she was gone. I put her hand on her chest. I rose and walked to the door, opening it, and telling the others that Grandma had passed. My father held me as I cried.

Again, I have no recollection of what happened afterward. I know I was there for both of my grandparents when they passed. I know my pain and sorrow was overwhelming. I know that I loved them, and they loved me until their last breaths.

I think those early life experiences shaped the way I react in emergencies because I do not "lose my head" during a crisis. My head is clear, and I think very fast on my feet. *"What do I need to do? How do I need to respond to what's happening? What questions do I need to ask? What next steps do I need to take based on what I hear and see?"* That is what happens in my head during any emergency, even when the emergency happens to me.

A few years back, I was in my back yard by myself, getting some oranges with
a pole. My husband was watching TV on his bed. We were alone at home. Somehow, when I pulled an orange down, the branch broke. I lost my footing and fell. Immediately, I thought to myself: *"Okay, this is what I need to do…now very slowly move your head, then your left leg, then your right leg. Now move your left arm…"* Unfortunately, when I tried to move my right arm, I felt a tremendous amount of pain. My cell phone was on a chair about seven or eight feet from me. My mind started to work the problem: I need to call the kids. If I stay here, nobody will know what happened to me.

Laying on the ground, I was looking at the ants scrambling around me, getting too close to my eyes. "You have to get up to get the phone," I told myself, crying out in pain as I attempted to do so. "Get up!" I told myself again, putting pressure on my left hand.

I was able to get the phone from the chair, and I sat down. I texted the kids, telling them that I had fallen and broken my arm. They immediately responded, telling me not to move and that they were on their way.

It took about 20 to 30 minutes for my kids to arrive. I was sweating profusely, and I thought that if I tried to get into the house, I wouldn't be able to climb down the stairs, as I'd probably fall. So I waited. Feeling dizzy and thirsty, I decided that I needed to distract myself, so I looked at my phone and started taking pictures of my arm and my face. I began laughing at my face, joking, telling myself that I was ugly before, but now I was even uglier! I was succeeding in entertaining myself and taking my mind off the pain.

When my kids ran into the back yard and saw me, one of them ran back into the house to get my ID and to tell my husband not to look for me because we were heading out to get some food. None of us wanting to worry him or get him excited.

In the hospital, we learned that my right elbow was broken into three places, and that I would need to stay in the hospital for the night. By the time morning came, the staff told me I could go home because the surgeon specializing in this kind of injury would not be available for three days.

My kids had left, so I had to call them to come pick me up. My arm was heavily wrapped, and I wasn't in pain thanks to the medications I was on. The hospital sent me home with instructions for the day of my surgery.

When we got home, my husband asked, "What happened to you?" I could see from his pale face that he was scared. I told him what had happened and what the plan was. I told him I was okay. He then got quiet and wanted to know why he hadn't been told about the accident when it happened. I explained that because we didn't know what I had done or what the treatment would entail, that we didn't want to stress him. I told him that I was here, and we know what happened, and we know what will happen next to heal me.

My husband went silent for about 30-minutes. Then, suddenly, he asked about what we were going to eat.

Days later, the surgery had gone well. My elbow was put back together using seven screws and some ligaments. And for the next few months, I had to take care of myself and take care of him. It was hard. The kids helped as much as they could, taking turns to take me to therapies and him to doctor appointments.

I wasn't in pain, and I only took one pill at night to help me sleep. And even when I felt pain, it wasn't at the level where I needed to take medications for it.

This time felt for me as if I were a child again. I could see what is happening to me, but it was more like I was looking at myself up on a screen in some sort of a movie.

I concluded that maybe all that happened in my past… maybe it was bad and ugly…but maybe it all has helped me to be able to manage the crisis I'm living through now with my husband. Due to my experiences, I'm able to stay open and keep my mind clear to deal with what's at hand in my life.

It's been fifteen years since my husband had his stroke. He has had his ups and downs. Little by little, he grows more fragile. He can walk but falls easily. His dementia and other health problems are advancing, and I am getting old and tired. It is such a heavy load to be responsible for another person and the pandemic did not help any because the circle of friends we had, little by little, disappeared. Some moved either to the places they came from, or to be close to their families. Others died.

As I look and see what has happened to my life in these past 15 years, I can't help but still feel not only frustrated but angry at him for not taking care of himself, for not being prepared, and for not thinking of us. Especially when he talks about his past and things that he was doing with his friends and co-workers instead of being with the kids when they were growing up. I'm angry. For him caring more about his family in Mexico than for the future of our own children...I feel resentment and anger. At him. At life. At myself.

I had worked so hard for my whole life preparing for the future to be good for us as we got older. And so much of what I had hoped for was now not anything close to what I had envisioned it would be.

When my children started pre-school, I remembered my own childhood dream of wanting to become a kindergarten teacher. I thought this even as early as when I was in kindergarten. To this day, I can recall my kindergarten teacher's name, her face, her white hair, and the wonderful way that she always treated me.

I'm proud to say that at that time, I already had earned my AA Degree from a Junior College. And I would volunteer in the classroom, too, while continuing my education to get a certificate to become a pre-school teacher. When my second child started kindergarten, I started to work as a preschool teacher. And even though I had reached that goal, I always thought about going back to school. Just a few years later, I did! My kids went with me to get all the information to apply to California State, and that's where I earned my bachelor's and also graduated with my master's in education...at the same time my eldest child graduated from high school.

Trying to be the best example for my own kids, I wanted to show them that when you want something with your heart, you have to work hard toward it, but you can make it happen. At the same time, I was trying to be a good teacher for my "other children" in my classroom. In preschool, teachers and parents work together. Implementing all I've learned, my work in the classroom is to also help parents see the importance of their role during the development of their own children for their future and for their own.

My husband, unfortunately, couldn't see all of that. He was too busy making his own future and helping his family in

Mexico. He had had his stroke one week after returning, and as I shared earlier, I had to battle to get what was rightfully ours. It took me five long years, but I finally did it, and I was able to get back the house in Mexico that was ours.

As for my daughters, I know that they have to make their own life. They have to work on their own futures. They get to make their own families, and have a right to be happy with their own partners. They are always ready to help me when I need it, but I try not to make them worry for us too much. And still, I hope for the situation with my husband's health to change for the better, sooner rather than later.

I also have hope that I'll be around to play with my future grandkids, if my girls choose to give me some! And for all of that, all I need to do is take care of Me, Myself, and I.

CHAPTER ELEVEN

Goodnight, *My* Mrs. Calabash— Wherever You Are

by Allison Beatrice Seton

Alzheimer's acts like a serpent's tail, flicking one person's emotional responses back at the other.
Dasha Kiper | Travelers to Unimaginable Lands

G randma asked me to marry her. To tell no one.
"Just you and I—let's run away together and get married."
Maybe it's why she is always asking if I am a boy or a girl of late. It must be the androgynous-gamine third-world look I'm sporting mid-life here.

My grandma asked me to marry her again. When a dreamier, sultrier moment of hers arises—it can calculate in an uptick in proposals.

We're driving in squash country Conejo Valley on the backroads one day, passing the childhood markers of massive old Oaks—drenched in light from the high sun, and she has decided we're on our way to see a property she wants to bid on. She says, "Don't get too attached—let's just look and see what our next

135

move will be or what offers they have." Our life runs hot. We open escrow twice weekly – per her slowly slipping mind.

She told me the other day that she is getting divorced, and things are tense at home. I'm hearing my 99-year-old Grandma Rosaleen channeling her thirty-year-old self, spilling the divorcee tea to her bestie. Yet, she's this centenarian, and I am her Granddaughter of forty-four years—and we are just on a drive for groceries rather than some scout to purchase a pocket listing for a pretty penny in the bushes of Calabasas.

When I tell her late one evening that I am almost forty-five (as is standard practice for her to ask, marvel at, and mock my age hourly), she throws her head back, laughs loudly, and so ruefully declares, "*I'm* not even forty-five yet!"; she pities me this woman, ever so ageist! Then, she demands her babies be brought in to be breastfed.

The dumbfounding beauty and painful richness of this is that I am literally bearing witness to this woman re-creating, re-living, re-imagining in real time all the things *I* so long to do in my own life NOW.

I daydream about what has become her lucid state of affairs. This time suspension and loss of her, and I having to re-dream up all of what she is pining for at the end of her days, is this uncanny, yet astonishingly fun, twist of this whole caregiving 'deal'. She has had two husbands, four healthy pregnancies, a year sabbatical in Surfers Paradise, Australia, endless real estate, parcels, and avocado farms from Fallbrook, California, straight down to Baja, San Felipe, and back up to wine country Paso Robles. And for me, the most coveted of all being the grand, great, & great greats she spawned from her brood, minus me.

I'm non-compete. Woman's got legacy...that's a Fendi. While I care for her, I dream back up her life with her—while fearing the lack of fortitude for my own.

I let her wax poetic on "going home." The little ones need her to make supper. Her son just left just a few short moments ago. Her parents are expecting her home and on the front porch by eleven. Her mother is sick. Her siblings Jasper and Margaret are arriving for brunch. This daily download from the clouds is impressive. Memory loss and dementia in any form can be devastating, but her world is still richly buzzing and fully alive. All senses blaring. All possibilities possible.

It's one a.m., my grandma almost asleep in the too-little, too-full bed we share — a cellular-level necessity to know her every move, and as the house falls still with silence, I rouse her just as she is about to close her eyes, and in the dark ask, "you want a warm chocolate chip cookie and water Rosaleen?... The babies are with Amanda—you can 'go home' in the morning—but I would love for you to stay the night with me."

"Oh, I would love that—don't tell anyone—they'll try to change it—or take me away," she purrs.

Her life is layered and renewed and created and designed and re-designed over and over and over again, all day, every day. It is a sort of homage to the love affair one has with one's own life. The always loving it and going for it. The stunning—unwavering love we have for those we love. The never wanting to leave them. The romance of nourishing your offspring with just a breast or a table of food. I see so clearly the reverence she has for the life she has led. The will to hold on to it. To wage war against her rewiring brain. The nuances and profound mysteries of dementia have brought about this spectacular show of force for how she feels about her life. Dementia might deconstruct, but it also decodes.

This new world order is often a hard (OK, soft) sublingual progesterone compounded pill for me to swallow. Well, it dissolves slowly under my tongue, kind of how our days feel as they mix, mesh, and mold into one after another. Slow, saccharinely sweet. My grandma's dreams, whimsies & desires are all the rage of a reality I crave. In a Pre-Caregiving, Pre-Pandemic world, I was on the brink of babyhood—having my follicles tracked and counted by fertility fan faves Huang and Wombach. Yet, thrust into this spiraling world of unknowns and variables I had not accounted for, I am supposed to do what? Wallow and wait for this woman's demise so I can figure out how to breastfeed my own? No.

Back at our shared cottage in what feels like the jungle of Tarzan, and mere yards from the Sepulveda Dam--I am sitting on the edge of our bed. As I get up from a sweet nothing conversation with her to fetch fresh peaches, golden kiwis, espressos, and olive oil-laden pastries from Proof (our favorite co-op bake shop in Atwater Village) —I begin to wail. I am weeping, wincing, and almost squealing in this high, breathless pitch, hoping the TV or the gushing water of the faucet drowns me out. Pouring out and over me is this grief. Deep guttural, dizzying, hyperventilating grief.

I've spent most of my life hunched over a deep steel kitchen or white porcelain sink of some kind. Sobbing. Trying to swim— but weeping from, and at—both beauty & grief—with an undercurrent of sheer fear of them *both*.

✱✱✱✱✱

Caregiving came late for me based on my grandma's actual need for it. She might have gotten herself to ninety-plus, but I've had a heavy hand in a hundred. I attest it to her tenaciously fierce nature—and perhaps it would have played out the same—but the 2020 abrupt reset and catastrophe that touched down also blew up and opened like a grenade my grandma's care. When she turned ninety-six, blowing out a ton of candles across a key lime meringue pie with a graham and white chocolate crust (yes, a white chocolate melted and now cold hardened addition of perfection), I asked her, "What does it feel like to be ninety-six?"

"The party's over," she declared, deadpanned with a smirk and wit so perfectly pitched.

I was dialed in to what the thirteen calls within thirty minutes meant from her, once the sun fell fast off the horizon. Where she had once sustained with plated lunches and meds, she now no longer could. Nothing frightened or cemented in me, her need for consistent care, then being awoken at two am, fully clothed and at the front door clutching a single taupe suede Oxford of mine and purse, in a full-blown state of demented delirium. I jumped between her and her escape. I pleaded with her. I begged her to go back to sleep. To relax. I told her she was OK. Circa two minutes later, my grandma grabbed at my face and scratched me from the very inside of my top lip to straight down the center of my chest bone. Leaving this huge V-like welted wound that withdrew blood and my sanity with it. I was heart shook. Panicked. My voice was hoarse and haggard from these initial days of little well-knowns and the novelty of newfound worries.

It was the start of the Pandemic's endless first summer, and I felt like I was hit with grief and tough decisions like never before. The losses of years past, of her mind, all the yet-to-be-determined potential losses within my body and life. So out of control was my capacity to do anything but try to contain her—keep us safe in any and all ways I possibly could. Not entirely—but in so many ways, I would be alone in this Pandemic. Her short-term memory only able to hold 'the world has a virus' for a few fleeting moments. Masks and the sourcing of all things Clorox were quizzical and non-important to her. I heavily envied this state. Gone were the days of endless reminder notes to eat, drink water, wash hands—not open the front door. Gone were evenings of returning home to her having bathed (she loved her baths), being happy, content, well-nourished, and watching television in the dim of our living room. Her ability to withstand, organize, and sustain life while I was gone had ceased. She couldn't be left. Left to her own devices. Left inside her own failing mind.

I had overseen my grandma's care for well over a decade—before she ever became someone who *required* care. I was proud of this. The notion that I could outsource her care, or even remotely feel I had the luxury to at her advanced age—was laughable. Fiscally, I couldn't afford it. Her mind medically was not going to allow for it. Well into her nineties, I could still travel internationally, stay active, date, and pop in to see Depeche

Mode at the Bowl now and again. I was looking to use my body. This hiker, want to be runner—very balletic Pilates-loving tennis fanatic (and moonlighting horse jumper) had been trying to 'preserve' her fertility—like it was a passion project. Always sort of the forethought to keeping the champagne flute out of hand and the pepitas and arugula overflowing.

But now, it was official. I was Rosaleen Carter's full-time caregiver.

Could I handle this? Her brain? Could I win against her brain? 'I have no network.' 'No guest house,' I kept repeating to myself on loop. No funds for a night nurse, a day nurse, or a four-hour respite. No kids for her to run around and expend energy after on a soccer field. No destination wedding in Serifos to live and breathe for, and what fun am I with NO babies!? No deliverables, as I called them. I needed to be practicing with this body of mine, and to go fast and hard at my life's work. I needed to loosen the grip on my losses and fall deep for their capital gains. The fruit of her wish for life has come with such a lovely luck and labor so equally tough, that this has felt like an extreme sport. Her mind the most unbearable, unbenign conquest.

What came next was a strong-armed education on what it is to be a caregiver in the truest of trenches. I won't rant on what it is really to be late-stage 'geriatric' in this country—or maybe I will someday. Think Noah's Ark. Sans any and all preparation. It was straight to the floods. What I could and couldn't do with my grandma became starkly apparent. Wildly heir apparent. I couldn't yell at her in front of a notary without being asked and then harassed to see my bank statements. I had to 'produce' her on balconies to one of our many different social workers of various counties and now of various states at the height of a pandemic. I took a private therapist call in her room—leaving her in the living room and thus near an exit—only to be startled by the pounding of a police unit thirty minutes later. They had my now very-in-distress-grandmother relaying to them she was being held against her will—and threw around the word 'hostage.' I called her everything in front of them. And didn't care. She had become my biggest threat of all. I self-declared her my little liability.

The rank and file of being the fifth born, fourth female grand baby fulfillment of the final filial fantasy (hers, not mine). Ha. Self-appointed and anointed. With I as her caregiver, as she has always been mine. Rosaleen is the protector, advocate, and warmth of everything promising and capable in my world. Dropped at the door of the hotel she managed across from the Huntington Beach Pier, I was seven days old, left haphazardly and rather comically by my surgeon father and soon-to-be RN mother, without so much as a bottle of formula or a change of diapers. Just a baby bundled and left in her care. Just that steadfast, fierce & and tough-as-nails matriarch. A life force of mine—whose care and overseeing will never be relinquished under my watch.

I intended to own her care like a couple of Panerai—stacked thick and tight on my right. And I have.

I had understood dementia to be memory deficient and non-neurotypical. Never did I expect such a distorted, illogical—all-decades-of-life-on-deck constant downloading of one's life. And the knowledge that, at some point, her life will end because she chooses to die and leave us is like the most radical and ideological oxymoronic kind of crazy to me. Tell me I've not worked this bloody hard to *lose* her.

Caregiving has been the most mind-bending mind fuck—and while I was built for the blows of her care, I am wildly uninterested in further unforeseen inevitable griefs; palliative care, hospice, morphine patches, or drips—I don't want any of it. Nor the brutality of this—inclusive of all the secondary fun losses. My fledgling, fervently fleeting, full force fading fertility of my forties. OK. Mid-Forties. Fuck. The Wim Hof freezing cold plunges (OK, the freezing setting on my shower and possibly a bucket of ice), endless dancing to Shakira's world tour with Meluma (have you seen him? not leaving him out), ballet in the kitchen, and up the hallways. Back-up dancing like I'm auditioning for Bieber.

The chasing of my grandma across a room—or a parking lot—containing her in small and vast spaces of this world. The demands. Don't get me started on the round-the-clock demands. The force of her voice when her brain surges to anger and agitate—when she is in angst–and just wants her damn babies brought to her breast. This woman. This nineteen-fiftyish housewife with a very before-her-time 'attachment parenting' style. The being up all night and massaging her. Giving cold water with antacids to counter late-night truffles against my better judgment —the monotony and brutal one-liner of 'I want to go home!' screamed and spit in my face countless times. Grating! I, being this reluctant and unknowing participant in a pact to be almost an extension of her—of her brain.

In turn, my brilliant 'neurotypical' brain rages against her disease and unease, against time and all odds. The agony of just piecing together dinner in a hurry or the rampant defeat of showers and soaked-filled variations of. The rush of everything to ease her anxiety. Am not sure how we make it to bed, heads on pillow—lulled to sleep by the valley's full moon and basin—the midnight mist and deep emerald ivy resetting for the dawn to come. It is a wonder we survive even a day. That I survive my periodic painstaking periods or menses or 'perimeno'—whatever this stage is—and the fright in me of having not front-loaded with a grip of Ibuprofen—and I am vomiting and going to the bathroom simultaneously. She calls me from this claw foot vintage tub to come to her. She is in distress. And so is her caregiver, who is forty-four on the floor and about to pre-decease her. And then what? They will come and find me and put me in a body bag and take her to some god-forsaken nursing home where she will see her own end in a calendar week.

I am in scalding water, incoherent—feeling faint. My prostaglandins misfiring magnificently, disrupting my entire life. My body drags itself to often a second or third shower. And I keep screaming that it's OK! I am OK! She will be OK! I make it to the bed wrapped in a towel, I've probably bled all over, feeling more drugged than she will ever be. Yet we wake and soldier on. Ever shocked that she didn't fall and split her head open or travel out two gates to the street—or break both hips.

Still drenched from water and pain—pretending to be this caregiver not about to die on her—I imagine I follow it up with: "Should I toss together a charcuterie board and piping hot shortbread dipped in dark chocolate to cap us off? She, of course, answers in the affirmative with an, "Oh ya!"—and so begins our day (of ordeals on ordeals on ordeals).

I'm always in this deep meditative state when it relates to my womb. The unknown of getting to use it—or even practicing to use it again. The madcap irony of being asked fifty-six times daily to produce my grandma's babies like they are ripe and ready in a Butler's pantry, prepping to take flight like a flock of doves fleeing an oven. Babies are an all-day affair. Hers. Mine. The lack of mine. When we head to the car after a day on the coast—she screams that I've left the baby on the beach!

My fanciful inquiries into my grandma's intuitive mind as to whether she sees babies in her crystal ball for *me*. She says of course. Hesitant twinkle in her eye. The cognitive, fully aware of my advanced age eye. I tell her how high-risk I am. All of this. This whole operation—occupation—full court home advantage plus thing we've got going is not for the faint of heart. I cry and weep at this existence. This moment of madness and magic that I will want for—for the rest of my days.

And so I get up from the bed upon which I've been taking stock of my life and tighten the towel around me. I throw on some solid Sting or Sade—Moby—to remind me that one of these mornings, I will look for her, and she will be gone.

Imogen—a Buckley version and verse of Hallelujah—and because I feel not 12, nor forty, or maybe both—but I often feel everything *but* the girl (or *a* girl-or gasp—a *woman*)—and so

I throw them on too. To ease our troubled minds. I throw it all on—amplifying our hearts as my grandma and I dance. I can feel the force in her arms and fingertips and the way she moves, watching her face light up in the glow of our well-dimmed cream string globes—humongous—planetary—earthy, and we keep dancing to a White Lotus Felix remix, and we are now in the drop–overwhelmed and in love with Sinatra sending us in the clowns and taking us to the moon. The theme song to Succession—watching her imitate the fiddling of a violin and conducting like she's a Gustavo. The Sopranos baritone "woke up this morning," and I am bouncing off the walls as if I am the chosen one. We fall a little too easily in love for cool cat Chet Baker. The Outsides 'Remembrance' pulsating & pumping jazz falsettos into our veins. We can sense the slow arrival of the birds with A Cinematic Orchestra— Barbra's Evergreen gets belted out—top of the lung—till my grandma declares, "This too is her favorite." To soothe and massage her brain and my vagus last nerve. To delight. To relish in sentiment. We dance balletically to 'This Bitter Earth.' I, then, crumbling in exhaustion from tears, my endorphins, and her endearing, unending love for me.

The 'Allison' she shouts for and pines for and asks for. "It's me, Grandma. I'm Allison," she says. "Alli b". Yes. Stating, "You're Allison Seton," as she lights up a Hancock Park night sky to me. She has been my ride-or-die. My advocate at every turn. My Mrs. Calabash long before we resided in the artist enclave of Calabasas and shortly after my Toronto stage intro to Durante. She has been my version of Elizabeth—set sail with me on the QE2—this Portobello Scotland-born Scotch-Irish miracle that made it across the Atlantic—who's been the overseer of our little commonwealth—my Canadian resident alien.

Most of what dementia is rarely makes news. There is an abundance of Instagram accounts on sundowning, shower refusals, and speech pathology. Our hours and minutes are nowhere to be found. A far-out galaxy of just us. Both of us heavily reliant on each other's brains and cognitive states. The reliance issues runneth over. She needs usage of my brain (or any well-working one nearby) to get her needs met—exhibit distress—to function and stay safe—and for me to fill in all her gaping gaps. I, held hostage by her shrinking hippocampus, constantly living in a state of fight or flight and what feels like existing in fifteen-minute intervals. What will her brain allow for? Today? In an hour? Tonight. We gratefully don't require Hoyer lifts, oxygen tanks, or to be at countless dialysis appointments, but her mind has been no less laborious.

This moment in time has made me feel like an often unfavorable advocate—a demonstrative Granddaughter of the Third Reich. An absentee friend to many I adore and love. An estranged sister and aunt. This was the rightful (albeit, er, slightly righteous) thing to do. This woman had done the work and manned the phones for us. Her care is far more harrowing, monotonous, and terrifying than this little tall tale. While I have been macro/micro-managing loss like a boss my whole life—this impending loss of mine, ours, the world over—nothing, and I mean nothing, will inform the second act of my existence as much as this.

I recently almost ran off the road heading up the Grapevine. I threw my hazards on, thinking she was about to open the car door from boredom, desperation, or hallucinations from a road trip to Canada of very little sleep. Her hand resting heavy on the handle—with an onslaught of verbal threats to do just that- I was beside myself. She won't wear a seatbelt. And what memory care unit of one (me!), and sans Seroquel (ever), will cop to this level of hazard and subpar care? Not I. There is no plan B. Tomorrow is a new day of possibilities and a more lucid, happier Gram. Hopeful. Exhausted. Ever fearful.

A visiting RN told me your Grandma is "really well maintained"—I was giggly. (my crypto caregiving currency increasing in real time, baby!) I am giving this woman the works. A thorough rinse down at every trip to the lou and a post-shower low setting blow dry if a hairdryer is on hand for her nether—personal valet and bidet. The stats don't lie. She's on three meds a day. Showers daily and wears cotton-ribbed hipster underwear to bed. No liner, ladies. Her hair shimmers from a box-bought dye (this strawberry blonde color—all my Vidal Sassoon fantasies of pretending to know how to cut hair, and mainly, to cut layers—is the Barbie dream I didn't think I had). She gets all my oils and fancy face creams pressed firmly into her ruddy, supple complexion—is given cold, crisp Italian water (if I've got it) when she wakes— full lymph massages for circulation I know nothing of how to execute—but do it all anyways. I could write a dissertation on just the care of her dentures alone—the bedside commode all night affairs—the endless falls which reached a tipping point, total pun intended. The laundry. The business of her. The paperwork of her. The PPE's and POA's and Advance directive this—and authorized representative of that.

Who will I be after this? When can I swim far into the lake and not check to see if she is OK on the shore? Not have to look back for a thumbs up from her son or my niece. To know that she is OK for three minutes of existence without me. When can I plunge into the deep of my mind and curation of life for longer than four minutes? What if I drown—or worse yet, want to? Who am I if I'm not being called to the rocky shore over and over by her? Who will be in distress for me? Who will want from me in this world—and will I want for a world without her? What will I dream of beyond my ovulating ovaries, past big loves, or all the unknown ones yet to land in my orbit? Sashimi. Oysters on the half from maybe a Lost Kitchen in Maine, cradled in an emboldened tart green apple vinegar, a scallion or two, a shiny shave of shallot. I'll dream of keeping everything retro 'fresh.' My losses won't have me—but will hold me. Sustain and inspire. Exalt. I dream of long-haul flights. Qatar—Majorca, Marrakech, Mozambique. Sleeping out under a Tanzanian sky in a world that doesn't know me yet.

CHAPTER TWELVE

After the Accident

by Kay Anonsen

O n April 21, 2002, at 11:00 p.m. my 44-year-old son was coming home from work on his motorcycle, going South on the 710 towards Long Beach when an Audi tapped his bike and tried to race him. Ronnie sped up to get away from him and ran out of road. He couldn't make the turn and had to choose between a guard rail and gravel. He chose the guard rail and went over it, flying off the freeway and landing 20 feet below on the 91.

Of course, I didn't know any of this. I was home, in bed watching T.V. staying awake until he came home, and pondering my problems – what to do about my job, stay until when? When can I retire? My son wants to buy a house next year and have me move with him. Do I want to leave California and move to Tennessee with him? I really need to do the housework. This place gets so dirty so fast.

My phone startled me. Who could be calling me after 10 o'clock? I answered and heard a woman's voice. It sounded like a party, like she was calling from a party, because there was a lot of noise in the background. I figured it was a wrong number and was prepared to be polite and tell her so. She told me my son had had an accident and was okay, but he asked her to call me. I thanked her for calling.

I figured he must have had a spill, and would pick up the bike, brush himself off, and continue home, where he knew I was waiting and probably worried. Really didn't consider the point that he had someone else call me. It just didn't register at all.

I checked Google maps though, just to see. He and I have location sharing and I could see his face on the map, but he wasn't moving. Finally, he started down the 710 and I thought, okay, great, he's on his way home. Then he turned right. I zoomed out to see what was to his right and saw the Harbor UCLA Trauma Center.

That's when I turned to stone.

I called the Trauma Center. "My son... I think my son is on his way there in an ambulance," I stammered out to the person who answered. The woman responded saying they were glad I called because he was coming in as a John Doe. I asked if he was all right, but she didn't know. I gave her his information. I called my sister and asked her to call everyone else.

I called an Uber because I couldn't drive. It started to pour rain as soon as I got in the car. When we got to the hospital, we couldn't find the door. Finally, we found a person who opened a door and told us how to get to the right door. When I got to that door, the security guard wouldn't let me in the hospital. He said I wasn't allowed because my son was in transit from Emergency to ICU and he couldn't let me in until he knew where to send me. I reminded him that it was raining out. He said he didn't matter. He said I could wait in my car or take a seat on one of the benches outside. He said it would be about 45 minutes. All the benches were filled with people sleeping.

I knew I didn't have the strength to stand that long because my knees were already buckling. I was starting to wonder if this was a nightmare and not real.

Then I got an idea. I called the phone numbers of people I had talked to in Emergency. From them, I got a number for the ICU. The nurse who answered seemed astonishingly kind. He told me to put him on speaker and bring my phone to the security guard. He told the guard that he had a place for me to go and to let me in.

THIS was the beginning of a year of learning how to get around "no"...

When I got past the security check point, I looked around and walked to the elevator. The guard said, "No, not that elevator, take another elevator." I couldn't understand what he said. Then another guard very gently told me to come with her and she would take me up in the elevator. I wanted to hug her and tried to explain to her the effect of her kindness. She smiled and told me to have a good evening.

The ICU nurse met me at the elevator doors and walked me past their security guard and into a staff room. He told me to wait there until someone came for me. I looked around at all the sleeping bodies in the staff room and sat in a small room adjoining it.

The Sherriff called me, returning my call, because the emergency social worker told me that is who has the information about the accident. He told me he didn't have any information other than that my son fell off the freeway and to wait for the traffic report. I was to call in the morning.

Someone came to get me from the staff room and brought me to another security check point, and I was finally allowed in to see my son.

There he was, lying in a bed, unconscious, with tubes and wires coming and going from and into his body. I looked down and saw only one foot protruding from the blanket. A resident came over to join me at the bedside. "Where's his other foot?" I asked. I was wondering why it would be tucked up underneath him like that.

The resident doctor said, "He lost his leg."

I swooned. A woman brought me a chair and a box of tissues. "I need a bucket, I'm going to throw up." This surprised me - not tears, vomit. She brought me a trash can. I didn't feel capable of sitting in a chair. I needed to lie down. I needed to lie down for a year. I needed to lie down and never get up again. I felt too small, too inadequate to know this, too weak to see the absence of a leg on my son's body. I felt this needs to happen to someone else, someone more capable of tragedy. What I really wanted was to just be able to lie in a bed next to his, and be with him, and never leave him.

I had to leave him though. All my life, since I can remember sweeping the stairs when I was 4 years old, I have tried to be useful. I don't like to end the day until I've recounted the use I got out of it. Why would I sit in a chair by my son's bedside in an ICU unit full of doctors and nurses, when his employer had to be told he wouldn't be going in today or for the rest of the run of the show where he worked? I didn't have phone numbers for anyone. I had to contact his closet friends. I had to go home and do that and come back to the hospital, and I had to feed his tortoise. Oh, and I had to tell my work I wasn't coming back. My sister told me our brother Bill was coming to where we were in Long Beach and would be here around 3 p.m. That was 12 hours away.

I had to get a bed for my brother's stay. Oh wait, no, that's right, Bill could sleep in Ronnie's bed. I had to change the sheets, and the living room was a disaster. There was no place to sit down. And food, I had to get food for Bill. I had to go home.

I Ubered home, and I watched the lights speed away from me, and the bridge soar up into the night sky. I couldn't close my eyes because I would imagine how it must have happened. And that he was there in the night on the side of a freeway with a smashed leg. Alone.

Anguish. I kept my eyes open and watched the streetlights until we arrived at my son's apartment. I went in, put on the kettle to make coffee, and found his carton of cigarettes. I set myself up on my bed and opened up my laptop. With 30 years of experience fundraising for the arts, I knew how to find people. I called and texted and emailed.

I let people pour their grief over me. And just to be clear, this is an awful thing to do to the person closest to the person who is lying in an ICU bed. Please don't ask us to take care of you right now. Please just tell us how much you love who we love and then ask how you can help. But I can't hold you. I can't comfort you. I have to go and have this conversation with about 10 more people. Then I have to go to the hospital while you get on with your day.

I had to find someone who worked on the TV show to tell them Ronnie wouldn't be coming back to work. I had to call his closest friends. I had to call my family. I had to call my work. I had to call his bank because his wallet was missing.

And in the middle of these calls, my son called me: "Hi Mom. I had a bad accident."

"I know, honey, I was there last night with you, but you weren't awake." This was the first of my long journey of feeling guilty for not being there for him because I was off doing something for him. "I'm just making some calls; I'll be right there."

I took an Uber back to the hospital. I hadn't slept, and so, again, I couldn't drive. I was 66 years old, and my son was 44. We were starting on a journey of his recovery, and I was going to soon find out that his amputated leg was the least of our problems.

For 15 months and four days, I've been there for my son. And today, he tells me he wants to go outside on his own for the first time: "Just around the block, and I'll come back through the ally so it's just half a block."

Half a block of treacherous obstacles. Cracks in the sidewalks, flower and tree cut outs that go right into the sidewalk corners, and you don't realize they're there until you trip over them. Even people with 20/20 vision and two legs do that. But I am the problem, according to him and both of my brothers. Also, I think the physical therapists and Ronnie have been discussing me, my fear of him falling, my fear of him getting hurt.

My fear, my fear, my fear.

I think my fear is reasonable.

During this past year of recovery, Ronnie's leg had to be amputated over and over again, farther up, to where he is now an above-the-knee amputee. And somehow, the optic nerves in both eyes were damaged in the hospital, so now he has only 18 percent vision. And, somehow, in the hospital, his left hand became paralyzed. I think the optic nerve damage was caused by the deep and permanent pressure wounds in the back of his head from not being turned when they put him in a coma. They put him in a coma because he had developed ICU delirium, misdiagnosed at first as alcohol withdrawal. And I think the paralysis is from the splint they put on his left arm after surgery to repair his broken humerus. It had dug into his left wrist and damaged the radial nerve.

I can guess what you may be thinking: SUE! Well, we tried. Unless you have really obvious and completely debilitating damage from something clearly caused by a hospital procedure, or you died, no lawyer will touch you. Plus, a suit must be filed within a year, and within that year, we were hurtling from one crisis to another, trying to survive. One infection after another after another, and they couldn't get his temperature down. Ice blankets. Ice bags on either side of his head. They kept the trach in, and when he was finally taken out of the coma, he couldn't speak. Then they couldn't find a rehab that would take him, because he'd had infections and now a trach and he was too young for skilled nursing so nobody would take him. And so, he lingered and languished, losing his will to fight.

An appointment notice for ortho follow up came in the mail one day when I was coming home from my daily hospital visit. So, the next day when I went to the hospital, I asked if my son could go to the ortho clinic appointment located in the offices downstairs. The nurse said, "Oh that's okay, we'll have them come up."

I responded with, "But he's been in bed for two months, and I thought it would be an outing, you know, somewhere else, somewhere to go."

The nurse gave me a startled look, as though this was only occurring to him now that Ronnie had not been out of bed in two months. Then he finally said, "Okay, when's the appointment. I'll make the arrangements."

During the second follow-up visit to ortho, one of the staff members said she couldn't believe he was still in the hospital; "What are they treating you for?"

"Nothing," Ron said. "I'm waiting for a rehab placement."

"You don't need to go to a rehab facility," the staff member scoffed. "Those places are just nursing homes. You need to get out of here. This place is intense."

Ron's eyes widened. His whole body seemed to react to what she said. As though a prison guard was telling him his sentence was up ages ago, and asking why he was still behind bars. As though DD was coming, and he was going to be liberated.

"Call medical services," she said. "Tell them you want to go home. Get your mother to fight for you."

And that is how he came home.

Now 15 months and 4 days later, he walks with a prosthetic leg that doesn't fit well and requires 15-ply socks, and the new socket hasn't been made because the clinic is down a staff person and twice canceled this month because of a "family emergency." He's had two surgeries on his hand and still he can barely lift it and can't turn it, and he says it feels like someone else's hand has been sewn onto his wrist.

And he wants to, now, for the first time since the accident, go outside and walk around the block, alone. And I am the only thing standing in his way.

My therapist says I must let him go, that it's his life, his recovery, and that my fear should not be a factor in any of it.

I have this trick I do now; I deliberately put a pleasant expression on my face, no matter what I'm feeling. I conjured up this expression and say what I don't really feel.

"Okay honey."

"You sure?"

"I'm sure."

I think my fear is a factor because he doesn't have to have any as long as I have buckets full. Once mine is removed, he has to feel fear on his own.

"Okay then," Ronnie stammered. "Well, I'll see you later. I should only be gone 10 minutes."

I listened as he went down the 18 stairs to the front door. I listened to the door open. I listened to him walk out and shut the door behind him. I clicked on the latest news of Harry and Mehgan and pushed all thoughts out of my mind.

*****

He's sleeping. It's 5:00 p.m.

Yesterday he did the same thing, took a nap in the afternoon and slept through supper. I had whispered to him that it was time for supper. At 7:30 p.m. I had again whispered to him that it was time for supper, and he got mad and told me to let him sleep.

This will be the fifth day he has taken a nap in the afternoon and slept right through a meal.

I listen at the door. No sounds. Is he sleeping? Or is it something worse. There's enough Diladud in there to kill a horse. Should I open the door? Should I call 911?

It's 5:23 p.m. I don't know why I'm crying. I know we're both a little depressed. I know we're a little depressed because there's nothing left to go after, no other intervention. He really is blind. The left hand really doesn't work. The leg needs a new socket, but he's walking well with it anyway. And there you go. The leg ended up being the best part of the accident. That sounds awful. It wasn't the best. It was just the least devastating.

It's so humid. I get on my bed to read a bit and the book is so disappointing. Full of accolades on the back. One guy even said he was ecstatic about the read. I didn't like it at all. Just miles and miles of descriptions. And no plot. Nothing ever happens.

And then something happened!

The shelf above my bedside table gave way, under the weight of the binders of the paperwork of the accident that I put there yesterday. I was so pleased that I had found a home for them, and they were still accessible, for putting papers in, appointment notices, correspondence from the insurance company. Bills.

Always when in a crisis, I get very calm.

The coffee cup from this morning spilled over everything. My water glass spilled over my library books. But my big glass of soda I had reached over and held so it didn't spill. I picked up everything. Got the basket I was going to throw out yesterday but didn't and put everything in it. I tidied up and saw the water damage to the Joan Didion book from the library. Why wasn't I reading that book anyway?

I should go out to the kitchen to boil an egg for salad, but Ronnie is still sleeping. Forget supper. But no, he'll wake up hungry and then what? Okay I'll fry the burgers and make the salad.

The Hummels broke when the shelf gave way, their legs broke. Ironic.

And my uncluttered desk is now cluttered again because that's where I had to put everything that was on the shelf.

Moan, moan, complain, complain. I'm tired. And it's humid. And it's dreary.

Zeke, Ronnie's friend, is only coming for 5 days, 3 really because two are travel days. Ronnie mentioned this today. And then he said it's probably because he was going to go back with them, and they'd have the real visit there. But he can't go back with them because he is still not able to be in the world, away from the living room, and the coffee table, where his meds are, and his pee jugs, and his world is finite and compact, and he can operate in it, knows where everything is.

When I went in to say hello yesterday, I sat on the edge of the couch, and he looked up but couldn't see me. He finally looked over and saw where I was, right in front of him. And he talks about working?! And going out on his own, to the park, to sit and read a book?!

Depression is sinking in because now we know none of that can happen, and there's no money either. Disability wants yet another doctor to look at him and this one not until August. I could vomit writing this. This gnawing worry about money, and what we're going to do.

I'll go boil an egg. That's what I'll do. The next right thing. But first, I have to clean the pot. Fine I'll do that too.

The egg is boiling in the pot on the stove, and I know I cried because of the Hummel. I broke the Hummel Mom gave me. I broke the Hummel that I've been carting around for years. Before now, it had a few knicks, but now it is broken clean in half, at the legs. Like my son. It's not that I am finally aware that my son lost his leg, but it was a heartless reminder. Whose heart was being heartless? Fate? Did fate break the Hummel's legs off? Did fate take my son's leg?

Fate isn't heartless. It is up to us to have the hearts. To have the heart to cook supper for a man who is sleeping through supper again. To make the salad, grill the hamburgers and put cheese on them and put them on a plate with cellophane and put them in the fridge in case he wakes up hungry later and is looking for something to eat. In case he is still alive.

I don't have the heart to do it is the problem. I don't have the heart to make supper or get up tomorrow and move the car for street sweeping and get it washed and go to Costco and start on the Medi Cal receipts. Or the next day, to go to the pain doctor and the Hangar clinic and come home and make dinner again, for a man who is sleeping. I don't have the heart to take the next breath. But I will.

I will take a breath in and let it out. Mt Everest isn't climbed in a day. I take the egg off the stove and empty out the pot and fill it with cold water. I give the tortoise some dandelion greens. She wants lettuce but we'll have watery poop all over the house tomorrow. I sweep and sweep and clean and clean and the next day it's all dirty again.

But these are thoughts. Not life. Life is in the cooking of the egg, the tearing of the lettuce, the slicing of the tomato. Life is in the sweeping and the mopping. Life is in hope. Hoping that all we hope will happen, will happen. The disability check will come, and it will be enough, combined with my pension, and we can both still work a bit at something or other. The mold for the new socket will eventually fit better, and he'll walk around feeling more secure. More of the hand will come back after the next surgery. By some miracle, the blindness will disappear as mysteriously as it arrived.

It arrived suddenly while he was still in the hospital. I noticed how he missed the table when he put his cup down. Again. We asked to see an Ophthalmologist. He came. He was in a hurry. He looked in Ronnie's eyes. He ordered tests. We never saw him again. We asked if we could see him again. We got a message from him that he saw nothing and to follow up with Ronnie's regular ophthalmologist who he had been seeing annually since he was diagnosed with diabetes.

But there _was_ something there, optic neuropathy. In both eyes. A couple of ophthalmologists later, I was told it was probably due to his vitals not being controlled when he had ICU tremors that were misdiagnosed as alcohol withdrawal. Heartless fate again? Or sloppy medical staff at a county hospital? And who cares now anyway unless there's some money in it. Hope. Hope that my letters will result in the hospital paying for the damages enough for us to get out of this one-bedroom apartment and into a house somewhere in the country that's cheap enough for us to live there.

This time last year, we thought we'd be moving to a beautiful home in a suburb outside Nashville, with enough space to not be seeing each other all the time, and enough land for the tortoise to live outside and eat grass and have her own little shed. After ten years of working so hard, he finally had enough money saved for a down payment on a house. Now look at us. I can't bear to throw out the broken Hummel, and I can't bear that they're in plain view and there's nowhere left to put anything.

Moan, moan, complain, complain.

Shred the lettuce.

There I did that. I shredded the lettuce into two bowls and gave some to the tortoise anyway. Hopefully she'll eat up enough hay with it so that her poop will come out in nice hard lumps that are easy to clean up.

He woke up! He wheeled out to the kitchen, and I said, "You woke up!"

He looked up at me and smiled. "Yeah, I had a great sleep but man that new dose of Seraquil in the afternoon is knocking me out! I got to get that changed."

"Are you hungry?" I asked this as he wheeled to the bathroom and he called back, "Starved."

"I'm making cheeseburgers and salad."

"Great," he said. "Wanna watch Boston Legal?

"Yes."

You see, it was nothing more than too much of a drug he probably doesn't need anymore, and now we'll have cheeseburgers and salad and watch Boston Legal and that will be wonderful. Lessons learned: Sleeping doesn't necessarily mean he's dying or wanting to die or killing himself in there. Sometimes a cigar is just a smoke. And even if he does, it's his life, his pain, his loss, and his grief. Stop purchasing more pain than you already have. I didn't lose my leg. I didn't lose the use of my left hand, and I didn't lose 80% of my vision. And I didn't lose my son. He is still here. Despite his tunnel vision, he can see me. He can give me a hug and tell me he loves me. With his prosthetic leg, he can walk towards me. Standing tall. We can chat about the big things in life and what's new on the streaming channels. We can enjoy a meal and we have started giggling a bit. We have a future. We have people to love and people who love us. We have today. The bills are mostly paid and there's plenty to eat.

There are all kinds of thoughts: *Even better is coming. Where there's life there's hope. Surely mercy and goodness will follow us all the rest of our days. You already have the watermelon, just remember to spit out the seeds.* Whoever said that couldn't possibly be talking about seeds this big. Or maybe. People have bigger seeds than these to spit out. I hope they have something as wonderful as we have right now, a shared supper and something to look forward to.

CHAPTER THIRTEEN

Through a Daughter's Eyes: Navigating the System

by Karen Klink

I have a special bond with my mom, I always have, even before she got diagnosed with dementia when she was 78 years old, more than ten years ago. Mom and I "get" each other. I often understand her when she doesn't understand herself. I love her fiercely.

As her advocate, I have fought the intricate maze of long-term healthcare for five long years. The system won. Isn't there a song like that? They may have won the battle, but I am not out of the fight. When I say "fight" I mean I "fight for" my mom. That is what makes it worthwhile. It is what makes my sleepless nights, my tears less painful. It makes my work fulfilling because I know I am helping not only my mother but countless others. There is a profound shift that occurs when you care for a parent. I found a reservoir of strength within myself. Emotions I didn't know I had coming up. I had no idea I could feel the way I felt, that I could care the way I did, or feel injustice the way I felt it.

I have been told I sound angry. I have been told I look angry. I have an angry tone, I have angry eyes, I have an angry face. What does that look like? It's my face for heaven's sake!

Am I angry? Yes, you could call it that, but I prefer the words "passionate and purposeful."

What kind of faces am I told I make? I think they are like the ones you see on emojis: The eye roll, the wide eyes, the wink, or the zipper mouth. "I can't help it, that is my face!" I explain. I can't help it if my eyes roll, or my hands fly up in the air when another ridiculous excuse comes out of a memory care executive's mouth. I might ask why mom's dentures are falling out of her mouth, or why the nurse can't tell that her hearing aids aren't working. I don't think I'm alone in wondering why the caregivers don't know her teeth are falling out of her mouth, or she can't hear, but maybe I am.

Now if you are shaking your head because what I'm writing here doesn't resonate with you, well then, you are incredibly lucky because you have never had to experience life in the long-term care system. I hope you never do.

If you did, you might hear from staff at your family member's care facility say things like, "She was fine before you got here," or "Your mom didn't tell us she couldn't hear," or a host of other auto-responses, and if you did, you might better understand why I might be a bit angry.

My mom only has top dentures so when they are not glued to the top of her mouth correctly, they flop around in her mouth both from side to side and up and down. Not only is it easy to observe, but it is disturbing to watch as most people's teeth don't move about in their mouths, get the picture?

My mom loves sitting out in the sun. It's one of the few things she still enjoys and something I would never want to deprive her of, but she's in a "memory care" facility for a reason; she doesn't remember how long she's been out in the sun and has gotten burned in the past. We pay a lot of money to the facility to make sure that doesn't happen. I expect them to limit her time and put sunscreen and a hat on her. But none of this happens.

"Do you know how long she has been out in the sun?" I asked the staff upon finding my mom sitting on the patio, her face red as a ripe tomato. The response has usually been a shoulder shrug. I am making a face; in case you are wondering.

My story, as with everyone's, goes back to my childhood, my life experiences, and my coping skills or lack thereof.

As an alcoholic from the age of thirteen, I didn't get sober for good until I was over 50. I couldn't take care of myself, let alone anyone else, and didn't want to. I was selfish and self-centered. I wanted what I wanted when I wanted it. I had little time for others unless I could get something from the situation or person.

Finally, I started to be able to feel my feelings, both good and bad, something that for perhaps 30 years as an alcoholic, I had run from for a long time. I got married, and currently, he is 85, no spring chicken…neither am I…although I'm 20 years his junior. When I was 45 and he was 65, the age difference didn't seem like a big deal, but now that he is almost as old as my mother, I see it a bit differently. I can't help thinking "Will I have to take care of him too in the future?" I guess I didn't think that through at the time.

My husband and I were vacationing in Hawaii in 2018. While coming up for air during a snorkeling excursion, we got a call from my sister who told us that my father had died. My father, with all his faults, was my mom's primary caregiver. A pivotal moment in my life. I remember thinking, "I need a drink," because, somehow, I knew this was going to be too much for me. I didn't have one then and haven't since.

Life from that point on has never been the same for me. I became a caregiver, an adult, a REAL adult. I never had to take care of anyone before, hell, I barely took care of myself, and while caring for my mom was never my sole responsibility, I felt in my heart it was. I am the oldest sibling, I am the "favorite" according to me and sometimes my mom! I have two sisters who help, but both have other responsibilities. They do their best, we all do.

Will I ever be all right with not bringing my mom home with me? Probably not.

So, when it came to mom, my sisters and I set out to find the "perfect" place. I probably don't have to tell anyone this, but there is no such thing. No one will take care of your loved one like you will. Of course, if you ask others – the doctors, the administrators, search firms, and social workers –they'll tell you that that's not true and that the problem isn't their level of care; rather, it's because I am impossible to please.

"Lower your expectations," my sister would constantly tell me. "Be in acceptance," said my Alcoholics Anonymous sponsor. "Nothing will ever change;" "You can't fight the system"; and the one I heard from others that hurt so much: "If you don't like it, then move your mom."

Do I listen? Sure, sometimes. But do I follow what I'm told? Not often. Instead, I question why, and I call out the bullshit. It has led me to become a very vocal advocate and activist for my mom and others like her.

When mom first moved into the last Memory Care, alarm bells went off for me, and reflecting, I should - oh how I dislike that word "should" - have taken her out of there right then, but we were in the middle of a pandemic and that wasn't practical. I am not practical, my sister is, and she was right I suppose. "The devil you know versus the devil you don't." Remember, this started at the beginning of the pandemic and not much was known at the start about the Covid 19 virus.

I remember back then; the nurses and staff would rely on my mom to tell them if she didn't feel well or needed something. Sometimes mom would be able to tell them, but a lot of the time she couldn't or wouldn't. I felt as if they expected a person with dementia to come up to the nurse and say, "Excuse me, but I have heartburn, and I have a prescription for that, can you give me some Tums?" or "I am feeling scared and anxious, can you reassure me and comfort me?"

My mom will tell her daughters, particularly me, things she will never say to a stranger. So, when she can communicate being in pain, anxious, agitated, or scared, it would be to us, and not to them. When I'd ask her why, she'd say: "I don't want to trouble them" or "I want them to like me." So, like it or not, I would be the one to have to pass along mom's issues to staff, and that earned me the reputation of being "the complainer" and not necessarily believed.

These professionals are supposed to be trained in dementia care, yet, more often than not, they don't seem to know how best to deal with some pretty common situations. My mom would forget that she needed her walker, so she would walk down the hall without it. Instead of bringing it to her, the caregiver would berate her. "Cindy, you forgot your walker again," or I would hear from my source that when mom was asking for her phone book to call her daughter, instead of dialing the phone for her, as they are supposed to, a caregiver would say, "You don't have a phone-book," which would just upset my mom. They seemed to make matters worse with my mother and invariably, they would have to call me or have me come there to de-escalate a situation that really shouldn't have been a problem in the first place.

My mom is not combative. I can calm her down in ten minutes. I think this might be true for many families, and it's another reason "family" needs to be present, in my view, no matter what. One of the most frustrating issues for myself and my sisters was the terrible communication at the facilities. Not only did they not communicate with residents and families well, but they also didn't communicate with each other. In our case, the administration kept the staff in the dark and the staff did not speak to each other, so when I had a conversation with one nurse or caregiver, it wouldn't be relayed to the next one which created constant tension. I heard comments including, "It wasn't my shift," "I wasn't there that day," "It wasn't in the notes," and "I will have to investigate it and get back to you" more times than I can count.

In 2020, 2021, and 2022, I contacted my local, state, and congressional representatives. I spoke to my congressperson and pleaded with them:

"It is beyond my belief that I must justify why my presence is necessary to care for my mother." This is how I started my pleas to my congressperson and to anyone who would listen. That is when I vowed that I would fight to make sure this would never happen again to my mom or anyone else's family member with dementia or needing a caregiver.

I wish I could say after that first year everything opened back up. Before the public health emergency, residents had rights, which included the right to visitors; those were taken away because "public health" was more important. That is what the Governor and the California Department of Public Health told residents and families. When vaccinations came, families were supposed to be allowed in, but that didn't happen. No one, not facilities, nor families, knew who to turn to when it came to rules or guidelines that differed based on location, the agencies in charge, and Covid status...and that changed almost daily. There were still restrictions on visitation, and we, the consumers, were at their mercy.

One time, I was allowed to see my mom in the morning in the facility, but in the afternoon I was not. "Was there a Covid case? Did the guidelines change? Who at the facility gave these instructions?" I asked, but I could not get a straight answer from anyone. This was a common occurrence. Standard procedure and communication were not their strong suit. I, on the other hand, am an over-communicator. Think about this, our ability to see our loved ones and advocate for them relied on what one administrator or nurse felt like saying on any given day, which could have been my mom's last.

In my efforts, I got involved in a grassroots group called the Essential Caregivers Coalition which is dedicated to establishing the role of the "Essential Caregiver" to prevent long-term care residents from suffering due to the effects of isolation during facility lockdowns. An Essential Caregiver is defined in our eyes as "an individual who provides direct care consisting of activities of daily living, emotional support, or companionship to a resident, and is chosen by the resident." As I became more aware of just how broken the system is, I moved on to long-term care reform in general. The pandemic had just shined a light on an already shattered system.

So, I set out to figure out how I could become an "Essential Support Person" or whatever term they were using. There is a definition for that in the Centers for Disease Control (CDC), Centers for Medicare and Medicaid Services (CMS) and state and local guidelines. The local guidelines states, "Patients/residents with physical, intellectual and/or developmental disabilities and patients with cognitive impairments should be allowed one essential support to be present in public health emergencies."

Mom called me, "I can't find my panties." This became a constant cry to the point that my sisters and I called it the "Ongoing Case of the Missing Panties"! This went on whether we were permitted in or not.

"We keep our panties in the top drawer of the dresser; can you please put all her panties in the top drawer of her dresser and let her know?" I was nice the first time I asked the staff, but no matter how often I asked, Mom's panties would be strewn in different drawers and even in her closet. It may seem like a silly need, but it isn't. And, jeez, doesn't everyone put their panties in the top drawer of their dresser, for heaven's sake? I went around taking an informal poll. Yep, everyone I asked responded in the affirmative. After two years of trying to get her panties in the top drawer – the laundry people just couldn't seem to figure this out, and the housekeepers and caregivers said it wasn't in their job description – we just gave up.

Sometimes, there weren't any panties at all. Every few months, several of them would mysteriously go missing, nametag and all. We would get that phone call. "Your mom needs more panties." I had to laugh…like I was a terrible daughter who didn't buy her mom underwear. I mean if they can't do underwear, I couldn't imagine them managing the hard stuff.

One time, I went into her underwear drawer, and someone had sewn her bra closed! They didn't do it to fix something broken or to help her get it on and off more easily. My mom has big breasts, so she can't step into her bra or put it over her head. She can hardly see. She could have hurt herself trying to get into the bra like that. This to me was either complete stupidity or, in my opinion, possibly retaliation regarding my actions.

I am an "Essential Support Person" – if only to keep track of a mom's panties – this role is needed. It is necessary. It is essential to the well-being of my mom and, I imagine, the other residents of long-term care, most of whom don't even have a visitor!

I set out on my mission to make authorities aware of this role, to get clarity on what it is, and to help enforce it being put into action. I drafted emails to all the regulatory agencies from federal to state to local. I went to the state ombudsman and my legislators. No one, not anyone would take responsibility or accountability.

"You have this 'Essential Support Person' role in writing in your collateral. Surely, you have a process?" I asked.

They answered: No, there was not. The California Public Health Department said since mom lived in an assisted living, this decision was up to the California Department of Social Services (CDSS). "Are you kidding?" I shot back. They said there is no process for this, and California does not have an Essential Caregiver Law in effect! They suggested I talk to the Department of Social Services since they were the licensing agency. CDSS said that this was a health issue and that they didn't have anything to do with health issues. They suggested we talk with the health department. In my eyes, being an Essential Support Person is not a health issue, and round and round in circles we went. I felt as if I was losing my mind and had to laugh because of how typical it all was of government and bureaucracy. This was two years into the Pandemic!

Of course, at this point, I gave up! Right? No! I finally found my area medical director at the Los Angeles County Department of Public Health. This wonderful human listened to me, heard me, put herself in my place, used some common sense, and figured out a way to help. The doctor said that since mom was in memory care and had a diagnosis of dementia, she had a cognitive impairment so she should be able to have an Essential Support Person. The medical director went out on a limb for me, and the facility wasn't too happy; they didn't want me around in the first place. This director wrote a letter on Los Angeles County letterhead that I was designated as my mom's Essential Support Person and should be allowed to visit and care for my mom during the pandemic regardless of outbreak status. By this point, visitation was allowed most of the time except for outbreaks. This letter allowed me to come in during those times, and I did.

I have to say that this woman gave me a glimmer of hope that there is some sanity in this broken system. She saw me as angry but saw through that my passion came from the right place. This doctor was an angel to me and unbelievably, she feels that way about me. I was able to connect this medical director to a couple of women I knew who had loved ones in long-term care who had similar issues, and she was able to help them also. That felt rewarding, and I am still in touch with these women, too. Unfortunately, this medical director was moved out of the Covid area. We continue to stay in touch and exchange ideas on how to improve the lives of long-term care residents and people who are vulnerable.

Perhaps, at this point, I should say that not everyone I encountered in the long-term care industry was bad, evil, or incompetent. There were some very caring and helpful people along the way. There were people and groups that I came across that I could not have made it through the last almost 4 years without, and I want to acknowledge them. First, my family, my husband, and sisters, then my comrades at the Essential Caregivers Coalition. I had a couple of mentors, Dr. Michael Wasserman, a Geriatrician, without whose encouragement I might have given up. Dr. David Grabowski, PhD. helped me see the bigger picture, and Tony Chicotel, attorney at California Advocates for Nursing Home Reform who got me out of more than one challenging situation, and my dear friend Richard Hsu, an Ombudsman. He is a true example of what an Ombudsman should be.

I've been told that one can't be a daughter and an advocate at the same time. While I agree that it's not an easy thing to do, I know that it IS possible AND very much needed. So, if you find yourself serving both roles, the following are some of the ways I found helpful in dealing with the challenges and issues. I am proud of what I did even if wasn't pretty.

My mom was in this memory care for two-and-a-half long years. It was traumatic for both of us, but she doesn't remember much of it. I can't forget. It still haunts me, though not as intensely as last year. Writing about it is painful. I didn't handle everything perfectly, that is for sure. In the end, I felt like I was losing my mind, I was so consumed with anger. I suffer from Post Traumatic Stress Disorder. The term Post Traumatic Embitterment Disorder – which is caused by a sense of injustice, humiliation, and a breach of trust – applies better.

There already were so many problems with the Long-Term Care Industry before the pandemic, Covid has made them worse. The solutions discussed in the press and elsewhere – more staff, better wages, and government involvement – are important but not enough. Transparency in ownership and better communication between owners, staff, families, and residents are crucial. Decisions should include all parties involved. I always say, "Families and residents deserve a seat at the table, and long-term care owners and staff should live in their facilities for a month."

From my perspective, and I am not alone, I have spoken to many family members and residents in long-term care who feel as I do. I offer some reflections and suggestions for how we could move forward:

— CLARITY & EMPOWERMENT: We need rules and regulations that are straightforward and comprehensible to the average person. The system often gives the impression to me that families are an inconvenience they would rather not deal with, leading to defensiveness on both sides.

— PEOPLE AHEAD OF PROFIT: There seems to be extraordinarily little proactive thinking from my experience. Common sense and even morals and ethics are lacking, and what goes on seems driven more by profit than doing what is right.

— SYSTEMATIC AND CULTURAL CHANGE: Long-term care requires complete transformation starting with how we even label things, "nursing home" has a negative connotation now, maybe changing the term would be effective, perhaps "supportive care home" or "extra care community." Stop calling them "facilities." And as it's said, this starts from the top down with our leaders. Leadership style makes a dramatic difference to both staff and residents. Think about "authoritarian" vs. "democratic" leaders: Inclusion matters.

— BALANCING INDIVIDUAL RIGHTS AND PUBLIC SAFETY: This is always important, but it should, in my eyes, lean toward resident rights. It is especially crucial during a public health emergency. As we say in the Essential Caregivers Coalition, "Stop protecting them to death." The role of Essential Caregiver (or now we prefer the term "Resident Designated Support

Person") must be recognized and enforced. If someone has a loved one in long-term care, they rely on us, whether it is a relative, chosen family, or resident representative. Advocating for guaranteed access will not go away.

The more my mom cannot communicate verbally, the more I am her voice. Cutting off physical communication between myself and my mom is unacceptable and goes against human, civil, and resident rights. You can train staff, but you can't teach empathy or compassion, which is what I find lacking. I can list all her needs they cannot fulfill, but I will start with love: Love that only a mother and daughter can feel, love that I have for my mom even when the time comes when she doesn't remember who I am.

I cannot write a conclusion to my story because it is still being written, every day. Sometimes, every minute is different when caring for someone with dementia. My mom is now in a Board and Care, which is a smaller facility. We had to leave the memory care for all the reasons listed above and so many more. The new place is not without its challenges, but it is so much better: More one-on-one care and easier to communicate with the management and staff.

I feel, though, that even when my mom's journey is finished, mine will not be, I will continue to fight for those without a voice, for the vulnerable, because it seems to be my calling and the right thing to do.

CHAPTER FOURTEEN

Remembering Mom:
A Time of Miracles

by Rowena Ilagan

C hristmas Day, 2020 was supposed to be a "typical" Christmas holiday for my family, with the exception of us wearing masks due to the global pandemic. I was looking forward to celebrating with my curious and talkative godchildren nine-year-old Emalou, four-year-old Ellie, and three-year old Acey and to carving traditional Honey Baked turkey that Dad often bought for both the Thanksgiving and Christmas feasts.

I had carefully wrapped the kids' presents a few days before and managed to hide them under the Christmas tree upon my arrival without anyone noticing. Emalou's leaked letter to Santa (my sister-in-law Min shared the letter with me on our Facebook family group, given I am the kids' "Naning" which is the kid-friendly name for "godmother" or "Ninang" in our native Tagalog) became my inspiration when shopping. I remembered Ellie and Acey wanting slime on their "wish list;" shoes and clothes on the "sensible" list. My niece Emalou also asked for new clothes, although being the most tech-savvy of the three, I imagined she wanted a new gadget for herself. She was never without her pink butterfly shaped iPad, playing computer games on home decorating or creating dance clips on TikTok. Dad took care of the sensible list by getting them fitting tees and nightgowns; I catered to their fanciful list by buying them ice-cream looking slime and walkie-talkies to indulge their chatty natures.

In all my 47 years of family gatherings, I was especially looking forward to this one. However, all those thoughts of celebrating and playing together went out the window when during breakfast, I saw Mom displaying a curious behavior. Usually, she had a measured way of eating: chewing one small bite at a time, as if chewing on thoughts along with the food that she was consuming. This time, however, I watched as her chin slowly fell to her chest instead and her eyes shut tightly like a clam, all the while still clutching a silver spoonful of warm oatmeal with burnt brown sugar in her hand.

"Mom," I said, shaking her shoulder, "wake up."

Mom tended towards daytime sleepiness with Alzheimer's, but it was unusual for her to be this sleepy, especially after having gone to bed nearly ten hours the night before. With my history of immune disease (I had been battling the CFS/ME or Chronic Fatigue Immune Dysfunction Syndrome for nearly nine years now and often developed infections as an offshoot of the illness), I knew that excessive sleepiness could be a sign of an infection. I feared that Mom might be in the midst of a nasty one, so I asked Dad to take us to Urgent Care right away.

Nearly four hours and a battery of tests later, my family got the startling news: Mom was positive for the coronavirus. Since her fate at Kaiser sounded grim and uncertain (with her being lumped together with dozens of other Covid-positive patients with no treatment in sight), I asked for her to get released right away. All we were given to take home was an oximeter to measure her oxygen levels.

That night, I took her vitals, offered her some food (low-fat milk and graham crackers, her favorites) and tucked her into bed. As a former lab rat (a chemist for UCLA, testing professional athletes in the NFL, NCAA, and Olympics for steroids and stimulants and later, a junior industrial hygienist for the government testing for occupational hazards and environmental exposures of City workers before medically retiring), I had read about and respected the CDC guidelines about quarantining 14 days, if results test positive. But in this case, I needed to stay overnight in Mom's bedroom. Because of Alzheimer's, she would sometimes roll away from bed and wander on her own in the hallway if no one kept an eye on her.

I was donning my half-face respirator and face shield from my industrial hygiene days, but my intuition niggled at me: it was just a matter of time that I would get sick too as I had been standing next to Mom (unmasked) at breakfast the day before when she was struggling to keep her eyes open.

In the days that followed, Mom continued to show excessive sleepiness and fatigue, even though her oxygen saturation levels stayed at 90 percent or higher. By the third day after our visit to the ER unfortunately, she had stopped wanting to eat. We all decided to take Mom back to the hospital then in the hopes that she might at least get some nutrients via IV. I placed a 911 call for an ambulance. Soon, there was a line-up of six-foot tall men clad in navy-blue, starchy uniforms and firefighter gear making their way through our living room hallway. I saw them pick up Mom from her bed and place her on a gurney; she stiffened like a human-sized doll. I fought back tears as they wheeled her away to the fire truck.

The Kaiser Hospital that she normally goes to for care did not have room to take her in, so Mom had to be admitted to Mission Hills, a neighboring community hospital. I felt uneasy already seeing Mom being wheeled away; even more so knowing that she would be taken to a hospital that none of us were familiar with.

I developed coronavirus symptoms just before Mom got taken to Mission, and I fought my own personal battle with the dreaded virus, with debilitating fatigue, muscle aches, nausea, and lack of appetite. Curiously enough, my breathing stayed normal, and my temperature rarely spiked which was surprising, given my history of immune disease. In between my lucid moments, Dad, my brother Erwin, and sister-in law Min would place video calls to Mom's room, and I would always shout out loud, "Mom! Mom! We miss you! Come home soon!" Her eyes would alternatively open and close again. She looked peaceful in her seafoam green hospital gown and her silver and black-tinted hair coiffed and combed to one side every time we had a video call with her.

Mom was nearing the 12-day mark at Mission Hospital when we faced the same nemesis again of her not eating. The doctors proposed putting a feeding tube to her stomach. I knew that her condition was starting to deteriorate if they were considering a long-term and permanent fix. Dad and my older brother Erwin drove to Mission that night and signed the consent form to place the tube. But the following evening, when the nurse had a video call with Mom, Dad and I saw Mom clutching a small tube in her hand and eating bits of the pink yogurt that oozed out of it. Mom was eating again! Encouraged, I sat up from my bed (still very weak from the coronavirus itself) and adamantly called out, "No feeding tube!" Dad and I both decided that we should bring Mom home and see if we can get her to eat again at home.

We got Mom back home at 10:30 that night and she initially had a burst of energy and appetite. She took bites of oatmeal that Dad prepared and even chided Dad, "What are you doing?" when he carried her entire body (just as a newly-married husband would carry his bride over the threshold) and tried to rearrange it squarely on the center of the bed so she would not accidentally roll off it. Seeing Mom acting like her old, humorous self before getting hospitalized buoyed our spirits, although unfortunately it was short-lived. She turned away when Dad tried to bring a spoonful of scrambled eggs to her mouth the following morning for breakfast. Mom stopped using words altogether, moaning instead and raising her arms over her head while she was awake. The nurse in charge told me that this was a sign of stress and anxiety. Desperate to help Mom, I asked the nurse what I could do, and she told me to increase her dose of Ativan for anxiety. To my relief, she finally stopped moaning, although I was so haunted by the sound that I would actually hear "phantom moans" late at night and I would rush to Mom's bedside, only to see her fast asleep. I changed out her undergarments, finding thin streaks of blood the nurses had told us about (which had initially delayed Mom's release from the hospital). I asked the nurse what this could be, hoping that it might just be from a hemorrhoid, but she said sadly, "your Mom is bleeding internally," which felt like a sucker punch to the gut. I called my friend Virgil (a medical genius of sorts) for some advice as he went through hospice with his mother Sandy who died of cancer, a medical emergency with his father Virgil Sr., and older brother Danny who passed suddenly in his sleep and had picked up lots of useful information from doctors as an offshoot of going through many medical maladies with his family. He asked me to take Mom's blood pressure before and after breakfast; based on that and other data, we could then determine where the tear might be. Encouraged that it might be in Mom's intestine and possibly operable, I called the doctor right away to see if we could take her back to the hospital for emergency surgery, but she simply said in a flat tone, "I wouldn't even bother." Her answer stopped me dead in my tracks. Virgil told me then, "Rowena, I'm sorry, but it's time to stop practicing medicine, and start preparing for the inevitable." Even with the doctor's answer and Virgil's advice, I still was resisting the finality of it all. It was just not in my nature to give up. (Maybe that stubbornness was coming from my own, almost decade-long personal battle with an obscure, misunderstood immune disease. I refused to listen

177

to primary care doctors, for example, who insisted that "there is no cure for CFS" when my very own experience with alternative medicine showed me otherwise, helping me get back to pre-CFS energy levels after years and years of treatment. Could my own plain stubbornness and dogged determination beat death too?) Virgil listened to my internal struggle and empathized with my feelings. "Did you read the Blue Book?" he asked gently. The hospice team gave me a thin blue booklet to read (the customary "Hospice Blue Book") which describes in detail the physical and spiritual changes that your loved one is expected to go through at various stages of the dying process. To me, it resembled a cross between a science primer and a mini-Bible book. Mom's extremities started to change slightly in color; her toes felt like they had been placed inside a meat locker and her nail beds took on a slight, purplish hue. She now spent more time sleeping, which, according to the Blue Book, meant that Mom had "one foot in the earthly realm, another in the spiritual one." Her mouth became permanently slack in the shape of an "O" also known as the characteristic "death O" that doctors use to describe patients nearing the end-of-life. When I described what I was seeing to the nurse, she said, "we're at that place now Rowena when we have to start getting her ready for her to go, maybe even days from now." She asked that I administer her "comfort meds" (morphine for pain and again, Ativan for anxiety) every four hours, regardless if it was past one's bedtime or not. I was still very weak as I had not shaken off the coronavirus completely and in desperate need of sleep and rest, but I was designated the "medicine giver" as I was used to measuring and mixing as the former chemist in the family. I would put on a fresh gown, mask, and gloves every time I entered her room and told her, "Mom, I am going to give you some medicine now to help you feel more comfortable," then put in drops on the side of her "O" shaped mouth. Sometimes Mom's lips would look chapped or patches of skin on her powdery-white face felt dry, so I would moisten a face towel to dab her lips or rub a bit of lotion on her face. Since Mom stopped talking days before, there was no way of knowing how she felt with these extra touches of care; I sought refuge in my imagination instead, thinking of how Mom might politely say, "thank you" at my efforts to make her comfortable and beautiful which was her usual demeanor in her lucid days.

About a week and a half after she returned from the hospital, Dad called me to Mom's room at about 5:30 in the morning and told me that her breathing had changed. I rushed in and saw Mom struggling to take deeper and deeper breaths, which the Blue Book said is what happens when death is close, perhaps within hours. I set myself down by Mom's side and held her left hand while saying repeatedly, "I love you, Mom. Thank you for everything you have done for me as your daughter. I loved having you as my mom." While I watched her chest shakily rise and fall, I started to think of all the things that we shared as mother and daughter. My earliest memories of her sacrificing as a mom were carrying our bulky, sky-blue suitcases (which matched our Catholic school uniforms), getting off the bus together hand-in-hand, and working our way (more like slithering through) the muddy fish market of seedy Metro Manila. Occasionally, she would buy me and my older brother Erwin an oil-stained paper bag of roasted peanuts or barbequed plantains from one of many Filipino street vendors while she bought and bargained for wares or food. When we immigrated to the U.S. as pre-teens, she spent evenings trying to teach us how to cook traditional Filipino dishes of chicken adobo or ground turkey menudo with chopped potatoes, raisins, and peas. (On my first solo trip abroad to Spain on an anthropology research trip, I actually placed a long-distance call to Mom to make sure I got her recipe for adobo just right to make dinner for my professor). During my first year with CFS (when my chemical sensitivities were at an all-time high, making me feel fatigued or short of breath while taking just a whiff of dust or second-hand smoke) and sleeping in our old camper van for some relief, she would visit me religiously in the morning to deliver a hard-boiled egg or toast for breakfast. When the tables were turned several years later, I started to look after her with her progressing Alzheimer's. Mornings were spent helping her in and out of her undergarments, walking a few blocks around the neighborhood elementary school together (and when that got too difficult, just inside our backyard with her right hand resting on my forearm and the other clutching a walking stick to "shoo" unruly dogs away), cooking simple meals of stir-fried chicken or veggie patties or heating up one of the pre-cooked meals from a Van Nuys senior center that she got delivered once a week. By far, our favorite part of the day was singing songs together while I played chords in our old organ or searched YouTube for karaoke versions. (I put singing in our daily routine when I learned that it stimulates the entire brain, perhaps even delaying the progression of the disease; I continued, however, when I saw how much Mom's morale picked up whenever we sang together). Her mellifluous alto voice would meld with my mezzo one while we took turns singing some of our favorite songs: the Beatles's "Yesterday," Dean Martin's "That's Amore," Doris Day's "Que Sera, Sera," Eric Clapton's, "You Look Wonderful Tonight," and Anne Murray's "Can I Have this Dance?" Mom remembered most of the lyrics to the songs, and for those few hours of singing, we would both forget about her illness. She would just be Mom, the one I sat next to for choir practice and mass at St. Jane Catholic Church for years through my teens and early 20s. She would giggle and talk about her teenage crush (who brought her cookies and teacakes) like a little girl, especially after singing a love song. All my thoughts of the past stopped abruptly when I heard Mom take in her last breath, and when I looked up, I saw a single, glistening tear drop from the corner of her left eye. The day before, the nurse overlooking Mom's care told me that sometimes patients who have been unresponsive for days will shed a tear if a loved one speaks to them, and that is exactly what happened with Mom. I thought it was her last, loving gift to me before she drew her last breath and walked completely to the other side.

The morning Mom passed away, I prayed to God, "Lord, please take this awful virus and sickness away from us. Take away all these awful memories of losing Mom. And please, protect us from more hurt or harm." As soon as I finished saying my prayers, I felt something stir and shift in the air. Frigid-cold winds started to pick up in spurts, alternating between calm and measured to strong and downright furious. I intuitively felt then that God was responding to my prayers. Scientists and the CDC touted open spaces as safer than indoor; ventilation helps keep viral counts low. I felt that the cold winds were God's handiwork at play. He was taking away the dreaded virus from our home and memories of Mom's suffering with it. I opened the windows to our house so that God would continue to "sanitize" our indoor spaces. Curiously enough, a picture that hung on our wall (showing a goldfish cowering in fear from a cat peering over the fishbowl) kept rattling with the wind. The message on that picture captured the fish's innermost thoughts: "The Lord will protect me." I felt that God was asking me to pay attention to that picture, to let me know that He was helping us through this horrible storm that we had just endured.

A few days later, we all did our Covid swab tests in succession. My last symptom of congestion cleared the day after Mom passed, and I tested clear of the virus. Dad tested negative soon after, and my brother (who I feared would accidentally pick up the virus from helping us clean Mom's room) also came out negative.

I think many of us in the early days of the pandemic had prayed fervently to God, hoping that we would not get sick with the Rona. God helped me weather the most devastating of blows: losing my mother to the virus. He not only facilitated the last bit of communication between us (with Mom's single tear) and protected my family but made sure that Mom and I would continue to keep in touch when she left the earthly realm.

I received her weekly delivery of cooked meals from the senior center the week she passed, and there was a flyer attached to the box about foods to eat to stave off the onset of dementia. I felt that it was Mom's doing, as she was a former nutrition major and cafeteria manager who constantly worried about my eating.

Around this time, I also rediscovered some old lab work from my doctor, saying that I carried the gene for late-stage Alzheimer's. Sending this bit of information with the weekly meal delivery was her way of taking care of me, even after she passed. I intuitively felt Mom's message to me, which often comes when asleep and dreaming: "Have faith and trust in God. I am with my family and feeling so blessed. I will stay with you and help you as much as I can." Mom may have been afflicted with a disease that affected her memories and cognition; the insidious, airborne virus accelerated the progression of her disease. But by asking God for help, I was able to survive the storm and share this story of faith and God-given miracles. There will always be storms, but God finds a way to help you through them.

CHAPTER FIFTEEN

The Space Between

by Mary Barbato

T his is me. You wouldn't know it, but I'm the face of a brain injury. They call it traumatic brain injury or TBI. Take that in.

I had a severe injury to my brain. My computer. The center of everything that makes you live, breathe and function had a traumatic big blow to it. So, as you would think, those functions were now not in my control.

Being told that meant nothing to me. Nothing meant anything to me. I was Barry White, even keel, just passing through life, numb. Sitting on a couch day and night with the only cue that time was passing being the awareness of the sun coming up by the gradual brightness in the room and the sun going down by the casting shadows on the wall. I just sat in bed or on the couch, day in and day out, not a thought I remember, in complete quiet. Unable to control my bowels. Unable to walk, talk, chew, read, write, or catch my breath after five short steps. My memory was shot, and I was in a constant state of confusion. Just sitting there, with not a thought of doing anything. 24 hours, seven days a week…like having a bad hangover and never, ever recovering from it.

They say I was lucky to be alive. Really?

I was 50 years old and had risen the ranks in the corporate world to where I had become the CEO of one of the world's most wealthy. But I was ready for my next life chapter. Up until that point, my life had been defined by my career. Unmarried, I loved my job. Some would say I married my career. The child of a mother who'd been invited to the Mensa Exam, I excelled at a young age and had recently been welcomed into the prestigious Deloitte CMO group. But once I hit 50, it was time to live a new life with balance. To do all the things on my bucket list that my career demands didn't give me time to do. It was time to take a position that would allow me to work to live. I was excited, happy, and ready for this new life. I would meet a man, have more dinner parties, and spend time with my family. Some would say I was skipping with the endless possibilities of happiness and the freedom that would come with it.

But in less than a minute, my life changed forever.

It was a Friday night in February just after 6 pm. The steady, cold rain on my windshield had me reaching for my wind-down-from-the-week warm and cozy hot chocolate I had just purchased and was waiting for me in my cup holder. I was anxious to get home to spend time with friends. We were going dancing.

I had stopped at a red light with two cars in front of me and a large refrigerator truck about a car's length behind. I heard the truck driver behind me laying on his horn. I lifted my head to look in the rearview mirror, but before my eyes got there, a car racing 65 mph swerved in between the truck and my car's rear end and hit me full force from behind. I didn't see it coming. I was a sitting duck. Then I felt the impact and my world went silent.

Later, I would learn the driver was a 29-year-old woman who was high, and who had recently had her license revoked for reckless driving.

She shouldn't have been on the road.

I shouldn't have a TBI.

Having a TBI is like having a circus constantly going on in your head. You are in a constant state of confusion, fogginess, and over-stimulation. Picture a three-ring circus full at the end of the performance with every member of the cast. The ringmaster is yelling, the trapeze artists are swinging, and the elephants are walking on their hind legs. The crowds are cheering as the clown cars come out and about 20 clowns file out with their horns and noisemakers. It's worse than the sound of an orchestra tuning up before a symphony. At the same time the amount of pressure from the injury makes you feel like you are going crazy as the imaginary vice on your head keeps getting screwed tighter and tighter until you're screaming in your head, but not a peep comes out of your mouth. There's not a sound in the house. All the noise is in your head.

This is constant. It takes every part of your being to stay sane. For you are caught in this world, and there is no way out. There is no pill to take. There is no surgery to fix it. Only the passage of time can heal a brain injury, at the speed of watching paint dry they say. You never heal back to your previous self. What you're left with is a list of disabilities and a consumption of sadness, exhaustion, fear, and suffocation of being caught in this semi-functioning body. It's at that point when you start to realize what has happened and the state you're in, that you have to fight to live. Because you ache to be dead.

The worst part of a TBI, if there is only one, is your loved ones and doctors don't understand what it's like to live in a TBI brain, so they are counter-helpful and hurtful. I liken it to being kicked when you're down, and then having dirt kicked on top of you leaving a bad taste in your mouth you can't forget. You hear the doctors say, "This is your new normal." Please help me understand what part of this is normal, I'd think. But I didn't want a new normal. I wanted my normal.

Someone once said to me something to the effect of "Well, let's hope those connections reconnect in your brain otherwise you're up a shit's creek". Please tell me how that was helpful. And not hurtful and anxiety-provoking?

I also got, "It's just like having a back injury. It's all how you look at it. Just don't make it more than it is in your head. You'll be fine." It's nothing like having a back injury. I can say that with confidence. I had one from the accident as well. And I'm not fine. How can they not see I'm not fine as I sit next to them with the darkest sunglasses, noise-canceling headphones, and a huge, hooded jacket with the hood pulled down low to try to stifle the stimuli of noise, light, and movement? Did they think this was normal? How nonchalantly they dismissed a major injury. My injury.

And the worst was, "Well maybe you shouldn't go because all the attention will be on you (because I'd be sitting there with my noise-canceling headphones, sunglasses, and hooded jacket and would need extra help)," after it was made clear what an inconvenience it was to go ten minutes out of their way to take me to see my parents. And from the same person, "Are you sure it's not all in your head"? As if I and the 12 doctors I was seeing were making this up and enjoying it. Of course, it's in my head...I would have said if I could process fast enough what he was saying. It's a brain injury! Again, so, so incredibly hurtful.

So, on top of being trapped in this body, misunderstood like you speak a foreign language, you're constantly being hurt by unthoughtful comments from the people who are supposed to love you. Try hard to understand you. Who should be caring for you. But are nowhere to be found.

But in their defense, people can't see a TBI, and doctors don't know enough about it, so the understanding of others is limited. The amount of help you receive from family, doctors, and friends is little. How can they help what they don't understand? Or want to understand because they might not be able to emotionally handle it. Out of sight, out of mind as they say.

I was fortunate enough to have a neuropsychologist who had made her life work understanding TBI patients and truly saved my life, a chiropractor nutritionist who worked with TBI players from the Minnesota Twins, a housekeeper who would change my soiled sheets each day, and my 77- and 80-year-old parents who would make the two-hour trek to come each weekend to stock my fridge with food for the week and make me a meal. I would greet them with a smile on my face and show them the coloring I'd done in my age 0-3 coloring book or the crown I'd put on the princess in my sticker book. My brain had reverted to pre-school level.

My mom would help me do a puzzle to help my brain heal, and my dad would take me for walks. First down the street, and eventually around the block. I couldn't go walking on my own. I wasn't steady on my feet, and I wouldn't remember my way home. They allowed me to stay in my apartment by myself because I couldn't deal with any stimuli, and I needed complete quiet and some semblance of normal. I knew I loved them, but the brain injury had taken away my ability to feel love for them. Beyond that, I had several doctors and therapists trying to help the best they could without knowing the most they could.

So here I am NOW. Fast forward five years to today. Five long years of constant caring for myself and being defined by my TBI rather than my career. I still have a way to go and several doctor and therapist visits, but I'm finally starting to do some of those things on my bucket list. I still can't feel love and joy, but I'm living and breathing well again. I can read, and write, I still search for words from time to time but I can talk (unless I have an "episode" from too much stimuli), I sometimes have trouble chewing, and unless you lived with me, or are keyed into me when you are with me, you probably wouldn't know I can't correctly hold and use a utensil in my left hand (my brain still can't figure out how to do that), and that I'm still a TBI patient with my list of disabilities. Life is going pretty well.

And then the accident happens.

He just wanted to ride a bike.

That's all I could think when my oldest brother told me our 84-year-old dad had broken his hip and was in the hospital. Later we would find out Dad broke his upper leg. Surgery, anesthesia, pain medications, and three screws later, Dad no longer remembered he was in the hospital. He didn't remember a lot of things. He couldn't walk, talk for himself, and was in a constant state of confusion.

Sound familiar?

It was when my brothers and I were visiting Dad late the night before surgery that we realized something was wrong. Out of nowhere, Dad announced to my brothers and me from his hospital bed that it was time to go to bed. My brothers and I, thinking that was Dad's way of telling us to leave, got up to go as my father threw back the covers to get out of bed.

"Where are you going?" we asked in unison.

"To bed!" my father shouted at us in frustration.

We all paused. "Where is the bedroom? I asked as I suddenly realized sadly what was happening.

"It's there!" he shouted again as he pointed to his hospital bathroom".

It was then that I restrained my father for the first time. There would be countless more times in the coming months as his leg healed, and Dad continued to forget he'd broken it.

I fought back the tears. Dad was no longer the same strong, smart man at that moment who had lived the American Dream and built a multimillion-dollar business over the last 63 years, still running the company up to that day. He was defined by his career. He loved it. But I knew at that moment from personal experience, life as he knew it had changed forever and his mental recovery would be long, devastating, and emotionally painful. I screamed in my head and later out loud from the bottom of my gut, "Nooooo!" as I fully took this in and fell slumped against the wall of my living room, falling to the floor uncontrollably crying with tears streaming down my face, reliving my nightmare.

"God, no!" I pleaded. "Please, please not my dad! Please, let no one go through the nightmare I've lived."

I was defined by my brain injury and he now by his fall. It was the only thing I thought about. Cried about. Got mad about. Couldn't live without. I had hope but couldn't imagine living a day without the reminder of my brain injury. My job was to get better and there was little I could do. So, I understood what Dad was going through. We were traveling similar paths.

I had been caring for myself since the accident. The irony is – for similar challenges my dad was now facing. I now find myself "in-between" in a caregiver role to myself and my father.

If you asked me when I was struggling to choose each day to stay alive – why the TBI happened to me? – when life as I knew it was gone forever, I wouldn't have an answer. As I look at my dad, I now know. Out of everything bad something good can come. I am my father's caregiver, advocate, strength. I took this journey before him so that he could feel compassion, understanding, trust that he is getting the best care, and know someone with personal knowledge of what he is experiencing and what helps in the moment, is walking beside him, understanding him. I come with experience and understanding like few others without cognitive impairments can grasp.

I was there to connect with him as no one emotionally connected with me. I wanted him to understand that I understood, because it was scary when no one understood me. That I understood also how devastating it is when you're not the same you know you to be. As it was devastating for me when my housekeeper found me crying in a corner from the horror of soiling my sheets yet again from not being able to control my bowels. I wanted him to know I was safe to confide in and I loved him.

Five years ago, my mom and dad would come to take care of me on weekends. It's now my turn to return the favor. I make lunch for my dad three days a week (but I describe it as having lunch with him, and I thank him for having lunch with me because I need it for my brain to heal). I encourage him to walk and ask him to take walks with me because it also helps heal the brain and keeps our body strong. I turn off the TV, and the lights, stop moving, and stay quiet so his head doesn't hurt like it does for me when there are too many stimuli. What a gift I was given so that I can be here for my dad better than if I'd never had my accident. The gift from my dad is that I'm no longer focused on myself and my brain injury, which has defined me these torturous years. I'm now focused on my dad, whom I love, which gives me the ability for the first time since my accident, to actually *feel* love.

✭✭✭✭✭

One year later, I'm happy to report both Dad and I are doing well. Dad's memory has come back, he's walking well, and he's returned to work. Just like me.

CHAPTER SIXTEEN

Raising Parents: The Highs and Lows

by Debbie Tynan

No one can possibly know what you're committing to when you step into the role of caregiver for your parent. The experience of raising my daughter, Emma, made me feel I could easily "raise" my mom, Dar. After all, I had witnessed my mom take care of her very independent mother, my grandmother, who lived to be 111 years old. Tongue in cheek, my mom frequently said about my grandmother, "It's difficult raising parents." I learned what an understatement that observation was as raising parents is emersion at the speed of light.

When raising healthy children towards independence, there are a gazillion happy and extraordinary milestones as well as phases before progressing onto the next phase. When it comes to your elderly parents, the status quo/no drama is always the ultimate goal.

191

BACKGROUND

My mom has a slow-growing benign brain tumor. Neurosurgeons removed what they could which included her entire hearing organ in one ear but were unable to remove what attached to the brain stem. Ten years after her brain surgery, the tumor grew so we decided radiation was the best "pick your poison" option to shrink the tumor. Every day for six weeks, I took her for radiation not understating the havoc the radiation would later cause. Over time, the radiation killed the retina in one eye and affected her ability to easily swallow causing dysphagia. The side effects of the radiation lessened her ability to be as conversational and chatty as she once was. Remarkably, her memory is stable, often sharing conversations out of the blue from months prior and I find those moments phenomenal.

Halloween 2017, my mom fell and broke her hip. Between the equilibrium part that was removed with the tumor on one side of her brain, and her broken hip which still hadn't healed as of 2019, she's a wobbly walker. Though she's fiercely physically strong, fear of falling and breaking another bone is her mental obstacle. Car and shower transferring is not easy which occasionally results in her slipping away from me. When I'm alone with her, I cannot lift her after she's gently slipped from my arms so the fire department arrives for a non-emergency visit. Knowing a crew is en route, my mom asks that I make sure she looks good as she anticipates a hot LAFD crew. Once they leave, it's back to business. No need to call 911 when your child slips but it's a different story when it's your parent who's on the floor.

BEAUTY and LOCKDOWN

At the start of the lockdown in 2020, my mom was all of 93 and refused to believe her beloved beauty salon was closed. And just like when little kids need proof, my mom was no different. My daughter Emma and I had to drive her around to prove ALL stores were closed including the beauty salon as she could not embrace that her standing hair appointment was suddenly kaput. I used to question why she insisted on getting her hair done every week when she didn't have plans to go out as, sadly, apart from Marilyn, most of her friends are gone. No more bridge games, no more book club. No more getting picked up by her friends to go to dinner and a movie. But I realized the beauty shop routine was stability and the only real routine she had left. Getting her hair done was something she looked forward to and it made her feel good. She had a countdown during the week for that Saturday appointment, always getting up early on the day-of so that she was on time. That appointment meant the world to her. Imagine my deer-in-headlights moment when my mom sternly looked at me at the beginning of the lockdown saying, "I'm not dying having a bad hair day!" My mom has never been a vain woman. It wasn't about that. She was grasping for the last stability of her routines. We improvised – I did her hair every week and we were incredibly lucky as her colorist was working out of her garage. Just like kids nagging, my mom wouldn't stop nagging me about taking her to get her hair colored.

My mom has immensely challenging medical issues yet still has her wildly clever sense of humor. Once when I told her she had been sleeping all day, she asked if she missed a meal. My mom, a retired LAUSD elementary school teacher, announced that she wanted to get a job, and when we asked doing what, she said, "I'm really good at doing nothing these days!" And as funny and witty as my mom is, she's as sweet and considerate as she's always been, like telling me at a doctor's appointment yesterday that she didn't know what she'd do without me.

HER CRUSH

My mom has had a forever crush on George Clooney so to help her concentrate on her walking, I enlarged a thirst trap photo of him that I found online, printed it, and then taped it onto her walker. I thought she'd be thrilled but instead, I got the disappointing side eye with, "Why didn't you put my photo next to him?" Now her photo is nuzzled into George's neck. Then she looks at their photo saying things like, "He doesn't have very much to say," and, "No one's ever spent as much time with me in the bathroom as he has."

George is on auto-record and my complaint is that he's only on five seasons of ER and not enough rom-coms. Once when we were scrolling through the guide, my mom noticed, "Sex Sent Me to the ER" saying she wanted to watch that show. I think my mom thinks it's an ER spinoff starring Clooney. When friends come over, we howl watching this crazy reality show while my mom is hoping Dr. Ross will be the attending ER doc. We did ask my mom if sex ever sent her to the ER – she said, "I'll never tell!"

ROUTINES

It's been seven years since she's been 100 percent dependent on me. My day begins while she's sleeping which is when I run to the market. My errands and appointments are time-sensitive. When I'm out, my daughter has my back – I wish I had the words to express my unyielding appreciation for her.

My mom's dailies consist of having her vitals taken twice per day. And mundane as it seems, her getting in and out of bed is an accomplishment, exercising, including a motorized mini-treadmill used while sitting, PEMF Therapy (Pulse Electronic Magnetic Field) used on various parts of her body, playing solitaire (with our help), watching the Today show and always going to sleep with George while watching ER round it out. Visitors are invigorating (including those firemen) and the more engaged she is with new faces, the less she sleeps. Often, I have to be creative motivating her to get back on the proverbial horse. One of her favorite books she read when we were little was, "The Little Engine That Could," so I tell her she's, "the little engine that could" which inspires her to push through whatever struggles she may be having. Thankfully she's stubborn, determined, and remarkably resilient - just like kids. And just like I've been a naggy mom to my daughter, I'm a non-stop nag with my mom nagging her ad-nauseam to drink her water. Frequently, I sit with her for hours telling her every few minutes to drink water and that's still not enough. For some reason, older people think when they have a sip of water that that sip is sufficient.

The side effects of IV antibiotics in the elderly are grueling. Sometimes my mom is not able to walk much less stand for a few weeks. The visiting physical therapists work to get her back to her baseline (standing and walking). That rehab cannot be easy for a 96-year-old but my mom has a strong-will mentality as if a pro athlete in training – and she never complains even when it can be painstaking just to try to stand.

I resisted buying an Alexa but now we can't go an hour without one of us giving Alexa a command or asking who won the World Series the year my parents got married or what the weather is in Omaha. Together with my daughter, we created a playlist of songs my mom loves which is why she's fascinated by Alexa. She's amazed with the round ball technology that's my mom's personal jukebox playing everything from Glenn Miller's, "In the Mood" to Sinatra's "New York, New York." And thanks to Emma, Grandma Dar is a Swiftie – her favorite T.S. song is "Enchanted." Music plays when my mom is awake and sleeping, and it's amazing to watch her sleep dance. The playlist is on when we're in the car and a couple of times, when she's been in the ER. Frank Sinatra said, "Music puts wings on the human spirit," and he was right.

Like little kids, my mom is obsessed with watching videos on my phone. She loves watching adorable Instagram videos with animals and babies.

Like kids of all ages, parents need consistent coaching, praise, and loving words of encouragement.

Just like with kids, every day, all day is spent making decisions, some critical where I'm second guessing, wondering, and hoping I'm doing right by my mom.

We have a rose garden, and my mom loves smelling the most fragrant roses – her reactions to nature's fragrances are heavenly. When the weather is perfect, she loves sitting in the garden, stimulated by watching neighbors walking their dogs and kids riding their bikes. The littlest things bring an immense amount of joy to people whose lives are challenged.

Emma created a genius hack to wake up my mom on days when my mom just wants to sleep (confusion and too much sleeping are often an indication of infection) by enticing my mom with her favorite food… ice cream! And, voilà! When we're really in a bind, our puppy gets the call for wake-up kisses. I am shameless to admit when my mom was once passed out in the ER due to an infection and the medical team came in to evaluate her, I told her that George Clooney just walked in. As if on cue, she woke up! The medical staff erupted with laughter then the ER doc apologized profusely for not being Clooney much less not resembling him.

Streaming is complicated (I wish there was one seamless remote) so we have to be with my mom to change channels and services which differs from toddlers being versed in tech. If we're not in the room when a show has paused or a movie has ended, she stares at a frozen screen until one of us checks on her.

There is a lot that goes into taking care of my mom and as new medical challenges arise, new details are added to her list of needs, more than I can explain to someone in ten minutes. It's not like telling the babysitter that there's pasta in the fridge, bedtime is at 10 pm, and where the post-it is with the WiFi password. Taking a geriatric's "babysitter" around the house, showing them all of the supplies, how to use various medical equipment, pills, and pill schedules, how to cut her food, how to maneuver and protect her when walking, etc., cannot be done in 10 minutes. To fully train someone, they'd have to shadow me for at least a couple of weeks and even then, my mom can have (temporary) new needs that arise like needing the nebulizer for a few days. The learning curve is tremendous. A few years ago, I had an epiphany... or more of a freak-out: What if something happens to me? What happens to my mom? What can I do to ensure she stays at home and gets the same care I provide without her feeling vulnerable or lost without me because she's dependent on me for EVERYTHING?

THE MANUAL

I needed a plan so that my mom would be cared for seamlessly. To make that transition as simple as possible for others to care for my mom, I embarked on an ongoing project creating a now 90+ page reference manual for caregivers to follow. It includes all of her doctors and their contact info, her prescriptions, her various diagnoses, exercises, menu samples, her favorite recipes as well as legal documents. I list protocols her doctors have in place such as when to take her to the ER.

If I could impart any wisdom from my experience to other family caregivers, it would be to create your own "how-to" manual. And it would be a good idea to discuss which protocols your doctors want to have in place for your parent in an emergency.

TIPS

- I can't say this enough: Get an oximeter. Get a blood pressure monitor. Get a thermometer.

- Use your smartwatch for vitals including the ECG app.

- Instead of those tiny plug-in night lights, get a Himalayan Salt Lamp.

- When my mom was in rehab, I got in trouble when I brought her mule slippers – mules are a hazard so we switched to closed-heel slippers and alternatively, heavy treaded socks when walking in the house.

- No more flare-bottom pajamas or pants. That style is an accident waiting to happen. The perfect alternative for men and women is joggers.

- Leather shoes are heavy so a safer alternative we love is the lightweight Allbirds which provide incredible support, and, they even make a shoe for the rain.

- When it comes to kitchenware, glasses filled with water or any liquid are a red flag for older people as they're too heavy to lift and hold as evidenced when my mom would accidentally drop glasses of water. We're grateful my mom was never cut. Stick with melamine cups, plates, and bowls.

- Flatware can also be heavy so I switched to a fun lightweight flatware and opted for the iced tea spoon as the longer handle is an easy grip.

- If your parent has high blood pressure and needs over-the-counter cough medicine, check with their doctor. Most over-the-counter cough medicines contain "DM" which can cause blood pressure to spike. We switched to Bee Keepers.

- Place treaded strips in the shower and/or tub.

- Check with Medicare about getting a shower chair and/or toilet chair. Add a bar handle in the shower.

- If your parent is using a hospital bed at home and the power goes out, learn how to bypass the electricity – be prepared.

- And, definitely, learn CPR.

CAUSE and EFFECT

I haven't had a day off in the seven years since my mom broke her hip. Of the few times I ran to New York when Emma was in college, those weren't days off. One night was always on the plane, and two or three nights were the most I stayed before rushing back home. I can't shut off my brain or my phone from my responsibilities – and the worrying. When away, there are endless phone calls and texts. Once when I was in New York, a PT called asking when I'd be home as my mom's blood pressure was high since she was anxious without me. Now it felt like my blood pressure was high as there was nothing I could do. In fact, I was angry as I literally had ten minutes left with my daughter before leaving for JFK and I wanted that time to be perfect but now those last few minutes were tainted with information I could do nothing about until I walked in the door nine hours later.

Emma's delayed post-COVID college graduation did not go as planned. My mom was at home in the care of competent caregivers so I naively thought I could relax and enjoy the weekend. We took the redeye to New York and I was exhausted as usual, not from jet lag, but from the emotional and physical toll of caregiving 24/7/365 without a break. The plan for the day of graduation was for me to take the 7 am train to her school so that I could save seats for our family and friends. I made the train and without realizing it, I got a seat in the silent car so there were no announcements for my stop. I was text replying to the overnight caregiver and by the time I looked up, I missed my stop! I panicked, and, as usual, because I'm laser-focused on my mom, I wasn't thinking clearly. I exited at the next stop where there was already a train going back in the direction from which I came. What I didn't know is that the train was an express back to Grand Central. I lost over an hour and a half of precious time with the clock ticking as the ceremony was starting at 9 am.

I couldn't conceal my location as Emma tracks me so our combined stress levels were elevated. I failed my daughter, myself, and my mission. What I should have done was Uber straight to her school from our hotel but didn't consider that an option as I've always taken the train. All of our guests and family had arrived, and they were saving ME a seat. Emma was sure that I was going to miss the ceremony. I had one assignment for this once-in-a-lifetime celebration but my only saving grace was arriving at school minutes before the ceremony started.

The reason I share this story is because my mom has been my priority, my sole responsibility, 1000 percent. My graduation fail led to my epiphany that I've been more of a daughter to my mom than I've been a mother to my daughter. I'll always feel haunted for stressing Emma on the day she had expectations of feeling euphoric – on the day she needed me most and on the day that I desperately wanted (and believed) that I would come through for her.

At home, Emma and I can't plan adventures together. One of us needs to be at home. Caregivers want a four-hour minimum and the costs are prohibitive so we bring the party to "Grandma's room," where my mom, Emma, the dogs and I hang out watching, "America's Got Talent" while eating ice cream. Though my mom is loyal to Clooney, Simon Cowell is a second-place distraction.

Spending quality time with my mom and daughter means everything, but it's complicated. I'll never get this time back with my daughter and it feels like time is running out with my mom. Emma has graciously accepted the sacrifices never once complaining as she loves and adores my mom – they have a loving, unmistakable bond – but the guilt... my guilt. I know Emma will forever cherish the time with her Grandma, and Grandma loves the attention from my daughter but it's hard, perhaps bittersweet.

Like the other caregivers in this book, I have a sibling who is busy. And, like the other caregivers authoring chapters in this book, most of us have been labeled, "controlling" and "manipulative" by our non-caregiving siblings and at least one caregiver has been called a "martyr" by her sibling.

No one thinks about the B I G picture when parents are healthy or the "what ifs" and who is going to care for your dependent parents and at what cost? And by cost, I don't mean literal but the heavy lifting and sacrifices.

Agencies in Los Angeles charge $40 per hour for caregivers. In our case, my mom needs 24-hour care. At $40 an hour over the last seven years, the caregiver tab would be $2,446,080 and counting. None of us contributing to this book is getting paid for our work as caregivers which is why the uncomfortable conversations need to happen in every family now so plans can be made in advance. Estate attorneys need to get involved. You'll need a Power of Attorney and a Medical Power of Attorney. There should be plans for the adult children and decisions about who will be in charge of caring for your parents. Similarly, you should make plans for your (adult) children in caring for you making concrete decisions now instead of when you're not capable. Will the responsibilities be split equally with your adult children or will they fall on one adult child? What are the plans and does everyone involved agree and understand? Put it in writing. But more often than not, the responsibilities are never equal especially when those responsibilities are not set in stone in advance. Not. Even. Close.

Know this: Caregivers are the backbone of long-term care services provided by family members. We provide upwards of $300 billion of value per year in unpaid care just in the US alone. Most caregivers are women: mothers, spouses, daughters, and sisters who are caring for loved ones without pay. *Source: Our America: Unforgettable.*

I tried working remotely but it wasn't sustainable. I'd be on the phone with a client and my mom would want water or a snack or needed me to change the channel on the television. Then there are the in-person doctor appointments all inclusive of traffic, sitting in the waiting room, and the visits which can take hours so there's no way anyone can take that kind of consistent time off. Aside from leaving the house for appointments, we have video appointments and physical therapy appointments in which I participate. In-between are phone calls with the doctors, and their staff, calls from various healthcare agencies, nursing, therapists, suppliers, and vendors. When home, I'm preparing my mom's meals and doing chores. Sometimes it's weeks before I get to the mail.

Paolina, the person spearheading this collaborative book project, has been exceptionally compassionate as I never made the deadlines I committed to for this book... my hours-long interruptions daily are endless. When I would finally sit down to write, I'd get a call, or my mom needed something. Then there's Rizzo, our puppy who hates it when I'm on the computer or the phone. My mom is a night owl so I could write after 1 am, but that means that I'm going to get little sleep and I need to be alert for a full day taking care of my mom. My reality is that I'm just not as reliable as I used to be for anyone other than my mom.

I have chronic lower back pain from helping maneuver my mom. Most often, I'm too tired to exercise. I don't eat as well as I should. I often cancel my doctor appointments as something comes up and I get distracted and forget to reschedule. I don't take care of myself as I should but I think about making changes and often that's as far as I get. Many nights I don't sleep, or rather I don't sleep enough so I've stopped making plans because I'm tired of canceling.

I miss vacations and going to exhibits with my daughter. I miss chilling with Em and the dogs at the dog park. I miss seeing friends – but I don't dwell on what I'm missing because someday it will be my mom who I'll be missing. My emotions are all over the map.

Even though caring for my mom is all-consuming, I'm the lucky one because of who my mom and daughter are – pure gems. My love and gratitude to them makes my heart explode – both are my greatest teachers and inspiration. I love, adore, admire, and respect these two strong, wise women infinitum. Our time together is a gift - a privilege. Every night, we share goodnight kisses, saying, "sweet dreams" and "I love you" followed by us saying to my mom, "See you in the morning," to which my mom ALWAYS enthusiastically replies, "Hope so!"

And THAT, my friends, is my inspiration to carry on for another day.

With love and support to you all for caring for your parents.
Remember to take care of yourselves.

CHAPTER SEVENTEEN

Adjusting to Now

by Anne Front

I blew out the candles on my birthday cake. I was fifty with a party crown on my head. It was plastic with jewels and feathers that made me feel grand. My family decorated the room with bright pink balloons stretched full of helium. The heat from menopause rose beneath my skin but didn't account for the feeling in my brain. My mind felt like it was on fire. It was like a new, creative spirit had woken inside me. I was starting a new job and focused on clear goals. Things that I had put off could no longer wait to be done. My new decade was coming in strong.

The next day, I found the balloons deflated with pink wrinkles, sagging towards the floor. The air had given way to gravity. I made a joke about the balloons being a sign of my aging body. Is this what the fifties have to offer? Little did I know that things were indeed changing. I was set on a course that would require all the helium and fire that I could muster. As powerful a new decade could be, it would bring me to a whole new terrain without a map.

I work with patients with serious illnesses. I walk along with them and their caregivers as the disease changes the fabric of their family. I love what I do and feel honored to be in the role of a professional guide. I thought I had it covered. I mean, helping people go through the difficult journey of illness and caregiving must give me the "get out of jail free" card. Right?

Apparently not.

The cancer diagnosis literally woke me up. My husband returned from an early morning doctor's appointment as I was turning over in bed, pulling up the covers for the last few minutes of sleep. He sat on my side and touched my shoulders. He told me the grim news that his physician found something and was very worried. He was scheduled for an immediate biopsy. The words circled around me. I couldn't breathe. As much as it was his life, the layers we had folded together year by year meant that if his feet faltered, so did mine.

It was the year before COVID closed the world down when my husband received the news and went for his biopsy. He was subsequently diagnosed with aggressive, stage four prostate cancer. We had two teenagers, one leaving home for college and the other soon to enter her senior year of high school. It was gravy time. We were close to the finish line of raising successful children. We envisioned what it would be like to have the freedom to get to know each other again. We fantasized about pursuing our personal and shared interests.

We made plans…

And then, well, as they say, "God laughed."

What I remember about those early days is not so much the drudgery of treatment – his daily treks to radiation for two months and the increasing fatigue of his new medication regime. It was the stark fear of unknowingness. That death was facing us in the worst possible way. As our lives were opening, the door was closing. The beginning of our illness journey felt black-and-white. We knew that the disease was terminal which meant that life was finite. We didn't know if the treatment would work, or how many months he had left. All we were certain of was that he was going to die. The sense of time was gone. We lived in the immediate, naked reality of loss.

My husband was offered radiation and daily medications. He was told that, although aggressive, the disease was moving slowly. That they could get ahead of it. The doctors threw out percentages as if he was a number on a spreadsheet. No guarantees, but time to get started. As much as we trusted the treatment team, the numbers swirled in our heads. Would he be here for graduations, weddings, grandbabies? How fast did we need to plan? How quickly could things change? What we didn't know is that for most, cancer doesn't act in one fell swoop. It was a series of step-downs, each phase different than the last.

Life felt entwined with death. Every beginning reminded us of endings. We had always imagined the ground was permanent and there to hold us. As the earth shattered beneath us, we would learn that we would find our footing only as we kept taking steps forward.

The day the city, the country, shut down because of COVID was the last day of my husband's radiation. His condition was too advanced for surgery, so this was his only option. The fear of starting a serious treatment gave way to a familiar routine. He worked a little, drove down to his cancer center, became friends with his technicians and staff, and drove back up the canyon to home and back to work. The treatment became a safety net, something that moved him forward, providing hope that this was just a dream. That with compliance, we might have a cure.

On the last day of treatment, he walked the once friendly radiation department hallway that had become desolate with COVID isolation and sterile fear. In retrospect, it was a reminder that the whole world was changing as fast as ours. He received a certificate of completion, a graduation of sorts. As we lost the stability of "doing something" to manage his cancer, we were distracted from the freefall of "doing nothing." Yet there was still something left to do. Bottles of his medicine came monthly in the mail. We bought extra pill organizers to fit the growing amount of prescription drugs. He used rubber gloves to handle the toxic chemicals.

We settled into the COVID routine and the routine of daily doses. Our son moved back home, losing his college freshman year. Our daughter lost the milestones of her senior year, time with friends, her prom and graduation. My father sequestered in with us, and we shifted from office work to working at home. Five people in a small house, filled with clouds of anxiety and loss, were traveling along a road of uncertainty. Not being able to escape our thoughts that became individual and shared.

We stared at the television screen reporting nightly numbers of hospitalizations and COVID deaths. Days were literally numbered as death screamed out to us right in the face. It was hard not to notice my husband's fatigue and increased naps amongst the terror of the day. In the early days, we wiped off groceries as we adjusted to masks. We watched Jeopardy! as a family and did puzzles. I learned to cook. Like his treatment had become a routine, so had our COVID days.

The sky brightened when COVID vaccines rolled out. We started moving in the world again. I decided to get my doctors' appointments done, screenings delayed for a couple of years. I sailed through my colonoscopy and drove to my mammogram. I came home to a message asking for a return trip. There was something abnormal on the scan. It turned out that my husband was not the only cancer patient. I had become one too.

My treatment was easier in some ways. The surgery and radiation were traumatic, but I knew the outcome was positive. It had been caught early and there was no spread. The scars reminded me daily of what I lost, and it was hard to remember what I gained. The gain being that my life was spared. With a five-year course of medication, I was told that I would be just fine. My doctor said it would eventually be a blip on the page of my life.

A blip? Working with serious illness and having a spouse that was facing his advanced disease every day, it seemed impossible that any experience could be so minute. It was unfathomable that I would get away scott-free while my husband would have treatment for the rest of his life. It seemed unbelievable that our second "get out of jail free" card had washed down the drain.

As I rebounded physically from my cancer, I adjusted to the daily medications. My husband and I laughed at our dualling hot flashes. We bought tornado fans. My pill box was smaller than my husband's, but it was a continued reminder that there were no guarantees. The fear burned my throat as I thought about our children being parentless. At least with one spouse, there's the idea that the other will be around for them. But two serious illnesses? The fear was palpable.

I've always been a crybaby. When I was a child, I'd run before my legs caught up. I'd fall time and again on the graveled sidewalk. Pebbles would imbed my skin that had to be picked out like surgery. Heavy white bandages covered my knees. The tears flowed easily with every injury, physical or mental. It was no dif-ferent when I learned of my cancer and went through the treat-ments. Surprisingly, I had somewhat held it together for the most part with my husband. But when our second diagnosis struck, my dam broke open.

It was then that I learned a new lesson about serious illness and families. As our family of four was closely intertwined, we felt each other's pain. That pain stacked up and had to pry loose. We were not healing or suffering as individuals. As a family, we shared the blood and scars between us. And it was becoming as toxic as the medications my husband was taking.

I got to a place where I felt like crying more than not. I would stay strong, get through my day as I helped others at work. But my body was tired, my mind consumed. I was tak-ing on more responsibilities at home as a care-partner. I took on more household chores and lost (most) of my indignation at my increasing responsibilities. My husband continued to do all that he could do (which was a lot), but his energy dwindled, and he only had so much to give. He was sore with body pain. He was handling his cancer with grace, but anxiety spilled out from his pores. As a family, we felt his losses and shared his fears.

Our illnesses had taught me that I couldn't ignore my body. The tears reminded me that I couldn't ignore my soul. How many times had I talked to caregivers about self-care?: That statistics show a higher likelihood of caregiver illness because of lack of self-care, deferred health screenings, and overwhelming stress. And here I was, fighting for my life. Not so much my physical condition because I knew that it was controlled. The cancer has already been removed from my body. I was existentially battling the sadness over my own illness that was wrapped around the grief I felt for my husband, and the intense pain I carried daily for patients and caregivers that I followed. It was like our cancers were fused and our blood flowed as one. It was like I would never fully breathe again, until I faced my grief.

I felt like the pipes in my body were clogged. I needed a way out. A place to care for my body and mind. Not as a recreational activity but as a lifeline. As little time as I had between caring for my husband, work, and children, I knew that I had no choice but to act. I joined a writing support group where I could express my feelings and not be judged. I reached out to friends and learned that I was not alone.

I've since gone on several day-long retreats. Some, where I sit quietly in meditation or sit outside listening to nature and feeling the breeze on my skin. Other retreats provided space for creativity. I spent hours collaging as a form of meditation. I harvested images from the boxes of magazines and drawings. I cut images slowly as if I was in prayer. I selected images that felt sacred. Some images scared me while others made me smile. One board is full of angels, warriors, and a child sleeping. I took with this an army of hope, strength, and dreams. Another is of a wrinkled woman strumming the guitar, a feeling of letting go. These images spoke to my soul.

I realized that I didn't have to interpret the ways I silently meditated. I let the collages hold me in a wordless hug. In silence,

I heard the trees swaying and let the outdoor breeze encircle me. I felt my breath ease. I learned mindfulness techniques which can serve me at home when panic sets foot or the care needs are overwhelming. My grief and my stress were often voiceless. With thoughtful, regular practice I started to attend to the deep emotional needs inside me.

I cried for a year until the tears became a trickle. The pipes were opening, and life was starting to pour through once again.

During that time, my husband was told by his doctors that he could stop the medications for his cancer. His energy improved and we felt like things were going back to normal. The stress abated as we built back our lives, our hopes, our plans. He went to his oncologist for a three-month check-up and found that the numbers had increased.

With more scans, we learned that the local metastasis around his prostate had traveled north to his lungs. The news was more dire. He had to go back on the medications right away. There would be no more breaks, no medication holidays. This was his new life. A life that would involve ever increasing fatigue and pain. His body once again would start to break down.

We walked the now crowded halls of our medical center. COVID isolation was over, but our journey was not. While my husband had his lung biopsy, I sat with our friend. Her presence brought me comfort. In planning to be alone, I wasn't sure I would welcome her support. But sitting with her, her gentle voice and easy laughter soothed my fears. Yet another lesson of letting help in. There are angels on earth, not always the ones we predict. But I had to be open to accepting what had been offered to me, which ultimately became my lifeboat.

With our friend, I shared the visitor badge. We took turns visiting my husband in the pre- and post- procedure rooms. We learned from the biopsy that there were too many small tumors to treat by surgery. That the cancer was going to stay in the lungs, and probably increase in amounts and size. He would be on surveillance until the numbers cropped up. I imagined a spreadsheet reappearing as we analyzed patterns and percentages. We would soon meet with the oncologist to talk about the next steps.

The next steps meant chemotherapy. Worries again surrounded us as we imagined hair loss, depleting energy, nausea, and toilets. Lots of toilets on both ends. The tricky part became realized as we learned that the physicians don't have all the answers. Professionally, as a palliative care therapist, I knew this. Personally, I was grabbing at words that would speak to our futures. As if the doctors had crystal balls and knew which path to follow. We were reminded time and again of patient choice. I felt confused and like we were at the beginning again.

"If the numbers stay low and you feel satisfactory, you can wait three months until the next blood work and scans. If they go high, we start chemotherapy. But if they stay low, the cancer may grow metastasize microscopically, undetected by machines and laboratories. When the cancer grows, the chemotherapy will be harder. But when you have chemotherapy, your quality of life will be worse." The doctors told us he could start right away if he was anxious about it growing. Or he could wait until things got worse. There were benefits and consequences to either choice. Choices bounced like ping pong balls getting whacked back and forth.

"Start to do things that you want to do that will make you happy. Fulfilled." The underscore was that life was about to get a lot more uncomfortable. We worried that once we started the chemo train, there was no getting off the tracks. The doctor assured us that my husband could start and stop as necessary. This wasn't about cure; it was about a balance of quality of life and quantity of days. Again, the decision was in the hands of the patient.

"What would you do?" we asked the doctors.

"It's up to you" was the typical response.

From there, we anticipate what is to come. I know the end stories from my patients and families. At some point, the illness will take hold and death will occur. The family left behind will be faced with the deep hole of loss. Regrets may emerge, unsaid words and missed opportunities. As much as we know the end, I also know the progressive losses to come even before then. They are already starting.

It feels selfish as I imagine what will happen after my husband dies. I feel like a cad. If I plan for his death, is that stealing his hope? Am I putting it out there to the universe that I am prematurely owning the outcome and therefore removing the chance of miracles? How do I balance trying to stay realistic, all the while accepting the mystery of what could be? How do I support his hope and shush my doubts?

We were sitting outside a shopping mall, watching people go by with bags on their arms or anticipation on their faces as they headed to the movie theater. Children were running ahead of parents and teenagers bumped into each other playfully. We shared a cup of gourmet salted caramel ice cream with bamboo spoons. We talked about our futures. Realizing that the threads were starting to unravel from one future to two.

My husband wanted to plan for our financial future. So that he could take time off to do things in whatever remaining time he has. There were unsaid words of also planning for the days when he becomes too weak to work. When I will have to take more time off from my job to provide care. Or if we must hire professional caregivers. There will be the day when we will need money to readjust to one income. Not to mention the time after he dies, when I will be alone in the house, bills needing to be paid. He was talking rationally as my blood pressure started to boil. I stopped hearing his words as the stereo in my mind blasted fear.

We ended up with a frustrating walk to the car. It took several days to resume the discussion. I sat on the couch with soft light illuminating his face. I was reminded of the person he is, the man that I love. As I connected with his humanness, I started to hear what he was saying. I realized that our communication, like cancer, is not linear. We must talk about difficult things together, so we don't have to carry them alone. It will take time with stops and starts, but we must stay open to the process. Open to each other.

Who wants to plan for the last days? But I know that if we don't have a plan, I will not know how to care for myself. I also know that I will regret not allowing him peace of mind to follow his heart in the time that he has. My logical mind understands this while my emotions heat up with fears of being alone. How will I be able to financially sustain myself, how will I know when to trim trees or how to talk to the car repair guy? The lessons will continue as we face uncertainty.

I used to imagine that death would have been as peaceful as Snow White falling asleep in the forest. I now know that there will be hospitalizations, medical equipment, endless nights, pain management and eventually hospice. Our future will involve incremental losses that will be messy and tangled. I know this because it is already happening.

And it was then that I learned the next lesson. I must remember that nothing is certain, there are no clear answers. Together, we must pick the treatment that feels right, seems reasonable. We have to freefall once again, into unknown territory. I have to find a way to let go of my expectations.

I don't know how long my husband will be in this world. I don't know if he will see weddings and future life events. I can't predict the future, but I can't hold onto the ocean waves. I must accept that they will come, and I will keep swimming. I've lived many years in the illusion of predictability. I believed that life was linear. I would graduate school, excel at my job, get married, have children and with my spouse, live into our old age as we chased our dreams together.

I am learning that the path I imagined has jagged rocks, hairpin turns and dark canyons that I must walk through. It is a new calling to trust that I will have the strength to handle what will come my way. I am also learning that things rarely change on a dime. Usually, even in moments, there is time to pivot. I am not alone, there are angels-on-earth to walk with me when I need help. I've had to find my breath and unclench my jaw. I feel my feet on the ground and let them balance me even as the earth shakes below. As I move into becoming an ever-increasing care-partner, so is my husband moving into becoming one for me.

CHAPTER EIGHTEEN

Mamma, in the Meantime

(excerpts from the book of the same name)
by Tony Luciani

I had an "aha" moment that changed everything between my mom and me. Up to that point, I was behaving like someone who was supposed to look after an old person, and that person was, well, behaving old. It's not unlike what a lot of people do, or think they must do, in a caregiving role with their elders. It can be a lonely time.

Then serendipity happened. There was a photo-bombing episode that awakened us. I was playing with a new camera, and my mamma couldn't wait for me to finish setting it up. So, without either of us realizing it, she photobombed the scene I was focusing (pun intended) on. It opened our minds to the possibilities of what could and should be. We connected on a level that we both were craving; something to play with and explore together. It gave Mom an outlet to express herself, and at the same time, it let me use my artistic creativity to visually describe it.

This beneficial relationship gave us permission to be ourselves.

My mother was at a crossroads of self-observation. She was still, at that point, aware of her cognitive changes, having been diagnosed with dementia, and found it disheartening to know that she was straddling the line of no return. She was fighting a losing battle with memory loss and with normal, everyday rationalizations. Mom was always one to be in control of her own decisions, so to be passive about clarity was difficult for her to accept.

My mother became genuinely rejuvenated with this project. Her days of just living developed into days of meaning and desire. Our collaboration gave her a sense of belonging and purpose. Mom became alive once again. Her smile returned.

And from the feedback of people worldwide, it was clear what we were doing was having even greater impact. The overwhelming online responses to the images we created validated our collaboration in its simplest form. People followed closely and absorbed every picture I posted as if it was their own experience. We were telling their stories as much as ours. It became an adventure for everyone who followed us on social media, and they totally climbed on board. That alone changed things for us both, as artist and model and as mother and son. With every image we posted, friends were made along the five-year-long journey. We didn't feel alone any longer.

I wasn't planning on this to be a project with my mom and me. I wasn't planning anything. I was just trying to get my mother interested in something to do, so I included her in my art-making.

At first, I was taking a few reference photos for a painting I was doing of her. Then, the modeling sessions evolved to stand-alone camera images. She would sit behind me in my studio while I painted, and this one day, the window light was just so perfect on her face. I put down my paintbrushes and picked up my camera to take some pictures. Mom's a natural model, and I saw that she was enjoying the role-playing.

My mother, Elia, never really showed her humorous side... until she began modeling for this series. It was a complete surprise to me. I imagine the photo sessions gave her a sense of "play." She understood it was all about her, and she ran with it. I tried to make the setups as fun as possible and always engaged with her throughout the process. Once we found something that clicked nicely together, our days became full of short waits for the next idea, and then the next. They were always there. The puzzle of life's pieces appeared.

The ideas started flowing. It became about storytelling. Her diary of sorts. The conversations we had, turned into ideas for visual snapshots. Some images were planned, and others developed on their own. They mostly all originated from my mother's stories. I would then get ideas. At times, those ideas shifted and morphed into a deeper sense of what was being told. I went with my gut in all cases.

As I became more comfortable with camera settings and post-work, the imagery developed into even more complex compositions. Mom's feelings of aging and memory loss were instrumental in deciding the direction this series was going. I was also encouraged by the many heart-felt comments people were posting, including those from individuals in photography forums online. I was capturing her memories, the ones she was losing to time. People related to the visual messages of frustration, annoyance and circumstantial humor. They saw themselves in where I am now as a caregiver. In a way, they all joined in with helping me look after my mom.

The purpose was initially to visually document my mother's life, by retelling her stories in pictures and having her express her present feelings. But, saying that, once they were posted online, the world noticed and began to connect.

There are many mirrors, doubles, and reflections within the project, and people have asked about the theme of self-image and the role it played. Mirrors are the reflection of the "self"... perhaps the soul. They bypass the physical and enter inside the person. I used mirrors to capture that feeling, internally. Mom looking into mirrors, playing with her double, and glancing at her reflections are metaphorically symbolic of the fact that that's how she wants to see herself. Her mind, because of dementia, remembers how she "used to be" not how she presently is. It gives her comfort knowing she can stop the advancing clock by reverting to moments of youthful recollections.

I also get asked why I chose to take the photos in black and white, despite the tone of the project being playful. Several reasons come to mind in response. Black and white, at least for me, suggests a stillness of time. The classical approach and mom's storytelling also seemed to fit together in concept. Most of the photographs are in black & white because, as an artist, my first love is drawing. It created the mood I wished to convey, reflecting my mother's life stories. Only a few images are in color because I needed that warm translucency to come through.

In art, the situation dictates the solution.

Ironically, the same holds true in life.

Helping with someone else's well-being is never easy. My natural inclination, however, is to assist whenever asked or needed. As a father of two children, my situation dictated the solution: I had no choice but to guide and nurture them. Same with my partner ten years ago with whom I shared the daily struggles of dealing with her cancer diagnoses by supporting her with unconditional love and understanding. Responsibility and patience are paramount in overcoming many of life's obstacles and their frustrations. Putting yourself in a dependent's situation can facilitate empathy. Perhaps, one day, you may need someone's guidance to make your life a little easier to cope. I want to believe in karma.

When it comes to my mom, and how at age 91 – still mending from a broken hip and now diagnosed with dementia – she moved in with me, I'll be honest, I didn't really know what to expect. But, again, the situation dictated the solution. And while I love every single moment of her life we experienced and captured together forever in these pictures, here are just three of my favorites (you can see our entire gallery by visiting my website: tonyluciani.com):

"Internal Reflection" started with mom looking at herself in the mirror and announcing how old she had become.....so fast! Time flew by. The idea was to present both sides of what she was saying, and emotionally revealing the feeling with one image.

I had mom holding the mirror up to her face and used a picture of her as a child in the mirror to show her as two – but as one person connected – yet divided years apart.

"No Escape from Within" – This one hit home with so many people for so many different reasons. Trying to visually depict Mom's internal struggles and to convey the sense that she had become her own prisoner had me playing with shadows. People are always trying to break away from an aspect of themselves, anxieties and worries they have, but they're tied to those worries by an umbilical cord.

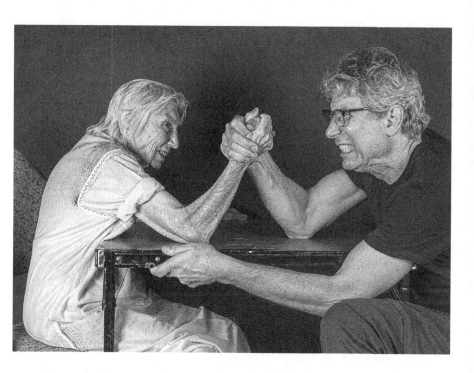

"Arm Wrestling" – Dementia is stressful. It's a lot of anxious moments and a lot of down, sad times. But it's also time of connecting on deeper levels, and a lot of life, love, and humor get rolled into that. I always tried with Mom to bring a sense of fun and play into our lives. This picture is from a time when we were sitting across from one another at a table, and I was taking pictures, and all of a sudden, I was inspired to challenge her to an arm wrestling match. Oh, how we laughed! She had such a great time, and I'll remember it forever.

However this project with Mom started, I know how it's unfolded: Through these pictures, we've been able to touch, grab, push, and pull people to places within themselves that are raw and real. My mom's diary has become more than art…it's taken on a life of its own and connected people in a way I, for one, never could have imagined. This opened up conversations about the urgency of a life about to be forgotten, and the need to embrace and live to the fullest every second on our own.

Artists are communicators. We express our thoughts, delve into our feelings, and hopefully touch others in beneficial ways. If we can accept the realities of aging without fearing it, we can respond lovingly to our elders. Ignorance only satisfies the moment, while experiences are without limitations. As artists, we can expose ageist attitudes by being true to each other, and helping to show the way to a better understanding that one day, we will be "them"...

I have always looked at people from the inside out, not the outside in. With Mom, it has never been a question of recognition or identification. I have always "seen" her for who she was, is, and will be, not from an outwardly physical sense, but from an internal connection. I have felt her and know her that way.

This project brought us together beyond just a mother and son relationship...beyond caregiver and care recipient. We understood each other from a creative endeavor, joining story-telling, family history, and artistic vision. And, by blending it all into one, we found a link that eluded us before.

It is my hope for all family caregivers that you find the link that connects you to whomever is in your life now so that you may be able to keep the very best of them with you forevermore.

CHAPTER NINETEEN

It's a Little Bit Like Marble Cake

by Mercedes Vega

*I*n an interview with Tim Ferriss, the well-known Dr. Gabor Maté, who specializes in addiction and trauma, described how a traumatic event can be either something good that should have happened but didn't, or something bad that should not have happened but did.

In 2015, I received a letter of acceptance to study abroad at my top chosen school. My older brother Manny was very happy for me and gave me the money to pay for my student visa, and to secure my flat in England, as a congratulatory gift. I was beyond grateful! This is just one example of my admiration for my brother's kindheartedness.

I still remember what should have happened but didn't. It was a very sunny Sunday, and

I was in a modern Buddhist temple, when I started to feel this pressure right between my eyes as we were all being guided through meditation. I kept getting images of being in this forest-like place surrounded by loved ones. When the Buddhist nun asked us to think of a place that made us feel at peace, I envisioned the previous Sunday that I had spent with my brother and cousin. We were at the beach, watching the sunset, and decided to go to Bubba Gump Shrimp Co. afterward. While at the restaurant we were celebrating the new chapter of my life that was soon to begin. I shared my plans to take a semester to do my thesis research in Central America. My brother, cousin, and I planned to meet up in El Salvador. I felt so hopeful and grateful at that moment; but then the meditation ended, and we were asked to share our thoughts about our experiences with others.

I looked around. The room was filled with golden Buddhist statues and burgundy drapes, the sun was peeking through the windows, and people were talking to each other. Even though I was there, for some reason I felt like I was outside this place, like I was watching a movie, not being able to connect with others. I sort of felt like I was invisible. I was a little freaked out, because this place was always somewhere where I could reset all my negative feelings and emotions; yet here I was, unable to shake this inexplicable feeling of being utterly alone.

I left the temple and started to make my way back towards home. I had promised to meet a friend at a music festival to film a video, so I made a quick stop. I was still not feeling that great: and in the middle of the show my phone rang. Even before I picked up, I had this bad feeling inside of me.

It was my sister's voice on the other end of the line: "Manny's in the hospital. He's been assaulted, and they said he's unresponsive."

My heart leapt into my throat, and my soul felt like it jumped out of my body, as my sister explained that we should all meet back at home.

I prayed silently: "Not my Manny, not now; I was supposed to see him, thank him. Oh God, please, please don't let him be hurt, in pain, or suffering."

I finally arrived home, but from that point on everything got complicated. Because Manny was the victim of a crime, the police were in the hospital. As a result, my family and I were not allowed to see Manny immediately...maybe an hour passed until they finally did allow us to, but it felt like forever.

When I first saw my brother lying there in the ER, I immediately knew that with every second without us at Manny's side he fell further and further into a more severe medical state.

"We encourage you to give up," were the words I heard coming from the trauma team.

What they actually said was more along the lines of, "There's nothing we can do."

In my heart, I knew it was not time for him to go. I said, "What does he have? I need a copy of all his records, labs, and exams right now." I pressured them to provide the paperwork immediately, and I learned he had a "subdural hematoma."

At the end of the night, getting practically kicked out – "visiting hours are over" – I went home to do some research on his diagnosis. I Googled various sites to find out how to cure it, fix it, and mitigate it.... It turns out that patients with this injury need surgery to alleviate the swelling.

I found myself with a great deal of pushback from several medical professionals who didn't think Manny was a candidate for surgery. I disagreed. My patient advocacy kicked in, with me threatening to report anyone who wouldn't at least consider this treatment for Manny.

Finally, three days later, in what should have been an immediate action, Manny got his surgery to alleviate the swelling.

My brother began to make a very gradual recovery. Every little bit of progress felt so big: one eye opened, then the other; he moved his fingers, then his arms; he followed us with his eyes; tolerated food; he could blink, and make sounds, etc. Each thing was a small blessing.

It was evident that my brother would need a lot of care, not just from the medical team but from us. I couldn't think of anything else besides him; all the memories from our childhood up until two weeks ago replayed in my head. The memories suddenly felt so vivid. I would walk through the neighborhood to go to my mother's house, and everything reminded me of my brother – the streets, the route I took. I would get flashbacks of him and me walking those same streets in the mornings on our way to school when we were in junior high. I would see him walking next to me, re-telling me South Park episodes he'd seen at a friend's house, who had cable at that time. I could see us both laughing – especially his laugh, his eyes squinting, looking up, wearing his uniform, a white long-sleeve shirt under his regular collar shirt, navy blue pants, and his hair combed, so perfectly parted towards the side.

Ever since I was a kid, I had never been an early bird. I hated waking up early in the mornings, and nothing or no one could get me up but my brother, who was always an early bird. He would tell me, "If you walk with me to school, I will tell you South Park episodes on our walk." I can't believe how much that worked. I would get up and be ready to be able to walk with him to school.

I decided not to go to England to study. I would stay by my brother's side and defer my dream of attending school and studying Social Ecology. Despite this being a dream of mine ever since I'd received my bachelor's degree two years earlier, giving that up for a while didn't feel like a difficult choice. In those moments, everything I cared and dreamed about became secondary. To me, the most painful part was not that I didn't get to go, but rather WHY I didn't get to go.

I have now been a caregiver for almost eight years. I didn't think of myself as such. I just quietly thought of myself as my brother's keeper. My mom and I are both Manny's caregivers; we are a team, and together we are slowly helping him recuperate and heal. I didn't think of myself as a caregiver, because he is in what they call a Skilled Nursing Facility, where he gets 24-hour care.

However, my mother and I have learned to do everything, from taking care of his hygiene to helping clean any medical devices, doing dental care, some physical therapy, etc. But most importantly, we do what staff can't: We provide him with the necessary companionship, love, and emotional support. We play his favorite music and movies, share his sense of humor, and even do things one takes for granted, like buying his favorite brands to use – *Old Spice* deodorant, to name one.

Our presence and care are not just part of keeping him company. Our presence is essential. My brother can't move much, or speak, and we have become an extension of him. With our intuition, knowledge, and strong emotional bond, we make the best medical and care decisions for him, always putting him first. Although he is not expressive, my mother and I read his body language, his expression, his mood, and his eyes. I have to admit my mother can be better at this than I can, but when it comes to my brother's favorite things – music, TV shows, and sports... that's all me.

Upon our visits, something I learned from my mother is to check my brother from head to toe and see if anything is physically bothering him. Unfortunately, because he's nonverbal, he can't tell staff when something is bothering him. Sometimes we've found wrappers, or caps from containers, that have been left behind. I guess it's not just that he's non-verbal – it's that some staff are not always careful. That is another reason that we, caregivers and family members, are essential.

Caregiving for my brother was like my little precious secret. I rarely shared this with anyone, and the only people who knew about this were family members and close friends. Going to see him was the highlight of my day. Before the pandemic and all the new restrictions they have now, I would walk through the halls after work, or after studying during my program – heck, sometimes after I went out. Whenever I wanted to see him, whenever I needed to see him, I would go just to check on him. As they buzzed me in (since they knew me at the facility), I would pass by and greet the staff, "Hey, what's up, how are you doing...long time no see..." Sometimes my brother would be sleeping, when he was fatigued, so I started cleaning and organizing his room to kill time. When I was finished organizing, and if he was still asleep, I would put on a PPE gown and squeeze into the very edge of his bed, with my legs sticking out, and place my head on his shoulder. I then just took a nap if I was also tired. This sometimes would wake him up, so I would play a relaxing meditation. He usually closes his eyes again until the end, when he hears the bell "ding." He just looks to my side and stares. `

Once he's up, this is "go time" for me. I clean his face and brush his teeth (something that some staff often miss). I get a playlist of his favorite songs, and we get to do some range motion on his arms and legs.

Since he suffered a brain injury, which can be similar to a stroke, his body became stiff.

Range motion, physical therapy, and massages are all necessary to help with spasticity. I tried to make it as fun as possible, while playing upbeat music. Time would always fly and before I knew it, eight hours had gone by. Before I leave, I always like to say a prayer and hold his hand. My brother usually falls asleep during this time; understandably after our day it can get exhausting.

I usually pack up my laptop, leave the radio on at low volume for him, and remind the staff to reposition him in two hours. Among all things, I also make sure to check his vitals at the beginning and end of my visit to make sure he doesn't have a fever or pain, and just to track how he's doing. I remove my PPE, and sometimes I keep my mask on and just sit in my car.

I am always left full of love in my heart. My brother cannot speak or move much, but he still radiates the same positive energy and love he's always had for others. Before I enter his room, and when he hears my voice, or my mom's voice, my brother perks up. His eyes get wider; they have this beautiful, soft look, and embracing him feels just as comforting as it did when we were kids. Even though he can't wrap his arms around you, you still feel that love and warmth around you when you hug him. Sometimes, he sighs and gives this look like he's filled with gratitude, and you just feel like everything will be all right.

My brother was a guy full of energy, always willing to lend a hand to help others with anything, and even to be a shoulder to lean on. He could rarely be still though: the only times I found him on the couch just relaxing was when he watched TV or his favorite teams, the Lakers and Green Bay Packers. I am joking: he was *never* just still during games – he was way too passionate about the team's scores to sit still. We all loved watching TV with him, especially comedy, because he had such a strong and contagious laugh.

Leaving his side is always the hardest, but like most caregivers we always have other things on our plate. To many of us caregivers, I think being able to care for our loved ones after they become ill helps us assuage the pain, trauma, and hurt of their huge health change. It's not just limited to their health. So many of us have to cope with *ambiguous loss*: they are with us, but we can't converse the same, we can't laugh the same, we can't eat at our favorite sushi spot, hike, or go dancing together with friends, and God, what I would give...to see another sunset together and make plans for the future....we miss all these things, but we don't let that overshadow the blessing of being able to have our loved ones with us.

Not caregiving, not being able to care for my brother, was so much harder for me. It was painfully traumatic. At the onset of the pandemic, those of us who have loved ones in a long-term care facility were banned from visiting them. To some of us, this was the first time in our lives that we were away from them for more than a couple of days. It was worse during a time of so much uncertainty, when their vulnerabilities and environment (their home) made them targets of this virus. All the fears one could think of flooded through our minds. We lost the limited amount of control we had over their health, and our uncertainty and anxiety just got worse. "Are they OK? Do they understand why we can't visit? Are they sad, depressed, feeling lonely?" were thoughts that often ran through our heads. I prayed that my brother never fell into despair.

We were allowed virtual calls: they would prop up the IPAD near him, and sometimes we could see him better than other times, depending on who was setting up the calls. I wanted him to be able not just to hear us but to see us, so he would feel calmer. During our video calls, I would remind him and tell him of things to try and comfort him, "Hi Manny, I am so sorry we cannot come anymore for now, but it will all be OK, we should be able to see you soon, in some way."

I never expected what would truly happen. Things became increasingly complex, as most will remember. After a year of only virtual contact, COVID-19 vaccines were approved, and public health guidance and orders were amended to mitigate the detrimental effects of isolation. But adherence to these changes was not equal, even as we became vaccinated. In our case, my brother's facility made it even harder for us to provide him with the same humane caregiving we had done before. His facility became very strict about family visiting in person, even as they claimed never to have had COVID-19 cases. They did not allow us to have indoor visits even though the public health agencies allowed for it.

When I saw my brother for the first time after one and a half years of him facing isolation, I was overwhelmed with emotions, so much so that I felt paralyzed. I desperately wanted to hug him, but at that time we couldn't, because vaccines were not distributed to everyone, and we had to be 6 feet apart. I didn't focus on those things; instead, I figured out a way to remain positive. I remember crying a few times and told him that my mom and I would be able to hug him in no time. We were only allowed a maximum of two hours twice a week for visits, and I made sure every second counted. I had to visit him in the activity room, a common area. This may seem insignificant, but it changed the entire dynamic of a visit because of having very little privacy.

So many times I wanted to talk to him and tell him how I felt, how much I missed him, how hard things felt without being able to see him, to hug him, and just to be next to him. Not to mention this perpetual guilt, that I never chose, of feeling like he had gone through things I could never know. I did what I could: I put my own emotions aside as soon as I stepped into the facility. I would walk in and take a deep breath, put on a mask, sanitize my hands, put on gloves, get tested for COVID-19, wait 15 minutes, and when I was cleared, I'd put on a yellow gown and would see my Manny, there waiting for me. "Hey, Manny! Are you ready for some music and range motion?!" Once I was fully vaccinated, I could give him a quick hug (our physical contact time was limited to seconds at that time), then I went about massaging his arms, range-motion, and our usual routine of movie watching.

Sadly, we only got to enjoy this for four months at most, before this particular facility decided to shut down again for months (banning in-person visits), despite never having had one single COVID-19 case. This time, for some reason it felt worse than the year when everyone was prohibited from visiting. Perhaps it was my confusion as to why they would still do this after so many data showing that isolation was killing just as many people as COVID-19 – in particular this specific vulnerable group. Especially after having so many of us fully vaccinated, it made me realize that isolating residents was at times out of personal interest and convenience for them. After almost six months of back and forth, and countless complaints to the department of public health, we got the facility to re-open and allow for adequate visits. My mother finally got to see her son, and care for him in the privacy of his room after almost two years.

However, this situation had left me very perplexed, not just with these structural systems, but with myself too. Five years before this, I was on my way to pursuing a degree in the hopes of saving our environment. After what happened to my brother, however, I switched my degree, in the hope of being part of saving him and others like him, so I went into public health.

Getting my master's degree in public health has opened up even more questions for me about our entire system: "Why aren't we doing more about these things? Why aren't we taking resident rights violations more seriously?"

I felt torn, like I had betrayed my loved one, but also like all the noise I made would cost me my opportunities in this field. During our last semester, one of the staff from our program had pretty much said that public health was a small field, where you can easily burn your bridges. "How can I advocate for my brother, whom I love so much, and not 'ruin' my career opportunities?" I certainly couldn't afford the mental health effects I'd endured from what had happened, and choosing to become a caregiver had sadly cause some gaps in my resume. It had changed so much for me. I had to make a choice, so I went for what was true for me, and remembered why I even went into this field in the first place.

"I will work to ensure that all people have the chance to live full and productive lives, free from avoidable disease, injury, and disability, and are supported in their pursuit of physical, mental, and social well-being." This is an excerpt from the Public Health Principles, an oath we take as graduates of the field. An oath that I strongly believe in and uphold in all my work.

My brother and all my experiences are what led me to change my field. Not speaking up would be betraying all of us – my brother, my family, and other residents and family caregivers.

In my journey as an advocate for residents in long-term care I was interviewed and featured in a couple of local news articles and on a radio station where I got to share my experience. All this time, it felt like I was in the belly of the beast trying so hard and so much to get out of that situation, but only making it out bit by bit.

I think I made the right choice. By sticking to my truth, I was lucky enough to find amazing caregivers – such as the Essential Caregivers Coalition (ECC) – fighting for the same causes and was able to connect with organizations like the California Advocates for Nursing Home Reform (CANHR). Recently, some of the ECC members and I were part of a policy access group, working on a state bill in hopes of preventing long-term care residents from ever having to face isolation, regardless of any public health emergency. In this policy group, I had the opportunity to share my testimony. I was as honest as I could be and shared my thoughts. I have always been against policy that is black and white. The truth is that family members or visitors, like me and my mom, aren't going anywhere. Also, we are very well-educated about health, and I think there is room to educate more people, just like we did during the pandemic, on how to practice safety measures when going into healthcare settings. There should not be a division between these settings, public health, residents, and families, especially because we all have the same goal, which is to keep our loved ones as healthy and safe as possible: and that includes having us with them, as long as we are adhering to safety measures.

After all of this, I decided to help myself, and after six years I finally joined the Family Caregiver Resource Center program at USC. This is why I get to tell my story, and you get to hear it, or read about it. I realized I had endured a lot as a caregiver – not from caregiving, but from the lack of structural support we have for people with disabilities, the elderly, and their caregivers.

I think of my life like this marble cake, with two very opposing flavors mixed together: the bad parts that should not have happened but did, the good parts that should have happened but didn't, along with the surprising beauty that came from it. Together they make this marble cake story where I am to accept it all and not pick out one over the other – because I simply can't.

Lastly, I had to remember one of my favorite quotes by Gary Snyder, that says: "Don't feel guilty [about the state of the world]. If you start to care for the environment because you feel guilt, your care for it will be unsustainable. If you're going to save it, save it because you love it...because it's the strongest force."

I try to remember these words when difficult things arise, especially during my advocacy, as my brother deserves to be cared for with love, and nothing less.

CHAPTER TWENTY

To My Husband, Dan, of 40-plus Years

by Ruth Kreshka Moran

Dear Dan the Man,

We were not so young when we met. I fell completely head-over-heels in love with you at first sight in San Francisco. A chemical weakening in my knees kind of attraction, lightning striking my heart. The complication was clear at once...you were my husband's best friend. A cliché. I was an older woman by three astounding years.

We travelled the country together presenting Shakespeare plays in college towns, driving a few thousand miles on each tour. You an Actor, Me a Tour Manager. After several years we three decided to make a change. I divorced my high school sweetheart; you and I moved in together. We relocated to New York City to embark on theatre careers.

We married, had two amazing children, the jazz babies, Ella and Miles. We made fantastic theatre. We collaborated with the cream of theatre and film community. Our luck was palpable. Usually one of us was working, allowing the other to take care of hearth and home. A balanced work and home life. We had meaningful juicy lives and a barrel of fun as well.

2001 brought the clouds. Sept 11 broke our hearts. Our city was badly hurt. Our children, both in high school, were challenged in ways we have never been. They came of age in a world suspicious of the immigrant, rife with security procedures, a lost sense of innocence, a communal grief.

And you were diagnosed with Parkinson's Disease.

Our marriage had been a strong one. We had the habit of mutual respect, support and love. We delighted in each other's triumphs. We held onto each other during defeats. Of course, we stumbled. Life left chinks in our armor, an indiscretion here, a clumsy forgiveness there.

I never questioned that we couldn't beat Parkinson's. I knew we had solved so many challenges together and that we could rise above this one, too. I stepped into the care partner role with gusto… educating myself on the complex array of symptoms and problems we might encounter in the future. I was present at medical appointments and gave kind support to you as physical challenges developed. We both agreed that the vast majority of dire predicted symptoms were not going to affect you. We were amused to think that turning over in bed or incontinence or on/off or soft speech or drooling or cognitive decline or hallucinations or compulsive behavior or anxiety would ever impact you. You were in tip-top physical condition. Your body and your voice were the tools of your trade. Your memory was outstanding, honed by years of use memorizing lines, blocking, actions, intentions and emotions. You practiced yoga and speech with a sensei's discipline.

We were correct for years. For ten years, the symptoms were so well controlled by our fantastic movement disorder specialist, Neurologist Alessandro DiRocco, that you appeared only mildly ill. Yet you felt Parkinson's inside you, *schpilkes* in your arms and legs, inner tremors, loss of power in your movements, occasional confusion when multi-tasking, compulsive computer use.

The next ten years brought us the suite of special gifts Parkinson's has to offer. Sleep disorders, vivid dreams, gait disturbances, balance issues, constipation, mild psychotic episodes. I recognized that the Parkinson's journey that I thought we had been on was actually just a beginning. I took early retirement from the academic job I had taken so I could spend more quality time with you before we were overcome by the disease.

As the end of the second decade approached, we began to see all the symptoms emerge that we had scoffed at years ago. My care-partnering became more care-giving. I gradually came to be assisting you with most "activities of daily living" which is the health care system's marker of disability. I ironically developed skills at nursing, an amateur at the profession that each of my three sisters' chose.

As symptoms emerged, a new bell was tolling. My dear Dan, you began to disappear. Slowly at first, then more rapidly, my dear heart, you became unrecognizable as my life partner, my hero, the one who sent lightning into my heart. I began to experience a relentless sense of loss, drip, drip, dripping, and growing into what I came to learn was anticipatory grief.

After twenty years of Parkinson's, I felt for the first time that I could not continue. At the same time, we had the opportunity to relocate with our daughter's family back to California. We said goodbye to the tiny East Village fourth floor walk-up where we had lived and loved for so long. The move was difficult for you. Shortly after we moved, Covid arrived. Again, we luckily were graced with timing that brought us away from the City during the years of isolation that the pandemic brought.

But I was drowning.

Rage, grief, guilt and stress were my frequent companions. I never was sleeping more than a couple of hours at a time.

I decided to try to find help outside of my family. For the first time I reached out to a support group, taking advantage of the Zoom meeting miracle that the pandemic grew. My sense of overwhelming stuckness as caregiver began to open up. Other family caregivers were willing to share their experiences, tips, humor, and fellowship. Together, we were a community of husbands and wives, sons and daughters, experiencing similar trauma, guilt, anger and despair. I was not alone.

From my first meeting with other caregivers, I was hooked. I felt enormous relief. For the last year or two, I have engaged with multiple support groups. I believe they are saving my life. I have a place I can vent and cry and be held and can hold. In the Parkinson's group, I bring experience that others need. I feel valued for it. I learn how to relax, breathe, laugh again. In the Dementia group, I am learning coping strategies as Parkinson's Disease Dementia comes into play at our house, and to laugh again and again. Together, we are engaged in online Palliative Care, which I know helps me, and I think helps you, too, my dearest. I have learned that an important way to live with you is to take the best care of me that I can, and to laugh.

I am working on allowing the dark emotions the space that they need and to laugh.

I am with you, Dan, even when I am furious at you for taking unnecessary risks leading to falls. I am with you, Dan, even when I cannot understand your garbled mumbling voice that used to read Shakespeare's sonnets so beautifully to me. I pledge that I will care for us both, the best that I can, and help us have the softest landing possible to this ride that is Parkinson's Disease.

Love,
Your Ruthie

CHAPTER TWENTY-ONE

The Addicted Angel

by Teri Wellbrock

I t was only a twenty-eight-minute car ride from the arrivals gate at Cincinnati/Northern Kentucky International Airport to Hospice of Cincinnati, where my eighty-seven-year-old mother was most likely telling another one of her dirty jokes to the nurse who had just arrived for the 7 AM shift change. Brushing the dog hair from my lap, having had my son, Jake's, seventy-pound pup perched on my thighs on the ride, I paused at the heavy wooden door of room 113 to take in one final calming breath as I prepared to step into chaos.

"TT! What are YOU doing here?" my mom exclaimed in combined disbelief and joy.

"I'm here to break you outta this joint, my sweet Momma!" I reminded her as I bent down to kiss her on her bruised forehead.

Her injury looked much worse in person. The purple pool of blood in her eye socket highlighted the once white of her eye that was now glowing red instead. As she struggled to keep that eye open, in what appeared to be a continual wink in my direction, I heard her sigh of relief sneak into the air.

"You didn't have to come all the way to Ohio. You have a job. You have a family that needs you. I'll be okay," she reminded me. Yet again.

"Mom, there was no way I was going to stay in South Carolina while you were lying here in a hospice room after that horrific fall." I kept my lecture tucked away as I replayed the phone conversations with hospital nurses from only a few days prior . . . *your mother is here at Mercy Hospital emergency room after tripping over her shoes . . . I'm here with your mom and she's sustained a pretty significant head trauma . . . we are going to go ahead and send your mom home.* Followed by more phone calls the following morning from the homecare hospice nurse and social worker . . . *your mom was sent home in an Uber even though she has brain bleeds . . . we've decided to have her transported to the hospice facility . . . she admitted to drinking alcohol prior to her fall.*

"Well . . . thank you for being here. I've missed you."

Jake came bounding into the room a few minutes later with Chloe in full sled-dog mode trying to make her way to GJ, short for Grandma Joann, or at least to the remnants of breakfast Mom was wearing on her faded pink sweatshirt.

GJ squealed in delight as Chloe's ginormous head plopped onto her, that tongue licking at some scrambled egg crumbles in the cracks and crevices of frail, wrinkly body parts, causing my mom to giggle even more. The door inched open as the chaplain interrupted the grandma/granddog reunion, and Chloe's attention was diverted to inspecting the scent of the stranger.

I expected my mom to be knocking on death's door after receiving the report only the day before from the hospice staff that she was spiraling quickly, and it might be best if I hop on a flight as soon as possible. Instead, she was her normal perky life-of-the-party-self trying to sit up in her bed so she could engage with her BFF of the day, the chaplain. As scripted, she began, "Anthony, did I tell you the joke about the nun and little Johnny?"

Jake gave his grandmother a quick peck on the cheek and let her give Chloe a good-bye pat on the head before leaving me alone with GJ.

"Mom, how are you feeling? How's your head? Those bruises look really bad."

"I have bruises?" she quipped.

"Mom! You fell into the corner of a table. You have a concussion. And brain bleeds. I still can't believe the hospital sent you home and tucked you into your bed unsupervised after that kind of an injury." Truthfully, I was not surprised, knowing her history at that hospital. I'm sure her chart had a big ol' "addict" red star on it. The routine was always the same. Go on a five-day drinking binge, don't eat, fall, call 911, and have Teri show up, with her superhero cape tied on tight like a noose, in order to save the day and clean up the mess, usually vomit, diarrhea, and urine in various places scattered about her tiny retirement community apartment. Oh, and blood. Always some blood.

I gently brushed her dyed blonde hair away from the blackening knot on her forehead, leaning in to study her more closely. "Does it hurt?"

"Oh, TT, I'm fine!" she said, brushing me off. "Where are you staying and how long will you be here?"

"I'm staying here. In this room. With you. I'll sleep on that couch over there by the window. And I'm staying as long as I need to stay. I already checked with the staff before arriving, and they will be bringing me a pillow and blankets."

Normally she'd have argued. But this time, she didn't. And that worried me on a soul level.

Visitors popped in and out over the next couple of days. Mom's friends from Guardian Angels Church, just a few minutes down the road from hospice, old co-workers, some of my friends who saw on my Facebook posts that I was in town, family members (some of whom we'd not seen in years), and nearly every day my mom's best friend from high school, Marlene, would call or make the drive from Kentucky, just across the Ohio River, to visit for a cackle-fest. Those two could talk incessantly for hours and never fail to make the other belly laugh. My cousin's husband, whom my mom adored as he kept her beat up little Toyota running all those years she ran over boulders or backed into electrical boxes in parking lots, brought her homemade ribs he'd cooked up especially for her with a little extra zing in the sauce, just the way she liked it.

* * *

Mom was an earth angel, who literally gave her coat away to a shivering teenager at a bus stop, who fed her poor elderly neighbors in her building by making vats of delicious homemade soups, who was always sending money to Save the Children and Salvation Army because they needed it more than she did, and lived her life shuffling the pages of prayer books when she wasn't telling her latest joke to the priest after morning mass.

She was also an addict who struggled every day to not give in to the taunts from the ghosts of her childhood traumas, begging her to sedate them with just one sip. But it never stopped with one.

* * *

My sister and I had been gathering every evening in the hospice room to reminisce, sing songs to Mom, play cards, and just enjoy being together as Mom dozed off from the pain meds. My sister had ended her much-needed and long-overdue estrangement with our mother upon receiving word of Mom's diagnosis of liver cancer and cirrhosis of the liver. We had decided to run a few errands, giving Mom the opportunity to visit with two church friends who had shown up for an impromptu visit. One of them was a drinking buddy and supplier (you know, the one who would drive to Kroger liquor store at Mom's request for a bottle of cheap vodka or expensive brandy, depending on the time of the month and if Mom had any money left until her next social security deposit). As we left the room, she was telling a joke.

A few hours later, upon our return, everything had changed. Mom was writhing in pain, moaning about her hands, her hands, her hands. I looked and her hands were swollen. She screamed in pain when I barely touched one of them. The nurse had no answer. The doctor, whom I never once saw in the fourteen days I stayed in that room with my mom, was summoned by phone, and he, too, had no answer.

We asked about blood clots, but that was disregarded. Mom mumbled, "The nurse told me it wouldn't hurt. But it did. It does."

Alarmed, I responded, "WHAT wouldn't hurt?"

"I don't know. The needle."

I wanted to find a staff member and demand someone explain to me what needle Mom was referencing and why she was experiencing such a sudden shift in demeanor. However, the little voiceless girl in me kept those demands confined internally. That same little girl who had been silenced by the violent smacks of a belt after Dad had been beckoned by the drunken slurs of Mom to silence the children. I was emotionally reeling from the fact that I had finally decided to leave the room for a few hours, leaving Mom with friends, joking and laughing and eating her tuna salad lunch, only to return to find her in agonizing pain and I could not find the courage to demand answers.

So, I did what I've always done, I dissociated and disconnected from my anger and heartache. Instead, I went into savior mode. Propping her hands up on ice packs and then heating up my rice bags to rotate between cold and hot compresses, I worked on easing the intensity of the pain, with some guidance from the hospice staff.

From that moment on, over the next several days, I sat helpless, watching her beautiful bright light slowly extinguish. Her blackened forehead/eye bruise literally slid down her face and landed on her neck. She stopped talking coherently, trying desperately to tell us something but was never able to complete the sentence. In the end, however, she was able to whisper, "I love you" and "I pray for you." I would play her favorite church music or opera arias, as I watched her neck arch and her breaths stagger.

* * *

I found myself time leaping to the 1970s with each labored breath. I could hear her gasped snores from her passed out position in the faded tan pleather recliner we'd inherited from an uncle, the seat of it held together with a strip of silver duct tape. Her glass of cheap vodka now watered down with melted ice cubes, the lemon wedge having made its descent to the bottom of her evening ritualistic chalice, awaiting the water beads slowly making their way from the orange lipstick rim to the *Good Housekeeping* magazine it had been unsteadily positioned upon, teetered ever vigilant by her side.

Suddenly the silence from the family room with its green shag carpet, pea green walls, and avocado green wall phone with the twenty feet of tangled green cord had my ten-year-old neck hairs raised to alert. Lying in bed, I squeezed my slumbering eyes shut even tighter, wishing and praying for the snores to start back up.

I knew she was there. Watching us. I could smell her booze-laden breath, mixed with heavy garlic from some fancy dinner out with her work friends. While she was out savoring filet mignon or a fresh catch seafood feast, I had dumped a can of SpaghettiOs into a pot in order to feed my sister and me, topped off with a bag of Doritos for dessert. Doritos I had bought myself at Lucas Food Mart using my babysitting money from watching various kids living in our apartment complex.

My eyes peeked open, against my conscious will, and my breath caught. Her eyes were blank. The butcher knife dangled by her side. My mind swirled with terror as I lay frozen under a thread-bare blanket, my little sister's seven-year-old leg draped over me in her slumber. The prayers cascaded from my chest in waves of pleading for protection. My eyes had squished themselves back shut, disconnecting from the reality that my mom was standing over her sleeping children with a knife in her drunken hand.

I cannot say how long she stood there as I left the scene mentally. A survivor skill I learned early on.

The next morning, she was yelling at me to *WAKE UP*, accusing me of being lazy, reminding me to brush my mousy hair and wear something with some color because I "dress like an old lady with boring colors." She had to get to morning mass at Guardian Angels Church early because she was the lector for the First Reading.

I guess she didn't stab me in my sleep after all. Just some morning word stabs instead.

* * *

Back in hospice, the days dragged on. My sister and I had prayed over her, had the priest give her the Last Rites, had all of her grandkids visit or FaceTime from out of town, and even given her permission to go. We talked to her about forgiveness, and even invited Dad (who had died in the same hospice facility in 2009) to come escort her into the next life. Yet she held on.

Sitting with my sister one evening, I had the ah-ha moment of what just might be the final piece of the farewell puzzle. I told her, "I promised Mom if she quit drinking, I would do a shot of booze with her on her death bed. I will bet the ranch she's waiting on that damn shot!"

* * *

Mom had been living sober for the past two and a half years (minus a fall or two off the wagon at Christmastime). I had walked away from her in 2019, after receiving a call from Mercy Hospital while on vacation standing in a parking lot in Estes Park, Colorado, asking me to pick her up from a detox stint.

Over those next three months, I cried daily, feeling the Catholic guilt weighing heavily on my heart for having abandoned her. Mom surprised us all by starting therapy, quitting drinking, and cleaning up her own mess. It was in those two and a half years of her finally stepping onto her healing path that I had the mother I had oh so desperately craved as a child. We blossomed not only as mother and child, but as friends who laughed together daily.

In November 2022, she received the diagnosis: Liver cancer and cirrhosis of the liver. And she took that as a sign from God that it was time to dive back into the bottle. Those dives eventually resulted in a drunken stumble late at night, alone in her tiny apartment, into a closet door, with her face hitting the corner of her bedside table as she descended. Bringing me back to Ohio for our final farewell.

* * *

We spoke to the nurse who said that she was most likely holding on for the promised "death bed shot". So, I hopped in my rental car and hit that Kroger liquor store I so despised and bought the tiniest bottle I could find of Jack Daniel's Cinnamon Fire, Mom's latest kick. The adult-aged grandkids gathered around her bed alongside me and my sister, and we took turns taking a little chug out of the bottle. I'm not a drinker so I touched it to my lips, as promised, and then we put it on a sponge that I put in Mom's mouth. For the love of all things holy, she perked up enough to suck on that sponge! So, we gave her a second "shot" and she sucked all of that out of the sponge, too! Wish granted, Momma. Wish granted.

On March 14, my birthday, Mom decided to leave this world with the most glorious smile I've ever witnessed radiating not just from her face, but from the essence of her being. That smile contained so much hope. I'm not quite sure what she was gazing upon as she released that final earthly breath, but I know she was being welcomed into love.

My mom and I now share a March 14 birthday. My earth-bound birthday and her heavenly birthday. I just happen to look at my phone and catch 3:14 quite often, and I cannot help but smile and say, "Hi, my momma. Golly, I miss you. And your silly jokes. I love you, too."

CHAPTER TWENTY-TWO

George Bailey and Me

by Paolina Milana

C hicago winters, when I was a kid, often delivered snowy stay-at-home days from school. Sometimes, we'd be lucky enough to learn of our school closing the night before from the local WGN station weatherman announcing it through the turned up volume on our old console TV. We'd wait in anticipation and cheer when "St. Lambert Catholic School" was called out (almost always one of the last).

My three siblings and I would huddle together sitting on our living room shag carpet, looking out our giant single-pane window at the glow of red, green, and blue bulbous Christmas lights poking out from the blanketed evergreens that fenced in our front yard. Dagger-like icicles that hung from the gutters of our roof seemed set on fire, glassy shards lit up by the streetlamp that stood out behind them on the corner of our lot. We'd wager which one would be the first to fall and cheer the snowplows that worked almost in vain to clear the streets, all the while using our fingernails to scrape the ice crystals that had formed in the corners of the window to make sure our view of what was going on outside wouldn't be obstructed.

Our family didn't have much money. Our parents emigrated from Sicily; so English wasn't our first language. Papà worked six days a week in his one-man barber shop. Mamma, while raising four kids and managing the household, set up shop at home as a dressmaker and seamstress. When we got sick, on the rare occasion that we went to the doctor, Papà paid out of pocket. Health insurance was unknown to us. Home remedies pungent with the sweet scent of their number one ingredient – garlic – usually exorcised whatever bugs ailed us.

Santa delivered one or maybe a maximum of two gifts each on Christmas mornings, and there were a few years when he skipped our house altogether. But I don't think we noticed all that much. Maybe it was because we never lacked for good eats. Our bellies were always full thanks to Sicilian feasts of Mamma's secret-recipe meatballs, Papà's Bolognese made with tomatoes from his beloved garden, and the annual chicken, ricotta, and Romano cheese-filled pasta pockets of homemade yum called *cappelletti* and seasonal fig cookies called *cucidati* they made together. We created our own festive fun. And regardless of the madness that insisted on residing in our home (as in Mamma's suspicions that the house may be bugged or that her family was trying to do her harm), love was always present.

One Christmas Eve in the mid-1970s, I may have been nine or ten years old, my papà and I sat together on our green and gold couch watching late-night TV. The plastic covers had been removed, part of our holiday traditions. My brother and two sisters had long ago gone to bed. Mamma had retired to the bedroom as well. Her head hurt. Her depression consumed her. And, unbeknownst to those of us in her family, the voices in her head were getting louder and meaner.

I snuggled close into the crook of Papà's arm. The black and white flicker of our TV bathed us in its light. My papà's bald head looked as if it had a halo of its own, quite fitting for whatever it was we had stumbled onto...some movie we had never before seen. It started with bells ringing and all sorts of voices praying for someone named George, a multitude of stars twinkling in the night sky, and then divine intervention showing up as constellations, the tiniest one representing an angel named Clarence.

It would be the first time the Christmas classic *"It's a Wonderful Life"* would air on TV and the first of many times that my papà and I would watch the story of a man driven to the brink of suicide after a lifetime of sacrificing his own dreams for others.

Little did I know then just how much George's journey would foreshadow my own.

"I'm shakin' the dust of this crummy little town off my feet, and I'm gonna see the world!"

If you know the story, you might recall the scene: 20-year-old George and 18-year-old Mary singing *"Buffalo gals won't you come out tonight..."* are throwing rocks at the abandoned old Granville House. For the past couple of years, George had been helping his father manage the family building and loan business, waiting for his brother Harry, two years his junior, to finish high school so that they could swap roles. Harry would take on working with their dad, while George would get the chance to start pursuing his dreams. In a conversation between father and son earlier in the movie, Papa Bailey shared his own dreams with George, letting him know that he wished his eldest son would choose to stay in Bedford Falls and continue his father's legacy. In his eyes, George was better suited to the role than his little brother, and he tells George that he was "born older" (the comment has nothing to do with actual years or birth order). In George's eyes, it's clear he's struggling with so many emotions including love and guilt.

During the first few annual viewings of *"It's A Wonderful Life"* both my papà and I would huddle close together, eyes glued to the TV screen, anticipating every single scene. Despite already knowing what was going to happen, we'd surrender to our tears and rejoice at the final tinkling of the Christmas tree bell.

"Look, Daddy...Teacher says every time a bell rings an angel gets their wings."

And why wouldn't we react in such a manner? The film had such an inspiring message about family and friends and the power that's greater than ourselves always watching over us, answering prayers.

By the time I turned 13, Papà and I had watched our favorite Christmas flick at least a half-dozen if not more times together, but my own prayers didn't seem to be getting heard, let alone answered. Mamma's schizophrenia had chosen me as its target with all sorts of accusations, including that I was promiscuous and sexually involved with my brother and Papà. The fear I felt for the Mamma I had – who resembled nothing close to Mary Bailey or even George's mom – caused me to distance myself more and more from her...and from myself and my own needs and challenges as a teenager who was becoming sexually aware and feeling as if I was "a bad girl" just as Mamma would say. I learned to stay small in the hopes of staying out of harm's way.

Year after year, little by little, the movie and its message took on a very different meaning for me. No longer was it one of hope; rather, I was aligned with George's despair.

Just like George, I, too, was seen through my own papà's eyes as having been "born older"; although *"piccola mamma"* (little mother) was the title bestowed on me at the age of ten, when I first began to take over household duties and traditional "mom" roles as Mamma's mental illness made it impossible for her to do much of anything herself.

Just like George, I, too, had a sibling, two years my junior. Mine was a timid soul, often in need of this "big sister" to defend her against the local bullies.

And just like George, I had dreams that one by one seemed to take a back seat to the dreams of others.

Our family needed money, so, of course, as a 7th grader in grammar school, I forged my birth certificate, pretending to be 15 years old and of legal age to get a job. Every Friday night,

Saturday, and Sunday, I worked at the local donut shop, unsupervised, and unprotected.

Our family needed someone to help with my little sister's schoolwork and getting her needs met, on top of additional work around the house, and helping Papà with his broken English understand complicated medical and insurance forms and navigate the labyrinth of healthcare and government systems. So, of course, during my sophomore year of college, I declined a scholarship to study for free in Florence.

"Tomorrow...I'd go out with my friends."

"Next month...I'd take time doing whatever, just for me."

"Next year...I'd make it MY year."

But my tomorrow, next month, next year never seemed to come around.

Just like George, my plans never materialized.

Mann Tracht, Un Gott Lacht – "*Man Plans, and God Laughs*" – the old Yiddish adage I learned early in life, and that time and again proved itself to be true – had me questioning my faith. So many times, I envisioned God looking down at me and my best-laid plans, wielding His magic wand to make sure they didn't happen, and laughing so hard at His handiwork that tears would be falling down His cheeks. It happened to Job. It felt as if it was happening to me.

I wondered if George ever thought the same thing. Surely, he must have when his father unexpectedly died.

Just like George, I, too, lost my papà. One minute we were talking, he was laughing, and the next second, he dropped to the floor. I was 25 years old when Papà suffered a massive heart attack...on the eve of my intent to tell my family of my escape to finally move out of my childhood home and into a place of my own. Hovering over Papà, his body wedged between the bathtub and the toilet, a trickle of vomit escaping his lips as mine covered his and I tried not to gag, I did my best to pump life back into him. But I knew he already had left me for someplace else, somewhere that had to be better than where we were. I stopped CPR, feeling his spirit gently pushing me back, telling me to let go.

Mamma stood in the doorway, tearfully begging me to do something. I did the only thing that came to me in that moment. I sat back on my heels and watched my papà's soft olive skin turn to a stoney ash. He was gone, and I didn't blame him. I would have left with him, especially since, somewhere deep within me, at that moment, I knew my fate was sealed.

How could I now leave Mamma and my younger sister to care for themselves? Neither one knew how to drive or balance a checkbook. Neither one brought in any income to help pay the bills. Mamma needed supervision to ensure she'd take her prescribed antipsychotic drug cocktail…Prolixin, Chlorpromazine, and Cogentin…along with her chasers to combat side effects, the names for which I can't recall. My sister, we would find out, had major learning disabilities and physical limitations that had fallen through the cracks because we all were so focused on Mamma's mental illness. My baby sister, the girl for whom I served as "little mother," struggled to cope with life's simplest things (from tying her own shoelaces to counting out the correct amount to pay for groceries at the checkout). Getting a job she could do and keep took a back seat to just helping her to survive *and* cope with her grief.

What would happen to them if I chose to leave?

"…but George, they'll vote with Potter otherwise…"

When his father dies, George is the only one who knows the business well enough to keep the building and loan from going under or from falling into the hands of the town's Grinch, the money-grubbing "old buzzard" Mr. Potter. Although George tries to stand his ground and announce to everyone that he's out of there and leaving on the next train to pursue his dreams, he just can't bring himself to do it. Neither could I.

Just like George, I felt trapped and as if I had no choice. And, yet we both chose.

George ends up giving his college savings to Harry for him to go to school with the agreement that once he graduates, Harry would return to take over the business and free George from his obligation to it. That never happens. Harry returns with a wife and a great job offer from his new father-in-law, and George can't find it in himself to thwart his little brother's chances at such a promising future.

My plans never materialized either. Following my papà's death, I found myself abandoned by my older brother and sister. Both disappeared, retreating into their grief. I was left to fend for myself and for our mother and sister. Even worse, when I would find the courage to ask for help, I was met with words that wounded me: *"Stop being such a martyr"* and *"This is how you get to live here for free."* So, I silenced my voice, stuffed down my own needs, again, allowing others to do what they wanted for themselves. I practiced becoming a robot. I steeled myself against any emotions as much as I could to make it through another day. My only comfort was food, and I swallowed back my emotions with equal amounts of it and booze. My weight soared...the scale, when I'd force myself to step on it, which only served to further my shame, swung its needle closer and closer to 300 on its dial.

Days into living life without Papà, I did my best to embody him: Mamma needed to be chauffeured to her doctor's appointments. Social security and social services for both her and my sister needed to be applied for and reapplied for. Hospitals and insurance companies were near-daily battles on speed dial. Groceries had to be bought. The lawn had to be mowed. The house had to be maintained with its utility bills and more needing to be paid. The funeral had added $8,000 to the tab, ironically the same amount Uncle Billy had lost that pushed George over the edge. I felt myself being shoved in the same direction, and my constant reminder of my failure to rise above became Papà's once thriving garden that I could see from my bedroom window. Weeds were choking the life out of it, and I couldn't figure out how to keep it alive. I barely noticed the same was true for me and that I was withering on my own vine, dying a little bit with every passing day. The only solution I could come up with to keep up with all of it was to ignore the evidence of anything being wrong.

I immersed myself in my writing at the newspaper where I worked. I excelled on the job. I tried to find joy in it, but success at that proved short-lived. I always ended up having to go home to the madness that awaited me. On the outside, I projected as normal an image as I could muster: Smiling, nodding, and participating in meetings that no longer mattered to me. I pretended they did. I went through the motions as if my life had possibilities, despite having come to realize it didn't. On the inside, I feared my thoughts, the voices in my own head berating, blaming, believing I was better off dead. Just like George, I was beyond discouraged and utterly alone, drowning in feelings I could not share with anyone and resigning myself to living a life of obligation and servitude disguised as my destiny.

My attempts at "keeping it together" were slipping. Mamma's voices had returned full-force. Her paranoid fears that we were being monitored and needed to whisper when we spoke escalated. She began, once again, to believe I was part of the conspiracy to do her in. Her meds were off and needed adjusting. As my thoughts were consumed with managing her mental illness, and not losing myself in the process, I failed to see the warning signs of what was happening to my little sister. In truth, I barely had time to acknowledge much more than her existence. Beyond making sure she was fed and transported to whatever social programs I had found for her; I didn't give her what she needed. I just didn't have it in me. I was down to the dregs, if even that. I didn't have anything left to give to myself, let alone to her.

After two years of spiraling downward further and further into my feelings of hopelessness, I knew something had to change or something bad was going to happen. That almost inaudible squeak within me whispered, "Get out." Slowly,

I sought to heed the voice and release myself from the life I was living. I secretly looked for somewhere else to call home. I even took a vacation with my BFF at the time, my first cruise to the Caribbean. And in those few days, I began to breathe, to feel alive, to think my future – not as their caregiver but as simply "me" – was possible again.

God, however, must have needed another laugh because the moment I returned to Mamma and my sister, before even unpacking a single suitcase, my 24-year-old-sibling greeted me with equal parts maniacal laughter and horror-flick-worthy rage.

"*Paola, siamo mezzi guai,*" Mamma choked out, her black eyes now doubled in size, full of fear, void of hope. She looked as if she hadn't slept the entire week I was away. And that was because she hadn't. When I asked her what she meant about us being "in the middle of trouble," she waved her hand in defeat, allowing my sister to show me.

Barreling down the stairs, she came at me. Instinct told me that if I moved so much as a hair, she would hurl herself full force at me, and I wouldn't win the battle. She screamed and shoved me to the side as she ran through our front door outside, across the lawn, down the middle of the street to somewhere I was certain even she didn't know.

Not again. My one single thought. It couldn't be happening again.

I could almost hear God's giggles.

As my sister exploded in her own psychotic episode, I called my brother to share what had just happened. His immediate response was that I had to be overreacting. He raced in his car to pick me up and go searching for our sister and to see for himself what I had clearly misunderstood. We found her, waving church bulletins and newspapers she had collected on her journey, pointing to words and pictures that had nothing to do with her, offering them up as proof that she was being celebrated by everyone in the know.

I could see it in my brother's eyes as he helped our sister into the backseat. Not again. It couldn't be happening again.

It was.

And when we drove to the emergency room, they were waiting for us. I had called ahead, before even calling my brother. Gone was the girl freshly back from the open seas. The robot in me had been activated. And just like when Papà had died, I already knew what was happening. Barely an hour or two later, it was my hand that committed her to a psychiatric hospital.

Even today, after all these years, when I close my eyes, I am brought back to that moment. I can still see the pen held between my fingers, shaking to sign my name to those papers, struggling to come to terms with the fact that my sister had the same mental illness, paranoid schizophrenia, as Mamma.

"Dear Father in Heaven, I'm not a praying man, but, if you're up there and hear me, show me the way. I'm at the end of my rope. Show me the way."

George takes on the responsibility of an $8,000 deposit that his Uncle Billy lost while on his way to the bank. It's not George's to own, but he chooses to take the wrap, falling prey to scandal and a likely prison sentence. He stops at Martini's Bar, drinks too much, and prays. The response he seems to get from his plea to God is a punch in the jaw courtesy of another patron at the bar.

Abandoned, discouraged, and confused about what to do, George concludes that he has only one option. He can see no way out...other than to take his own life in the hopes that his family will survive with the money they'd receive from his insurance policy.

Just like George, I, too, prayed. And just like George, I, too, would feel as if my prayers went completely unanswered or were answered with a punch in my gut. I had nothing left in me to give. I could no longer see a way up out of the hole I was in. None of it was mine to own, but there was no one else stepping up to hold the bag.

I was now living with and caring for two family members, both diagnosed with paranoid schizophrenia. Surrounded by so much madness and keeping it all secret, I was losing myself completely. I lashed out at home and at work. I was becoming a danger to myself and others. And in my clouded thinking, I had concluded that my only option was to take myself out along with my mamma and sister. I couldn't just "pull a George" and throw away my own life, I *reasoned*, after all, who would care for them after I was gone? It was the right thing to do. Or so my muddled mind decided.

If anyone had told me back then that I would come to a point in my life where I would plan out and nearly succeed at murder-suicide, I simply wouldn't believe it. But that is, indeed, what happened.

The "how" of my plot doesn't matter. After all, "*Man Plans, and God Laughs*" – and just for the record, I didn't end up killing myself or anyone else.

What does matter is that, just like George, I, too, encountered an angel.

On my dark night of the soul, the night I had decided to act on my plans, I wanted one last moment to myself doing the one thing I had come to love. After a full day of work at the newspaper, I stopped on my way home at a local health club where I had been freelancing for added income. I didn't visit it for a final workout. The place had a giant jacuzzi, and in that pool of water, my very overweight body could feel weightless and free. It was the only place at that time in my life where I felt even a moment of peace. I wanted that just one last time.

I soaked for hours imagining what was to come. I thought about leaving a note, what I might write, or if it even mattered. Before I realized it, I was the last person left in the club, other than its owner, Margie. When she came to tell me it was closing time, she must have seen something in me that no one else before her had. Whatever it was, she refused to let me out of her sight, forcing me to have a chat with a friend of hers whose office was just down the road.

Lynn was the woman I would meet that night. She was my Angel Clarence. Margie would leave me with this licensed therapist. I had agreed to give her 30 minutes, after all, I had a murder-suicide schedule to meet. Lynn sat across from me in her Captain's chair, while I sank into her marshmallow-leather couch. Every ounce of me felt exhausted, deflated, and ready to go to sleep forever.

"Margie tells me something's going on with you," this pixie-sized girl-next-door said.

I gave her my usual response, shrugging my shoulders, looking down at my hands folded in my lap: "Nothing. Nothing's going on."

And Lynn replied with four little words that would begin to bring me back to life: "Tell me about 'nothing'..."

George never left his hometown of Bedford Falls. Time and time again, he put others ahead of himself. And life kept offering up alternatives that, at least in the moments they were presented, were things George desired. Marrying Mary and starting a family, for example, is one of those. In his day-to-day life, he still thought of what he had intended his life to be, even putting together miniatures of the towns he wanted to create. But at his breaking point, he loses control, smashing the models of bridges and buildings he had made in his earlier years. I imagine George thought what I did: Why bother...? It's over. Life holds no further possibilities for me.

George and I were wrong.

With the help of his Angel Clarence, George got to see how his dreams HAD materialized. He had built up the town with "the prettiest little homes" people could afford to buy and live in without being shackled to massive debt or being in servitude to Mr. Potter. He created a community...much bigger and more meaningful than just erecting a skyscraper in some anonymous city. His life had touched so many others in a way he never could have imagined and, seemingly, with far more impact than if he had chosen to leave right after high school.

With the help of my angel Lynn, my dreams, just like George's, also materialized in ways I could not have imagined. In my case, I did end up leaving home. I trekked cross-country from Chicago to Los Angeles with nothing much to my name, leaving everyone and everything I knew for the unknown, heeding a voice within beckoning me to go. My leaving allowed me to be a better caregiver to my family and myself. It empowered me to find MY home and my purpose, beyond the tiny window of possibilities I alone could envision. I now help others turn their own trials into triumphs by telling their own stories. I inspire others to see themselves – all of who they are…good, bad, and everything in between…as powerful and worthy…just by being.

Did I abandon my mamma and sister in order to live my own life? No. But I did give myself permission to prioritize me. I let go of the idea that I had to sacrifice myself to benefit them. I learned that it wasn't "either/or"; rather, it was possible to give to them what I could AND give to myself what I deserved.

Ironically, stepping away from circumstances that were pulling me under resulted in others in my family rising to the occasion and taking more of a leadership role in our family caregiver duties. It also allowed me to have a more authentic mother/ daughter and sister relationship with my mamma and younger sibling. I no longer viewed them as burdens; rather, I could engage with them with more love and compassion, acknowledging and respecting them for being their own people…good, bad, and everything in between.

What a gift I had been given.

Me and George Bailey.

CHAPTER (BONUS)

I started this book with a Foreword sharing mostly how it came to be and what it has become. I couldn't very well end it without a little something more for those of you who have made it here to the end. So here are a few inspiring quotes and more to help you on your family caregiver journey.

"If Your Compassion Does Not Include Yourself, It Is Not Complete."
~ *Jack Kornfield*

"There are only four kinds of people in the world — those that have been caregivers, those that are caregivers, those who will be caregivers, and those who will need caregivers." ~ *Rosalynn Carter*

"Caregiving often calls us to lean into love we didn't know possible."
~ *Tia Walker*

*"Self-compassion is simply giving the
same kindness to ourselves
that we would give to others."*
~ Christopher Germer

*"A hero is an ordinary individual who finds the strength to
persevere and endure in spite of overwhelming obstacles."*
~ Christopher Reeve

*"It's not the load that breaks you down,
it's the way you carry it."*
~ Lena Horne

*"If caregivers are not healthy, mentally well-balanced and
spiritually sound, then those for whom they care will suffer."*
~ Leeza Gibbons

ABOUT THE AUTHORS

(in alphabetical order)

Kay Anonsen

Kay Anonsen worked for many years as an actress and then decided to pursue a Master's of Psychology. Her arts and research background developed in her a great ability to write proposals, and she spent 25 years developing programs and raising funds for the disenfranchised. Her son moved to Long Beach and when she came to visit him, she fell in love with everything about it. She went home, retired, moved to Long Beach with only two suitcases, and she has never looked back. When she has nothing else to do, you can find her at the beach in her chair with a book in her hand; otherwise known as paradise.

Mary Barbato

Mary Barbato spent over 30 years writing strategy decks, newsletters, press releases, articles and various other forms of content for Fortune 500 companies. She then rose to the position of CEO for one of the wealthiest men in the world. She has won numerous awards for content and web creation and has also produced and edited one season of dLife, a television magazine show on life with diabetes, for which she won a Telly. Her career ended when she became a caregiver to herself and later to her Dad. She has spent the last 6 years recovering from a brain injury and has made it her goal to educate those who care for brain injury patients (whether it be from an accident, stroke, or dementia) to enable them to better understand and care for those who suffer from these horrible conditions. She also hopes to bring comfort to those that are going through their own care recovery journey with a traumatic brain injury. She currently lives in the Berkshires with her cats Masala and Dosa, coaches soccer at her old high school, and is restoring an old 1902 Victorian and an 1888 Post Office. In her spare time she consults directly with C-Suite executives in healthcare. You can find more on Mary on her LinkedIn account at https://www.linkedin.com/in/marycbarbato/.

Shunese Coran

Shunese Coran, a serial entrepreneur and strategist, discovered her passion for geriatric care and supporting vulnerable populations while caring for her grandmother. She currently manages a non-medical home care agency for seniors and individuals with developmental disabilities. Shunese also provides consulting services to small startup businesses, crafting impactful programming and support services tailored to empower vulnerable populations. In honor of her grandmother's legacy, Shunese founded Catherine's Family Child Care, offering community support and a nurturing environment for children and families from her childhood home. Her true dedication lies in helping individuals reach their full potential after adversity and trauma. Currently pursuing certification as a Grief Counselor, she aims to provide a safe and empowering space for children and teens navigating grief and life after loss.

Jeanne Erikson

Jeanne Erikson is the primary family caregiver to her mother, 95, since her first stroke in 2007 and second stroke in 2022. She is a former Certified Nursing Assistant who worked for five years as a Care Manager and Activities Assistant in a facility assisting late-stage dementia residents. She successfully works with groups of seniors or individually implementing activities and cognitive stimulation programs. As a private caregiver, she has a passion and love for seniors, working to ensure their independence and dignity as they remain in their homes. She has a B.S. degree in communications from Cal Poly Pomona University.

Enma Espinoza

Enma Espinoza was born in South America. Enma is a loving wife, mother, and grandmother. She enjoys having her cup of Cafecito calientito (hot coffee) with hazelnut and cinnamon every morning. She decided to participate in this collaborative book project because she considers herself a voice for

Frank, her beloved husband who lost his ability to speak in the early stages of dementia, and she wanted to share their beautiful love story "Loving Frank, Loving Me" as well as highlight the importance of practicing self-care. Enma enjoys nature, visiting botanical gardens, forest bathing and trying different kinds of food from all over the world. She loves venturing into unfamiliar places and continually learning new things. Part of Enma's weekly routine is prayer, gratitude, reaching out to friends who are going through a tough time, especially caregivers as well as joining caregiver support groups in English and Spanish and virtual and in person programs that are available for older adults at the senior centers.

Anne Front

Anne Front is a palliative care therapist and educator on topics of serious illness, caregiving, grief, and advance care planning. She is not only a professional realm of palliative care but is also a cancer survivor and spouse to a cancer thriver. She feels honored to walk alongside those facing their health challenges and the ones that love them. She is also committed to her own self-reflections as a means of making sense and meaning to her own illness and care partner journey. Through her personal and professional experiences, she uses the wisdom of stories to inform her writing, counseling, and palliative care coaching. Anne can be reached at www.anne.front.com

Rowena Ilagan

 Rowena Ilagan has been working for years as a scientist to support her chronic writing habit. She is a native Angeleno with short stints in Salt Lake City, Utah (testing athletes during the 2002 Winter Olympics) and Mallorca, Spain (doing anthropology research at an artist colony). Creative writing and social science research in cultural/religious anthropology or ethnobotany are some of her interests. However, her lived experience as a chronically-ill patient with CFS and Multiple Chemical Sensitivities and as a family caregiver (mother with Alzheimer's, older brother with a stroke), prompted her to seek part-time work in dual tasking (teaching fitness with cognitive stimulation) to stave off dementia onset in older adults, participate in Caring Across Generations (an advocacy fellowship fighting for caregiver rights), and pursue this writing endeavor in a book for carers. She hopes to enter grad school in public health or cognitive psychology and learn a healing modality such as speech language pathology with applied linguistics in the coming years. When she is not taking care of her brother, his 2 year old Corgi-Shepard Chandler Bolt, or working, Rowena loves to relax with a good book, movie, or game. She is an introvert forced to engage in extroverted situations (activity direction, party planning) more often than she likes. Rowena is often found learning new dance routines, coming up with games, or collecting funny jokes/memes for her classes and social media channels.

Tracey Y. Jones

Tracey Y. Jones, a devoted daughter and primary caregiver, has courageously supported her father through his battle with dementia since her mother's passing in 2015. A proud Angeleno, Tracey hails from Los Angeles, specifically the area formerly known as South Central Los Angeles.

In the late 1980s, Tracey broke barriers as one of the first black women to enter the male-dominated photography industry. Her talent in capturing beauty and emotion through her lens earned her apprenticeships with renowned photographers. By the early 1990s, she founded her own photo studio, creating a diverse portfolio that included celebrities, rising stars, and families. Transitioning into the early 2000s, she excelled as an award-winning project manager in the entertainment and advertising sector, supporting innovative concepts. Later, she explored the death care industry, as a community counselor.

Tracey is a compassionate advocate for the welfare of others, with a strong history of community service. She served her local community as a Neighborhood Council Chairperson, demonstrating her dedication to community development and well-being.

Currently, Tracey holds a prominent position as a founding board member of the Greenmount West Community Foundation in Baltimore, Maryland. In this role, she contributes to initiatives that enhance the quality of life and opportunities for individuals and families within the community.

Driven by her family values, dementia awareness, and a creative passion, Tracey is on a mission to transform her life experiences into compelling narratives, as an author, to empower and educate others.

Parissa Kermani

Parissa Kermani has over 30 years' experience in the spa industry having managed practices with revenues of over $8 million a year. For the last 6 years, her life's journey took a detour from this path when it became one about all things "family". She is currently the manager for her brother's medical practice while she was also the caregiver to her Mom. After her father's numerous ICU admissions over the course of 10 years, Parissa devoted some of her time as a volunteer at Cedars Sinai Medical Center in Los Angeles as a way of expressing her gratitude for their care of her father. Her newfound passion is that of writing, starting with her chapter in this book. Her story is about the beauty and brutality that a caregiver experiences. She hopes that she can inspire any caregiver reading it to realize the undeniable importance of self-care in this role, to have them take stock of what they do and determine what they will need to change in their circumstance to save themselves. All the while recognizing the beauty and honor that there is in providing this care. Parissa lives in Burbank, CA. She has a love of Pomeranians, traveling, and gardening.

Karen Klink

Karen Klink wears many hats: a devoted daughter, essential caregiver, tireless advocate, and fierce activist. She has spent the last five years of her life determined to make the lives of her mother and others like her better. She is passionate and purpose-driven, unwavering in her pursuit of positive change in the Long-Term Care System. So, when asked to share her journey, she thought, "Why not?". She writes with a fire and an authenticity that mirrors her actions. Karen's altruistic spirit began after quitting the rat race, after 25 years as a trader in the stock brokerage industry, she then volunteered in a variety of causes from politics to championing the special needs community. Karen feels this short chapter is just the beginning of her writing as she continues with her ongoing changing relationship with a mom who has dementia and the needed transformation of the system. She lives in the small community of Hermosa Beach with her husband where she finds peace and gratitude in the ocean and music.

Tony Luciani

Tony Luciani has been a full-time painter for over forty-five years, graduating from the Ontario College of Art (Toronto, Canada) in 1977 with honors. Still relatively young at twenty-one, he continued with his fifth-year post-graduate study in Florence, Italy. It was there that he found maturity as an artist while observing the paintings of the Renaissance Masters. Returning home, Luciani was immediately accepted for representation by a well-respected and established Canadian art gallery.

In defining his work, Luciani prefers to be placed in a tradition of figurative art, which is interpretive with focused observation.

In 2014, Tony Luciani included photography as a means of his creative expression. The ongoing series depicting his aging mother, who had dementia, has garnered him many accolades and a multitude of prestigious international awards. This recognition has further enhanced his artistic reputation globally. A world-wide assemblage of media, together with a massive online audience, pinnacled when, in 2018, Luciani stood alone on stage at the Boston Opera House in front of 2600 people and gave a moving TED Talk about the artistic collaboration with his mom.

Most recently, Luciani's painting, 'The Dressmaker', oil on canvas, won the prestigious FIGURATIVAS 2019 International First Prize Purchase Award at the Museu Europeu d'Art Modern in Barcelona, Spain.

Tony Luciani's art can be found in private, public, and corporate collections worldwide. He is represented in Canada by Loch Gallery in Toronto, Winnipeg, and Calgary. Learn more at www.tonyluciani.com and www.ynotphoto.com.

Paolina Milana

Paolina Milana is an award-winning writer and empowerment coach who helps people turn the trials of their lives into triumphs – either through coaching them in the writing of their books or through coaching them in manifesting and co-creating the professional and personal lives they dream of having. Her "Madness to Magic Method" teaches those of us who weren't born yesterday, especially the professional "do-it-all" women among us, how to use storytelling techniques to overcome adversity, build confidence, foster connections, and drive more business. *"Your life isn't a fairytale, but you ARE the hero of your own story"* is a favorite mantra of hers. A former Chief Communications and Marketing Officer with journalistic roots, Paolina has risen to the top of the corporate ladder, has had five books published, (four of them award-winners, including *"Seriously! Are We THERE Yet?!"*), has built her own six-figure business, and devotes herself now to helping others reimagine their lives, write their next chapters, and become the heroes of their own journeys. Connect with her at powerlina@madnesstomagic.com.

Tonya Mills

Tonya Mills was born in 1966 in Galveston, Texas. She began using her love of reading as an escape from her childhood abuse, leading to a love for writing poetry. In June of 2022, her poem "Lost Souls" was published by Silent Spark Press. During her teen years, she was a caregiver for her mother, who suffered from depression. Tonya moved to North Texas and became a solopreneur. She met her soul mate and lives in a small town with their poodle, Aleister. Tonya resumed her role as a caregiver during her mother's senior years as she suffered from many illnesses and recently passed away from them. She is passionate about writing and is currently working on a teaching memoir. In her spare time, she loves having parties, going on paranormal ghost hunts, and traveling.

Ruth Kreshka Moran

Ruth Kreshka Moran has helped bring the words and works of Sam Shepard, Joseph Chaikin, Eugene Lee, Beth Henley, George Walker, John Patrick Shanley, David Henry Hwang, Reinaldo Povad, Truman Capote, Samuel Beckett and many others to New York's theatre community. From 1998 to 2014, she served as Director of Production for Columbia University's Graduate Theatre Arts Program and Head of the Stage Management Program there. She co-produced *Me to Play*, a documentary about two actors with Parkinson's Disease performing Samuel Beckett's Endgame, now available to stream on Prime, Fandor, and elsewhere. She has been care-partner to her husband Dan Moran for 22 years.

Mercedes Negrete

Mercedes Negrete comes from a large multigenerational family where the traditions were always cherished and followed, and where marriage, good or bad, was for a lifetime. The only way to leave was if one of the partners died, I left that years ago. Mercedes followed her dream by going to school, first to learn English and then to get her high school diploma, and, ultimately, to earn her Master's Degree in Early Childhood-Primary Education...all while working and raising her family. Mercedes' children went into a head start program which she claims was the "light" she had been searching. She started to work as a preschool teacher when her youngest child started kindergarten and received her Master's when her oldest child graduated from high school. Mercedes worked for the program for 21 years in different positions: Teacher Assistant, Teacher, and Education Facilitator. Her calling and her heart, however, were always in the classroom, working with the children and their parents. After her husband's stroke, and with Mercedes, herself, becoming ill, she left her position and ever since has made it her full-time job to keep her husband alive and the household running smoothly.

Makeba Pease

Makeba Pease often refers to herself as a well-qualified Uncertified Nursing Assistant with an MBA. She never expected that she would have to put her 25-year career on hold to care for her mother, but she dove in headfirst to become her primary caretaker. Without training or assistance, she toughed it out through the hard times and learned to navigate a system that was not designed to support the commitment required to care for an aging parent. She told her story to give a voice to those that require care and those that commit to the care of a loved one. It is her hope that those in the struggle will feel supported during the times they feel alienated and defeated. Her prayer is that those who read her story will read between the lines and put the documents in place to ease the financial burden and put the safeguards in place to protect the ONE or the FEW that stand tall in the fight for the voiceless that require care, that can't speak on their own behalf and didn't leave a big bucket of money for long term care. Without that bucket, a committed volunteer is required. She is glad that her mother has HER. It has required an entire shift of mindset for the commitment.

Allison Beatrice Seton

Allison Beatrice Seton resides in California, with a heart that is half always in New York, and half in the deep of the Canadian Rockies.

Susan A Shoemaker

Susan A Shoemaker worked as a nurse for more than thirty years. Her experience was in Behavioral Health Case Management as a Staff nurse at state psychiatric facilities and drug and alcohol rehabilitation centers. Also, she spent many years working with the community as a Public Health Nurse for the state of PA, educating the community members with various outreach programs and medical clinics to teach health and safety to other healthcare members and facilities in her area. Susan was a

Volunteer at the Women's Resource Center, assisting with domestic abuse and violence issues. She also holds Certificates in Emergency Management and Mental Health Emergency Management.

Mother of 3, Grandmother of 5, and Great Grandmother of 1, she has personal knowledge and experience in caring for family members with Mental Health illnesses and drug and alcohol addiction, as well as caring for parents with physical conditions. She is currently retired from her nursing career, but not life.

Susan decided to share her caregiving experience with others who may benefit from realizing they are not alone in dealing with this sometimes-heartbreaking illness. Susan can be found on the Facebook page personally and for this group.

Wendy Lew Toda

Wendy Lew Toda is a multi-disciplinary artist, poet, coach and retreat facilitator, creating at the intersection of grief and joy. She is currently the primary caregiver to her parents and supported her auntie's care for her late uncle. Wendy's work has been shown nationally and published online and in print. She has written poetry since childhood, following her fascination with naming and expressing the complex wonder of our lives. Her persistent love for finding just the right words to capture an experience underpins her growing curiosity in poetry as medicine for our souls. Giving voice to her stories in this manner is a personal creative practice. It is one of the ways she tends her own self-care in the land of caregiving. Wendy's poetry introduces the beauty of joy to grief, inviting that beauty to be a clear and kind resource of strength for healing and new wholeness. She hopes her fellow caregivers might notice echoes of their own experiences reflected in this chapter of poetry and find hope in remembering they are not alone. Learn more about Wendy: www.wendylewtoda.com.

Debbie Tynan

Debbie Tynan's must haves are love, humor, car-dancing and good friends.

Climate-conscious, she's worried about our planet surviving. She wants future generations to enjoy the fresh powder she's savored when skiing the Rockies and Alps.

Before she was a mom, Debbie worked for the magical world of Disney. In the summers, she was a camp counselor for kids battling cancer and HIV/AIDS.

Debbie's a dog lover and grandma to fur babes, Woody and Rizzo. Gardening is her therapy, she's an arts and culture enthusiast and is curious about everyone's story. She believes our passports should look like your favorite, shabby cookbook.

Mercedes Vega

Mercedes Vega recently completed her Master's in Public Health but still considers herself a Sociologist at heart. Growing up in an economically diverse city like Los Angeles, she witnessed many inequalities in her community that invoked in her a passion for social and healthcare justice. She discovered her love for literature, creative writing, and poetry at an early age. Still plagued by the challenges of writing for self-expression "because writing makes it real" according to her, she's decided to finally share a piece of her life with the rest of the world. When she's not writing "venty entries" (a private series dedicated to venting about the world!), Mercedes enjoys writing and translating Spanish poetry written by Central American writers to English in her personal blog, (https://lucyavega86.blogspot.com/) for others to enjoy. Her inspiration comes from her Salvadoran mother who gave her books in Spanish that depicted true stories of civil war survivors, whose native words often resonated and touched her young soul. Her love for her roots and dedication to family is reflected in this beautiful collaborative book, where she shares her and her mother's journey as caregivers and the ripple effects these sudden changes can have in one's life and in the rest of the world.

Teri Wellbrock

 Teri Wellbrock is a trauma-warrior, having survived and thrived after learning to cope with her C-PTSD symptoms and 25 years of severe panic attacks by utilizing EMDR therapy, personal research and learned coping skills along with a foundation of faith and positivity. She is currently an audiobook narrator; and writing a book, *Unicorn Shadows: From Trauma to Triumph – A Healing Guide*, about her multiple traumas, with the intent to help others reach their own joyous and peaceful existence via her "story of hope". She also speaks publicly at trauma-recovery events about her triumph over trauma. Teri is mom to three beautiful children (ages 30, 27, and 17); graduated magna cum laude from the University of Cincinnati with a Bachelor's Degree in Psychology; has written a children's book, *The Doodle with the Noodle*, with her daughter, about their Therapy Dog, Sammie the Labradoodle; has created the Sammie's Bundles of Hope project (bags filled with trinkets of hope donated to children with trauma history); and is producer and host of the top 2% globally rated show - The Healing Place Podcast. She maintains a blog at www.unicornshadows. com and writes a monthly Hope for Healing Newsletter. Her life purpose is to make a positive difference in the lives of others and shine a light of hope into dark spaces.

ACKNOWLEDGMENTS

This work was made possible thanks to a grant from The Picerne Family Foundation. Thank you goes to Executive Director of the Kenneth A. Picerne Foundation Victor Nelson who chose this collaborative book initiative to be part of the Foundation's Artists Outreach Program and who has shepherded this project from start to finish. In addition, sincerest thanks to St. Barnabas Senior Services (sbssla.org) and to the Los Angeles Family Caregiver Resource Center at USC (losangelescrc.usc.edu) – the two non-profits that helped in connecting us with family caregivers who wanted to share their stories and participate in this endeavor.

One of our chapter authors is Tony Luciani (TonyLuciani.com/photography) who is owed a big thank you for granting us permission to use one of his beautiful photographs on our book cover.

What you hold in your hands came together as a real book thanks to the donated cover design and manuscript formatting services provided by Matt Stone and the team at 100covers.com.

Thanks also to the writers who helped us edit this manuscript especially Sara, Brenda, and Adam. And in the end, what you hold in your hands came together as a real book thanks to the donated cover design and manuscript formatting services provided by Matt, Shanna, and the team at 100covers.com.

We couldn't have done this project without so many people lending a hand. Sincerest thanks to you all.

And to every family caregiver who stepped forward to share their story in this book…you are giving a gift to yourself, a legacy to your families, and a promise to others. Your stories matter. YOU matter. And I thank you for being part of this collaboration.

Made in the USA
Las Vegas, NV
10 June 2024

90953033R00164